MW00714103

A FAMILY GOES TO WAR

ALSO BY RICHARD S. JACKSON

The Third Thorn: A Collection of Recollections
  Onota Collections, 1992

*The Best of Friends: Adventures with Goldens
and Other Family Members*
  Fithian Press, 1994

A Gap at Green Hills: A Novel
  University Editions, 1999

The Boyajian Papers: A Novel
  Onota Collections, 2000

A Family Goes to War

RECOLLECTIONS AND LETTERS FROM WORLD WAR II

Written and edited by

Richard S. Jackson

2003/ONOTA COLLECTIONS/YORK HARBOR, MAINE

Copyright © 2003 Richard S. Jackson
All rights reserved
Printed in the United States of America

Published by Onota Collections
Post Office Box 78
York Harbor, ME 03911
1-207-363-2706 or
1-772-231-0061

ISBN 0-9705722-2-0
Library of Congress Control Number: 2003105721

Printed by Morris Publishing
3212 East Highway 30
Kearney, NE 68847
1-800-650-7888

*This book is dedicated to the memory of James Monroe Mathes Jr.,
who lost his life in enemy action in the English Channel aboard
PT-509 in August 1944. As a lifelong friend, a college roommate
and brother-in-law, I was aware that Jim was not only a
leader of men, but that in death he took with him
not only an insatiable thirst for life
but also tremendous promise.*

CONTENTS

Introduction

MY FIRST CHILD, a son, was born on May 3, 1943. It was, of course, an active period in the history of our country. The United States was engaged in World War II. The opposition was Adolph Hitler and his Nazi legions who had taken over the German government, and indeed, threatened to take over all of Europe. Our close ally, Great Britain, was being severely punished, and was in danger of being invaded. At the same time, Pearl Harbor, the main base of the U.S. Pacific Fleet, had been attacked by a surprise thrust of the Japanese on Dec. 7, 1941, that President Roosevelt described as a "day that will live in infamy."

Mindful of the history that was being made during those days, I started writing letters to Richard S. Jackson Jr. whom we called by the cuddly name of Dickens. They started with a description of the activity that took place as my wife and I hustled to the hospital at 2 A.M., when pre-birth cramps had become consistent, and they ended with the conclusion of the war in 1945. It was my excuse for a journal. I wished to capture the excitement of the times. As an officer in the Naval Reserve, I had an active role in the war, even though, as it developed, I was never stationed outside the confines of continental U.S.

The letters to Dick Jr., and eventually, to his sister Mary French, whom we called Bonnie (born May 11, 1945 in Seattle, Wash.) formed the core of this book, because they described not only the events of the time, but my reaction to them. I had intended to eventually put the letters together in book form to present to both

Dickens and Bonnie. In rereading the letters, I realized that they were too personal, even for the recipients. Gushing first words, overly cute descriptions of baby's first actions or reactions, are difficult to turn into readable tales. But my descriptions of such as indoctrination training in Newport, R.I., work at the South Boston Naval Yard, V-J Day or even a trip across the country by train, seemed worth salvaging.

But this was hardly heroic fare. Among the notes and letters I had carefully preserved was a most bountiful source. There were letters from brothers in a landing boat regiment in the Southwest Pacific, a bomber wing in Italy, and armed guard duty aboard a freighter plying the Atlantic. I acknowledge the wisdom of my Father and Mother, the recipients of most of these letters, who had them copied and passed about from brother to brother, no matter where we were located. And then there was a multitude of other letters from friends and relatives. My close friend, college roommate, and brother-in-law, Jim Mathes Jr. wrote marvelously descriptive letters from the English Channel before, during, and after D-Day, until he was lost aboard PT 509 in a clash with German E-boats supporting their control of the Channel Islands. I am beholden to Mary Chapman Watts, Jim's widow, who supplied copies of his letters and details of her search for him when he was declared "missing in action."

I acknowledge the assistance of Bud Brett, who was one of the first of our group to enter the military and who wrote tirelessly of his experiences on the USS *Honolulu* before and through Pearl Harbor. I had in hand exciting letters from my friend, Fred Borsodi, who left Hartford to fight in a P-40 against Field Marshall Rommel, the "Desert Fox," and his Afrika Korps, during the pivotal African campaign. A mutual friend, of Freddie's, and mine, the late Bill Webster, wrote frequently of his experiences as a test pilot with Curtis-Wright Aircraft in Ohio. I further acknowledge the assistance of Jean Loomis, widow of Chet Loomis, Johnny Cooney, the widow of Dinner Cooney, and the gang at the Aetna Insurance Company who wrote me letters. And, of course, I acknowledge the role of my late mother, who was so active as a nurse during the war.

Mother's letters and Dad's add to the flavor of this book, as do those from Jim Mathes Sr. and my classmate Herb Mattlage.

One might wonder about the lack of footnotes attributing various facts to a distant source. This is hardly necessary, as each person, for the most part, was living his or her letters and quoting only themselves.

I must bow in the direction of Alamogordo, N.M. where Brother Jeff is not only a frequent contributor to this book by letter and recollection, but performs once again as my primary editor. How, at his advanced age, he remains so adept at adding commas, providing synonyms, and all the other necessary grammatical nuances, I shall never fathom. Also, thanks go once again to my wife, who has a sharp eye indeed, and without whose help I could never proof the galleys.

I would be remiss if I did not thank Eric Larson for his understanding and assistance in providing the camera-ready pages, and once again, the folks at Morris Publishing for bringing this book to a successful completion.

Prologue

IN THE UNITED STATES World War II was like a malignant growth. Its tentacles reached into almost every family, snatching at young blood in the bloom of manhood and sending them overseas to the battles. Mothers, fathers, sisters and younger brothers were left to worry and brood. They could do no more than pray for a speedy conclusion to the war, and for the safe return of their loved ones.

Our family was no exception, nor were the families of friends whose sons kept in touch with us. The four Jackson boys were in the service before the end of hostilities and our mother worked tirelessly in a hospital as a Red Cross nurse's aid throughout the war. The following letters and personal recollections reflect the flavor of this war from its simplest and less heroic phases to some of its more exciting episodes.

A FAMILY GOES TO WAR

CHAPTER 1

THE BEGINNINGS

IN EARLY 1940, Hartford, Connecticut was a very pleasant city in which to live. I had just joined the Aetna Insurance Company in an executive training program. I moved into a house off Farmington Ave. with six other bachelors. We were looked after by a black retainer who cooked and did what cleaning he thought necessary, which was limited but sufficient. The draft law had been passed and it was necessary for everyone 21 years of age and older to register and receive a draft number. Each day the newspaper printed two or three full pages of serial numbers. It was incumbent upon everyone registered to check the numbers; hundreds of numbers daily. If one's number was published, he was expected to appear at a designated staging area within a few days' time. This meant that he was a private in the Army of the United States. The first men were drafted on November 28, 1940. It was a deadly serious lottery. I saw some of my friends troop off to the military.

By the fall of 1940, when my fiancée, Mary French Mathes, had been graduated from Vassar College in Poughkeepsie, NY, we were married. The ceremony was in Greenwich, Conn. on September 14, 1940.

Our first year of marriage in Hartford was pleasant and busy despite the draft hanging heavy over my head. We rented an apartment at 19 Willard Street, just off Asylum Avenue, a main street that ran to the center of the city. At the Aetna I moved from the underwriting department covering the State of Texas, where I had worked under a couple of delightful Connecticut Yankees named

Mason Greene and Art Ives, to the Special Risks Department under the tutelage of Corporate Secretary John Downey, with other departments in between.

We were off on ski weekends in the winter months, and in the summer played tennis on the private courts of friends, and swam in their pools. Our social life was brisk.

With a Dartmouth classmate, Buzz Waters, I helped introduce Kingswood School to lacrosse. We started the Hartford Lacrosse Club and both played in positions of our choice, since it was *our* team. Always a defenseman in high school and college, I chose to play close-in attack and managed to score my share of goals, something I'd always wanted to accomplish. When Buzz went off to Marine training after the first year, I continued coaching at Kingswood a second year. In the summer I kept in shape on the tennis court playing on the Aetna tennis team in the Insurance League.

Soon after arriving in Hartford, I had enlisted in the Connecticut State Guard as a private, B Company, First Battalion, First Military District. For some inexplicable reason, I had resigned as of May 29, 1941, obviously well before the infamous act that precipitated the entry of our country into war. Perhaps my resignation was based on my concern that the Guard would be automatically enlisted in the U.S. Army. If I was to serve nationally my preference for service was the Navy; and indeed, it looked as if I was to serve.

There was hardly any doubt that the USA was headed for war. President Franklin Delano Roosevelt spent a great deal of time communicating with Winston Churchill in England. The sympathies of FDR, and those of the great majority of Americans, were clearly with Britain. The president sent a number of four-stacker destroyers to England, which earned mixed reviews from his countrymen. But most agreed that Hitler's Germany had to be stopped.

Indeed war was inevitable and every thoughtful person felt it. Some, such as my close friend, Chester S. (Bud) Brett Jr., who lived across the hall from me in Dartmouth's Lord Hall, opted for the military directly after graduating from college in 1940. He was in the first class of "Ninety-day Wonders." These men went into naval training on a grounded naval vessel called the *Prarie State*, shored up on the east bank of the Hudson River, at the edge of New York City's West Side Drive. Shortly after the completion of his training, he boarded the train for Los Angeles, Calif. and penned this letter to us. He was to be one of our most consistent correspondents during the early hostilities.

Santa Fe
The Chief
November 29, 1940
Dear Dick & Math,

You will never know how sorry I was not to be able to get up to see you before I left. Time just flew by, and before you knew it, I was back in Boston... At the present time I am somewhere west of Chicago. I have to report at San Pedro and then out to Hawaii to take over duty on the light cruiser USS *Honolulu.*

I got my commission okay, in fact I stood 58th in my class, Not too bad...

...I am not terribly enthusiastic about the whole thing for I have no idea how long I will be in it. I hated to leave Boston—awfully hard saying goodbye to the family...I am going to have a couple of days in Los Angeles before I report, so I am planning to have a right good last fling. I have heard that the battleship *Tennessee* gets into San Pedro on the first, so I'm hoping that maybe Web will still be with her, and I'll have a chance to see him...

...Good luck and I hope it won't be too long before we'll be together again.

Ever,
Bud

The above letter from Ensign Brett was followed by this one sometime later in which Bud refers to the fleet being on a war-time basis. With the clarity of hind-sight one wonders why our fleet was surprised by the Japanese attack on Pearl Harbor which was to take place in December of that year.

Bud also refers again to our mutual friend, my classmate, Bill Webster, another resident of Dartmouth's Lord Hall. Web was serving on the battleship *Tennessee* in 1941 after having received his wings from the Naval Air Station in Pensacola, Fla.

U.S.S. *Honolulu*
March 27, 1941
Dear Dick

How glad I was to receive your letter tonight. We sent one of our planes in to Honolulu this afternoon as we are now some 100 miles at sea. It seemed so good to hear about all my friends in the East and especially about Math and you. Sounds as if you had gotten in some wonderful skiing and how I envy you. And now you speak of spring. I wouldn't notice any difference for it has been just like what I have always known as summer ever since I arrived out here…

From everyone I hear of friends who have been drafted. I feel rather lucky that I am where I am, in spite of the fact that if we go to war the Navy will most likely see far more action than the Army…

…Maybe I should address you as coach. I think it is swell that you have the opportunity to take that lacrosse position and have the chance to do a little exercising. I miss it terribly, because we don't have much chance to get exercise on board. Also interested to hear of your progress in the insurance business…

…I am, by now well settled on board my ship. The *Honolulu* is a light cruiser of 10,000 tons with a heavy armament of 6" guns. There are about 45 officers on board and due to the fact that she is a flagship of the cruisers of the battle force we also have an admiral and his staff on board…

…The Navy is very much on pins and needles and every day are adding precautions. At all times we operate under war conditions. This means darkened ship at all times while under way. Absolutely no lights of any kind on the main deck and above including running lights. All ports are closed tightly with nothing but a battle circuit supplying lights below decks. This war-time cruising also means plenty of watches besides the regular officer of the deck watches. We keep some part of our five-inch battery manned at all times. My battle station is what they call sky forward. This is a director which houses a range-finder and a range-keeper which combined automatically compute and send to the guns all information which is necessary to lay the guns on the target. It is very complicated and I still understand only about half of it. Except when at general quarters (when the ship has all guns and battle stations manned) I am control officer in the sky forward. I haven't as yet had control of the battery while firing. Besides this battle station I have numerous duties on board. I am a junior division officer that entails many petty duties. Also I am a junior lookout officer. They are really keeping us busy. Besides all this I have to keep a gunnery notebook which means that I have an assignment to do every week and I must also do a day's navigation at least once a month.

At the present time we are as far at sea as we have been in the past week or so. We aren't due to return to port until the end of next week. It is beginning to get rather boring because we aren't going anywhere in particular—just cruising around in an assigned area standing by for an instant call. Up to now we have had two periods of fleet maneuvers and are due to have another the first of the week lasting until the 4th. During these maneuvers all the ships of the Pacific Fleet that are in these waters get together and divide up into two forces. They carry out bombing, submarine, and destroyer attacks. We do all right until it comes to repelling the planes and I really believe that a ship is almost helpless against any kind of strength in the air. During these periods one is very lucky to get even three hours sleep.

In a way I am interested in my work but speaking generally I will be very glad when the whole thing is over. I like the navigating and standing deck watches but the gunnery part involves a mechanical mind. Two or three times I have had complete control of the ship. This means making turns and changes of speed. Since the majority of times we are in company of some other ship, it really requires skill, which I sort of lack as yet, as you must keep station and distance at all times…

…It may be conceit but I think that I am doing the best of any of the reserves (7) on board and consequently I think that I may be sent to gunnery school this spring. These are usually held on board some ship so it wouldn't mean that I would get back to the States. But it might mean that on completion of the school I would be sent to some smaller ship as gunnery officer. Time will tell.

Dick, you don't know how mixed up I am about life in general. Here we sit, just waiting and waiting. I have a feeling that one of these days we will wake up to find ourselves at war and headed for some unknown destination. It is not the thought of war that moves me but the feeling that I am just marking time and not getting anywhere. I should be at home working for Chester S. Brett Inc…Hell, I'll be an old man by the time I get at all settled. Of course, I'm not alone in the situation and maybe shouldn't be kicking, but to me the Navy or the war is not my life or my future, but just a spot in which I have been waylaid. I am ready for what the war has in store for us and I am ready to start action any day and get it over. I must confess I am not absolutely ready to go home because I would like nothing better than the chance to see some more of the world. I have seen about all of Honolulu I want…

…I imagine that you have seen Web so that all I have to say is old stuff. I tried to look him up when the *Tennessee* was last in. I found out that word got out about his marriage and that he was therefore given his walking papers by the Navy. I'm curious to know his status now as far as the Navy is concerned. Keep me posted if you hear…

…The family is still at 138 Marlborough Street and would just love to see you. They have beds for you and Math. Don't hesitate to do it. Just let them know ahead of time and they'll be waiting…

Until later,

Bud

Bud Brett was sent to gunnery school aboard the USS *Boise*, another light cruiser similar to the *Honolulu*, the following June. This dashed his secret hopes to be transferred to a smaller ship in the Atlantic.

Bill Webster did indeed get ushered out of the Navy when he advised his superiors that he was married to Bunny Dorman, whom he had courted while at Dartmouth in Hanover, NH. It was easy for a pilot to get bored on a battleship where their work, generally a mail run, was almost incidental. Shortly after his dismissal he signed up with Curtis-Wright Aircraft Corp in Ohio, as a test pilot.

On December 7, 1941, we were on one of the Hartford Golf Club fairways, playing a neighborly game of touch football, when word was received by a blaring radio that the Japanese had attacked Pearl Harbor. War was declared and it rocked the nation. Life changed drastically that very afternoon. It made the work at the Aetna more of a chore than a job, and I noted that I was moved rapidly from department to department as people went off to the military. It obviously meant that I was "cheap and available" labor where needed rather than a junior executive learning his trade.

A few weeks after the Pearl Harbor attack I heard from Bud Brett in the form of a brief postcard. Bud recollects on that fateful morning he was the officer of the deck. He was looking forward to being relieved of his watch, and going ashore for a noontime beer party being arranged by the ship's supply officer. He would change into civvies, jump into his 1931 Model A Ford, and join the party. It was a Sunday morning; not much was going on.

He was equipped with a long-glass which he used to spot Top Brass in approaching motor launches. He wanted to be ready for them just in case they desired to come aboard the *Honolulu.*

The morning calm was suddenly shattered, as Bud saw planes that appeared to be dropping from the heavens. He first saw them as they dove down toward the battleship *Pennsylvania,* which was in dry dock nearby. He could see the red circles on the wings and immediately dispatched a Marine messenger to advise his skipper. He recalls saying, "Tell him that planes with red spots on their wings are attacking Pearl Harbor!"

After the initial assault by dive bombers, torpedo bombers immediately followed. A destroyer that was tied up at the same pier brought down a bomber with its 50-caliber guns, and it dove into the water next to the *Honolulu.* The plane sank even before it had a chance to burn. The plane was later brought to the surface and the two pilots were still at the controls. The plane was taken to Ford Island and one of the *Honolulu*'s pilots managed to get a piece of the wing. He gave half of it, including part of the red circle logo on the wing, to Bud, who sent it home to his father. It has since been framed for a keepsake.

Following the torpedo bombers skimming across the harbor came the horizontal bombers that dropped the big 1,500 to 2,000 pound bombs from some 3,000 meters up.

By this time, Bud, with his long-glass, was following their progress. "I actually saw a bomb come down," he recalled, "and it looked like it was headed directly for us." As he followed it with his glass, the image became so large, he lost it. A fraction of a second later the bomb smashed through the 18 to 20 inches of the dock, and exploded a few feet from the ship's hull. It ripped a gaping hole in the forward part of the port side below the waterline. The crew, who had started hurriedly readying the ship for the sea, had yet to cast off the electric lines to the dock. The ship lost power when the crushing of the bomb severed the connecting lines. Thus, there was no shipboard power, since the internal power of the ship had not yet been effected.

Bud was relieved as officer of the deck by the executive officer, and hurried to his battle station in the forward battery of five-inch guns, high in the superstructure. His efforts were primarily nullified by the lack of power, but the *Honolulu* was spared any further damage.

Three hundred and sixty Japanese planes had attacked the Pacific fleet, the Army aircraft at Hickam Field, and other nearby military installations. A total of 3,607 American servicemen were killed in the attack, and 1,145 were wounded. About 100 civilians were killed or wounded. Two battleships were destroyed; three more were sunk and later refloated; two others were heavily damaged, and one lightly damaged. Two light cruisers besides the *Honolulu* were heavily damaged. Three destroyers were put out of action, a repair ship was badly damaged and a mine-layer was sunk. The attack destroyed 174 Army and Navy planes.

Bud recalled that after the attack when the officers had collected in the *Honolulu's* wardroom to have an earned sip of coffee, the supply officer returned to the ship and told the gathering, "Oh, by the way, the beer party has been postponed."

After the completed emergency repairs on the battleship *Pennsylvania*, and a destroyer, the *Honolulu* went into the dry dock to receive a brand new bow, preparatory to a trip to San Francisco for full repairs. Bud's comforting postcard reached us just before Christmas.

Dec. 21, 1941
Dear Math & Dick
   Two weeks since the first attack and I'm very much a healthy man. Sorry I can't tell you about my activities but the censors just

don't go for it. Maybe some day…Am wondering if the Jackson
boys will be called in now. Write me and let me know all the dope.
Suggest you send letters via clipper.

As Ever,

Bud

Another very welcome letter came from Herb Mattlage. Herb was a
long-time friend whom I first met as an opponent on the football
field as a high school freshmen. He lived in Douglaston, NY, not far
from my home in Plandome on Long Island where I had grown up.
We later proceeded to the same college, Dartmouth, where we were
football teammates. Herb had opted for the Navy after graduation,
and was serving on the ill-fated USS *Arizona* on Dec. 7th, 1941,
which was badly mauled and sunk with a loss of most of the crew.
We had heard dire rumors.

January 18, 1942

Dear Dick

Thanks for your letter. It must be a very helpless feeling to be so
far away wondering if a fellow is still alive or what happened. The
reports about me were not true because I managed to come
through a lot better than you heard, but it wasn't easy. I was right
in the middle of it. Only one thing saved me from a lot of trouble.
I happened to stay ashore Saturday night with three other fellows.
This got me back toward the ship after the affair was well under
way and it was possible to see what was coming at me all the time.

I was out in a motor launch in the middle of Pearl Harbor,
headed toward the *Arizona* when the second heavy attack started,
and if you don't think that was a warm spot!! Well, I looked around
and took in all the action until a Jap plane almost landed on our
boat—it seemed so close that I could have reached up and touched
it. Then I hit the deck and stayed there for a few minutes. It would
be foolish to say that I wasn't scared because it was a terrible experience.

The whole affair was something that I couldn't comprehend. It
was so far out of my imagination that I didn't think to be afraid until I thought of what might happen if one of those little pellets
dropping out of the sky hit me. Then, after I realized, I reviewed

my entire life and thought of all the pleasant things that had come
my way.

I'd like to tell you more about the nasty business but the censorship is mighty strict and they'd be sure to cut the whole thing up.

I am safe and although a hell of a lot of shrapnel and other assorted bits of ironware came my way, nothing seemed to find me
for a resting spot. I've seen Warren Flynn, Bud Brett, Paul O'Brien,
Robin Hartman and a couple of others from Dartmouth. All fine.

Best,
Herb

Back in the mainland the country was arming rapidly, and military
dress was the popular sartorial fashion of the day. College graduates
were making the rounds of recruiting offices in search of commis-
sions as officers.

I made some sorties into New York offering my services to various specialty branches of the Navy where I felt I could be the most
effective.

An earlier attempt to get into the *Prairie State* V-7 program was
too late. It was filled up with a waiting list as long as the arm of
Frankenstein's monster.

I remember one interview with Lieutenant Commander Jim
Crowley, one of Notre Dame's fabled "Four Horsemen," and subsequently the football coach at Fordham University. He was fleshing
out a unit to go to flight training and fly bombers. I was rejected as
being too large.

One day, on just such a mission, I was in the back of a long line
snaking through the fifth floor corridor of a downtown New York
building. It was my custom to try and approach a yeoman and ask
for the names of the interviewers on the very slight chance that I
would hear a familiar name. This day, a yeoman advised that Ensign Jacquelin Daniel was one of the interviewers. Bingo! There
could be only one male Jacquelin Daniel in the world, and he was a
classmate of mine, and fellow football player at the Hun School. I
had later played against him in Palmer Stadium in the 1937 Prince-
ton-Dartmouth match-up. I sent in a note, and was immediately
jumped over the rest of the line. Jack sent me off to another inter-

viewer, who was a crusty, elderly fellow, who gave the feel of a neo-phyte naval officer.

It was a perfunctory interview. Apparently he was attempting to fill some sort of a security need for New York civilian shipyards and docks. It was not my cup of tea, but beggars can't be choosers. I recall one question he asked.

"If you had to reach a blazing fire four decks up on an ocean liner, secured at a dock, what pounds pressure or force of water would you need to reach the deck?"

I thought it a hypothetical question and felt cornered. But I didn't hesitate. "Roughly 500 pounds," I said.

"Good enough," he said, nodding his head vigorously. Obviously neither of us had any idea of the correct answer. "You'll be hearing from the Navy shortly." Then addressing the yeoman he called, "Next interviewee please."

My physical exam in the same office was negative. It seemed I had a pilonidal cyst, and the military, at that point, did not welcome anyone so inhibited. I was told it was a condition that, if inflamed, can be of such painful intensity as to render a sailor useless. Discouraged, after being on the brink of success, I decided, with the help and advice from my wife, and my parents, to have the operation to remove the cyst. Generally such wounds were left to heal from the inside out, which took a matter of over a month. I was concerned that the Navy would not have the patience for such an operation. But my surgeon suggested that in a matter of a few weeks the wound could heal from the outside in. So he sewed up the wound. In due time, I passed the Navy's physical.

On Monday, August third, I received a document from the President of the United States. It said, "To all who shall see these present greetings: Know Ye that reposing special Trust and Confidence in the Patriotism, Valor, Fidelity, and Abilities of Richard Seymour Jackson, I do appoint him Ensign in the Naval Reserve of the United States Navy to rank from the Fifteenth day of July, 1942." It was signed "For the President" in the scrawling old-man signature of Frank Knox, Secretary of the Navy.

CHAPTER 2

INDOCTRINATION

BUD BRETT remained a steady correspondent. In his July letter he comments on those close to me. He writes of his own parents' war work, something not unique to many parents considered too old for the draft but who felt the urge to help in the war effort. Pearl Harbor had brought the country together, a rare condition for a country that is powered by competition. My own mother was already volunteering as a Red Cross nurse in the Meadowbrook Hospital in Mineola, L.I., NY.

Bud mentions Jim Mathes, my brother-in-law, who had been my roommate at college. He was a leader who was always very much in the forefront of things. He simmered under his current inability to gain entrance into the military because of a chronic kidney problem. He watched his friends troop off to war while he, with his wife Mary Chapman, went off to a school of agriculture in Farmingdale, NY, on the end of Long Island. Bud mentions my brother Jeff, one of my elder twin brothers. He worked in our Dad's insurance brokerage house in New York City, and had volunteered to serve. He had been rejected by all services on the grounds that he was not physically fit. What Bud cannot mention is that his ship, on convoy escort duty between Australia, Somoa and the U.S. until late May, had traveled north for a two month operation off Kodiak, Alaska. She was eventually to screen the first American landings in the Aleutian Islands.

USS *Honolulu*
July 3, 1942
Dear Dick

At last we got some mail, the first since my last letter (Apr.28). What a God send mail is. It works wonders for the spirit. I received yours of June 1 and one each from Mother and Dad. They are well entrenched at Harwichport (Mass.) by this time. As you noted they are working hard and I guess will continue their work at the Cape.

I've been much interested in following your effort to land something in the service. I do hope you get your commission and that you would be pulling your share but still be able to be with Math. I know what a painful thought it must be to think of leaving her...

...Congratulate Jim on his progress in agriculture. It would certainly be foolish for Jim to throw himself in with the service after the trouble he has had. And isn't it too bad that Jeff can't land something, especially since he is so anxious. It seems sort of funny since we supposedly need men so badly. Maybe his time will come yet.

Mother enclosed your nice letter within hers. She thought I might like to read it, which I did. She was tickled pink to hear from you and is hoping that you and Math will be able to make it to Cape Cod this summer for a visit, but I suppose that gas rationing will pretty much restrict your travel. I get a kick out of Mother and her work. She said she has received her button denoting 100 hours service and really feels quite proud. One night she received a call at 4 A.M. to report and be ready to leave at 5:30 A.M. for Providence to give out food, etc. to men fighting a big fire in a lumber yard. She said it scared her but thrilled her no end.

You may now address me as Lieut.(jg). Yes sir, I have been promoted and that means about 50 odd bucks a week. I'm really salting away a nest egg for after the war. I'm putting away about $60 per month and hope to average about $150...

...We've been at sea for forty days so I have no more news. Please give my love to your family and Math.

As ever,
Bud

On the 8th of August I reported to the Naval Training Station in Newport, R.I. along with some 2,000 fellow officers just a step away from civilian life. I caught a train in Grand Central Station, in

New York City, and was extremely self-conscious in my brand new dress blue uniform with the brass on the sleeves and on the cap brilliant in the morning sun. The terminal was awash with sailors, many of whom courteously saluted, and I kept a good eye out for those who outranked an ensign to offer my salute. It was nerve-wracking. I ran into Robb DeGraff, a Dartmouth classmate, equally resplendent in his new uniform, and another Dartmouth '39er, Ensign Irv Naitove. Irv had been serving for a few months at a station on outer Long Island, and was extremely proud of the slight greening of his tarnishing gold brass, an indication of military experience. We were all headed toward the same indoctrination.

In Newport, we were assigned a barracks, a bed, a battalion and a battalion commander, a company, a company commander, a platoon, and a platoon leader. Our schedule was strict. We were up at 5 A.M. and, in formation, were taken for a run of over a mile. We were led by a chief petty officer, one of the ex-football players from the large mid-west colleges. A quick breakfast followed before some heavy marching around the training station. This generally was concluded with a gunnery course, or one on seamanship or even one on the social aspects of being an officer and a gentleman.

There was the occasional night shift, when we stood watch, mostly guarding against prolific rats that were as big as cats, and were busy socializing during the night hours. But mostly we marched, frequently along side companies of young seamen who made up the major population of the base, some 80,000 strong. They would hiss just loud enough for us to hear, "Goddamn Golden Boots." This expression was apparently prompted by the tan, or golden puttees laced around our lower legs, that were worn on the march. Although on the base we were forbidden to wear anything but khaki uniforms without shoulder boards, our obvious standing as officers was probably part of the golden implication. Normally the only indicator of rank was the stripes, so technically we did not outrank the seaman without our stripes.

Every five days we were allowed to entertain guests or wives at the Hostess House, just beyond the fence of the compound. My wife, now showing very early signs of her pregnancy, had made the trip to Newport and was tucked into a tiny boarding house room surrounded by other base wives. Every other week we were allowed off base, with our golden stripes restored, for 24 hours of freedom.

Math wrote frequent letters home to her mother, who naturally was worried about a daughter in her first pregnancy.

Newport, R.I.
Sat. Sept. 26, 1942
Dearest little Mrs. M.

Newport certainly is a busy place. My train was an hour late to Providence, but it didn't make any difference to me as I got to Newport well before 5. And you will be pleased to know that I didn't have to carry my suitcases once. I even had the taxi driver carry them up here, in 24 Greenough Place, to the 3rd floor.

Thursday evening, Mary Lou Fox drove us out to see her husband, Bill, and Dicksie. Dicksie had a cold—the tail end of one—but seemed to have shaken it pretty well by yesterday. We could only see them for a half-hour but it was good to see darlin' Dicksie for even that length of time…

…My room here at Weinberger's is still a myth. The woman in it isn't moving out until Monday, but Mary Lou Fox has been wonderful to me and I'm very comfortable staying in her room. We couldn't see the boys at all today to speak to, but this morning five of us wives drove out to watch Captain's Inspection. All the boys looked so neat, except for their queer little leggings…They really looked very impressive—and only with two week's training. I was amazed. Their marching is wonderful. Once while they were at ease Dicksie had a chance to look around for a short grin at me. I was so proud of him…We hope to see the boys tomorrow P.M., but everything seems to change at a moment's notice, so we can't ever be sure…We're having a most relaxing time and live for phone calls from the boys. Plans can never be made for more than a half-hour in advance as they can't be sure what's coming next. Seems rather poor organization but of course this is the first time they've had the indoctrination course here at Newport, so it's all new and mistakes must be corrected as they go along…

Lots of love to all,
Math

Another letter from daughter to mother was written on October 21st. It was full of little housekeeping notes such as laundry and the knitting of socks, etc. but there were a few illuminating items affecting the lives of the camp followers. This one includes a big bust.

Newport, R.I.
October 21, 1942
Dearest little Mummy,

It was so good to hear your voice last night and we're all so excited about the delicious chicken in store for us. You are so sweet and good to send it…We get so sick of going out to meals when the boys have such short leaves. It seems as though most of the leave is spent in a restaurant waiting for food to come. So Sunday we'll have a gay time…Chicken and salad here in our room in the evening—Becky, Mary Lou, Bill, Dick and I.

You asked about having Mrs. Weinberger cook a chicken here for us. The reason I said no, so quickly was because she never uses her oven, even for herself. She keeps all manner of things stored in it.

Dad phoned this morning about our B-gas ration card. I hope he found it…I asked him to send my Riverside Trust Company savings account book, as they say I must send it to get my savings out…

…The other evening Natalie, Helena, Becky, and Mary Lou were all in my room. Becky was sitting in one of the beds—and Natalie hopped on with her. Crash—Bang! Down went the bed. Mrs. Weinberger came running upstairs fully expecting to find broken limbs strewn about. No one was hurt. I apologized to Mrs. W. and she said it was all the fault of the furniture company. She said she couldn't be having her guests risk broken limbs, so today the furniture company came and strengthened all the beds in the house. It was the second bed to go down. Becky's went before…

…You wrote and also said on the phone not to go out alone after dark. Goodness, dear, I never do. None of us do. It just isn't done. We have so many of us that every place you go, there is always someone else ready to go. And at night, there are at least always four of us gals together. And then, we only walk home from supper in the dark. We're always home evenings early. We have such fun here in the evenings—knitting, writing letters, playing cards, listening to the radio, and chatting that there's no temptation to budge…

…We've been working at the Red Cross lately, making bandages. It's kind of boring but I felt guilty doing nothing at all.

Lots of love to all. Be a good girl and take good care of Little Mrs. Mummy.

Math

The food sent by Mrs. Mathes was a tremendous hit and served for any number of meals for the camp widows and their husbands.

We were already looking toward our next billet. Math wrote her mother on the 29th of October, "I am disgustingly and exceedingly healthy. So is Dicksie. I sort of hate to think of leaving Newport and all those swell girls, but Mary Lou and Helena will probably go to Washington, and maybe we will too."

There were many letters from the Aetna Insurance Company, because any I wrote to the company were passed from department to department and yielded an amazing return. Here is a letter from one of my closer associates, who had past service as a chief petty officer in the Navy.

Aetna Insurance Company, Nov. 10, 1942

Dear Dick (Sir, to you)

…It really doesn't seem as if you have had time to have done all the things you talk about in your letter. I got a big kick out of your waking the cooks, when on watch. From experience, I know how you felt when your order first began to take hold. The big question down in your boots is "what do I do if they don't pay attention to me?" But that deep voice of yours ought to get 'em…

…Jim J's boy Stewart, left in the draft yesterday and Jim is really broken up about it. They really are taking the boys now and I heard today that one insurance company was told by the draft board officials to prepare for all married men without children to be going by the end of the year…

You don't have to tell me, for I know, that your training isn't a life of ease. The simple fact of breaking away from home and all the things you hold of value is in itself far from pleasant, or reassuring. The unfamiliar environment and at times stupidly queer rou-

tine you are suddenly thrown into does not make for pleasure. And
finally you are supposed to absorb Annapolis in three months so to
speak. That means the hardest kind of work…And when you are
through the indoctrination period, then you have just begun.
Sounds tough and it is tough…But it's worth going through even if
you get nothing out of it except mental and physical discipline. But
you will get more out of it with your natural ability, your interest
in everything around you, your knack of making friends, and last,
but not least by any means, your very keen sense of humor and
imagination.

Dick I can't remember all the people who have asked to be remembered to you, but there are loads of them…

Here's wishing all good things for you.

Art

I heard from the president of the Aetna Insurance Group Companies, Mr. W. Ross McCain. Here are some excerpts:

The Aetna Fire Group
November 17, 1942
Dear Dick,

Your newsy letter has been received, and I am very glad to learn
how well you are getting along. The Officers and people in the
office are very interested in our sailor and soldier boys so I am taking the liberty of passing your letter around.

We are beginning to feel the strain of the war effort in more
ways than one. We are losing a number of employees. I believe the
company as a whole has over 300 out and we expect this to be 500
in the very near future.

They are making quite a drive in Hartford for company organizations to subscribe 90% of employees on a salary deduction basis
for the purchase of War bonds. Our companies are now over 90%,
being somewhere in the neighborhood of 95 or 96%, perhaps even
higher…

…Our marine losses were very heavy and will cost us a lot of
money this year. But it looks as if the new men whom the government has been training, like your own good self, have finally gotten
the submarines under control on the Atlantic Coast. So we are in
hopes that the losses are going to materially decline.

I was under the impression that you were going into some form of insurance work in connection with the Navy, and I am wondering whether this type of work has been postponed.

Sincerely,

W. Ross McCain

President

It was interesting to me that Mr. McCain was under the impression that I was going into some form of insurance work in the Navy. It would appear that some Navy recruiting officers had the same impression. Fire control, of course, means the control of the guns' fire, and is the heart of naval gunnery. But to the ill-informed fire control means controlling fires, which process, in Navy terms, is properly called "damage control."

By early November our Newport training was drawing to a close. Admiral Van Buren, Chief of the Department of Naval Ordnance, appeared from Washington, DC with a young Lt.(jg) at his elbow. The Admiral was on hand to address the 200 or so ordnance men in camp. We had all been O-V(P), (provisional), at the outset, but with the completion of the 90 day training we had been promoted to O-V(S) ordnance volunteer specialists.

The admiral was long in the tooth, and his speech, though designed as pep talk, fell slightly below expectations. He offered to answer any personal questions after his lecture, and so a long line formed.

"I was an English major in college, Sir, and worked in a fire insurance company before enlisting, but I know something of boats. I was brought up on the water. I don't see how ordnance can use me. Can I transfer to D-V(S)?" This was the designation for deck volunteer specialist, in brief, sea duty.

"Noooo. We need you to keep back those big forest fires in our ammunition depots out in Utah," the Admiral retorted, waving his arms dramatically as he kept back the imagined flames.

Each man was scheduled to visit with the Admiral's aide to discuss his next assignment. I explained to the young lieutenant my personal desires to go to sea, and my doubt as to whether my background suited me for ordnance. When I described the admiral's comments to him, he chuckled and said, "well, the admiral was not far off. We can always use a certain number of English majors to do security work and similar tasks. I can guarantee you that you will not end up in the gun factory in Washington where we are sending all your engineering classmates."

My orders came through in a matter of days. I was directed to the Naval Gun Factory in Washington, DC on November 9, 1942 along with 197 engineering classmates, and two fellow English majors.

CHAPTER 3

THE GUN FACTORY

THE NAVAL GUN FACTORY in Washington, DC, was bustling with energy. Our class of 200 men were introduced to the massive 16-inch guns. Some of the barrels were being forged in the factory, some were having liners inserted into the barrels. We made a side trip to the Aberdeen Proving Grounds where we watched the guns blast their projectiles out to sea. The ground shook and the air was split with the sound of thunder. One often wonders if all hands at sea were duly warned. We felt for any unadvised shipping in the area of the target.

Primarily we went to school. Our instructor was an English major left over from the previous class. The engineers were amused at the simplicity of the material presented and laughed their way through the course. It was all new to me and the other English majors taking the course. I marveled at such fundamental things as worm gears and was enchanted by this new world of physical science. I played back to my instructor all he had taught me, right out of the text, which earned me a top ten ranking in the class of superior engineers.

Math followed me down to Washington when I had secured living quarters. And this is what she had to say to her mother. Her reference to her sister Fuffy's party was a pre-nuptial gathering. She was to marry Frank Gerrity of Boston, soon to be Ensign Gerrity.

Washington, DC
November 27, 1942
Dearest Little Mrs. Mummy,

I wish you could see our little home. We're as cozy as two little bugs. And it's so nice to be on the same rug. Do you realize I haven't had my man coming home each night since August? Newport was, of course, nice because I had so many swell girls to fool around with and it made every 5th day come a little sooner. Here it is nicer because I have my Dicksie every evening from 6 P.M. on. And the days haven't seemed too lonely…Dick's friends, from Newport, the Deweys, should be moving in to the room next to ours this weekend. It isn't vacant yet though, but it will be nice to have his wife's companionship when they move in. We're pretty far from Mary Lou Fox who is also here in Washington.

Monday evening we arrived in pouring rain, got unpacked and settled. It was so wonderful to have Dicksie meet me at the train. Then we met John Willard from Hartford in town at 8:30 and went out to Cacky and John's apartment for supper. He has a law course in the evening, hence the late dinner…After eating, they drove us on to the center of town from where we took a bus home. We got here at 11:30, in the dark and rain. All the houses on the street are exactly alike. I wish you could have seen us going up to each one and peering at the number to find which was ours.

The Navy Yard is in southeast Washington, a questionable residential area. We're a good distance from the Yard, and surrounded by housing developments at DuPont Village, just on the edge of DC. A good spitter could spit over into Maryland. All the little houses are made of brick and vary only in doorways or other tiny differences. The girl, Edna McKinney, who owns this house is about 32, very talkative, but nice. She leaves early and comes home late. She's going to a welding school and looking for a defense job. Her side-kick, Margaret, is younger and home more often. Her job is a "folder." She folds speeches for the Senate, and works in the folding room where others do the same thing all day. During the busy season she worked from 8 A.M. to 10 P.M., but now she's laid off. I guess elections being over means fewer speeches…

…There are a lot of children in the neighborhood, some cute, some aren't. Ours will be cute. We'll think so anyway…

I wish you could have been a fly on the wall at our Thanksgiving

dinner. Dick got home about 5:30 P.M. and we went into town to
celebrate. The big city swarms. It's fun to go by the Capitol and the
White House. We went to a place called O'Donnells—delicious
food. It was crowded as most good places are. We waited for a table
and finally were seated on the second floor, right near the stairs. It
was like Grand Central Station; people coming and going all the
time and all looking to see what we were eating.

The head-waiter gave our waiter orders to man that station,
meaning serve us. But he didn't man the station very well. He
seemed confused. We had our soup served with dessert. But the
whole thing struck us as funny...

...We hate to miss Fuffy's party. If it weren't for the baby I'd, of
course, come up both weekends. I mentioned the probability of
going up for the 20th, and staying over until Dick came for Christmas. His face fell a mile. He looked so hard for a place for us to
live. No sooner does he find one and gets me here, than I suggest
going home. He's so good and I hate to disappoint him, I know
you and Fuffy will understand...

Dickens is kicking—enough so that Dick has felt it. He's kicking now so I must get my lunch. He must be hungry, and so am I. I
feel wonderful.

Dick is working nights this week to get material for his thesis.
Now he's gathered enough to write it. Wants to have it off his mind
before Christmas.

Lots of love from us both to all,
Math

Finishing in the top ten of my class qualified me for a special fire
control school, across the river in Anacostia, commencing on January 6, 1943. It was comforting to have my wife in Washington,
though our quarters that I had secured in the rooming house were
hardly palatial. But she had miraculously located a furnished apartment, almost on the river, in a place called Fairfax Village in about a
month's time. True, we inherited a bevy of cockroaches that we
chased into the apartment next door, until they were dispatched
back our way by our neighbors before the day was out. And there
was a sole bedbug that we captured during our stay. An oddity in
our life, we kept him alive but secured in a box.

At school we were under the tutelage of a chief petty officer. It was obvious to me that I was well out of place in such a gathering, but there was not much I could do about it other than to try and apply myself to the mysteries I was confronting daily. I recall so vividly hearing for the first time about synchro generators and synchro motors—ad infinitum. Finally, bursting with despair, I said, "Chief, I am sorry I have to ask this, but just what is a synchro motor?"

"Ask me anything you want," said the chief, as my more enlightened classmates snickered. "A synchro is the same as the old selsyn." He went on with the explanations of the marvels of the synchro. I remained in the dark, never having heard of the *old selsyn*, until a classmate later gave me the necessary information.

* * *

Another letter came from the Pacific fleet. Bud Brett had responded to my latest, advising him of my commission as an ensign. He also recounted his first stop off in the States at Mare Island (San Francisco) since leaving for Hawaii in 1940.

On November 3, the *Honolulu* had departed San Francisco, escorting a convoy to Noumea, New Caledonia. Later that month, the ship left Espiritu Santo, a port in the Vanucatu Islands south of the Solomons, where they joined Admiral Wright's Task Force 67 to reinforce positions on Guadalcanal.

U.S.S. *Honolulu*
November 22, 1942
Dear Dick,

Congrats on finally getting your commission. I know that I am very tardy in answering your letter. Imagine that it must feel awfully funny being separated from the Math kid but from the sounds of things it won't be long before you will be together again. I am very anxious to hear of your assignment. Knowing you the way I do, I can well imagine how happy you are now that you are settled...Do you think that there is really any chance of your getting sea duty? It would be something if we should some day meet up in a foreign port.

...After a total of about six months at sea without seeing what one could call civilization, we finally got back to the States. God,

Dick, you can't imagine how good it seemed. I didn't have time to tour east, but the family did make a quick trip out to the coast. Their stay was long enough for us to get caught up on the latest gossip…Until you have been separated involuntarily from your family, you can't imagine what such a visit means to a fellow. I thank my lucky stars that I have such a wonderful family.

I had a seven day leave and they were with me for about six days. The rest of the time there was a party every night. These short stays in port don't do your health any good. Met lots of gals but none that gave me much of a thrill, other than at the moment. So I left just as free as when I entered…

Once again we are on our way. Where and for what purpose or for how long I can't say. My work has just about tripled since I joined the ship. I now have my own division of 170 men and such an outfit can really keep you busy. The navy out here has really done a bang-up job. Plenty of action and so far…we have come out on the top.

I feel so terribly guilty when I sit down to write. I have so little to say and yet I do love long newsy letters. Write soon, and a Very Merry Christmas to you and Math, to your Mother, Father, Jeff, Harry, Betty, Tom, Jim and Chap, Mr. & Mrs. M and the rest of the clan.

As ever,
Bud

My brother Jeff was the first member of our family to enter the Armed Forces by a matter of 11 days. He wanted desperately to enlist following the Japanese attack on December 7th. The Army was accommodating. He received a draft notice and reported to a Mineola L. I. location, with his "hand luggage containing toilet articles." His physical exam revealed a "left inguinal hernia" and he was rejected and classified "4F remediable." This meant an operation by an Army surgeon at Uncle Sam's expense, or his own physician at his expense. If he opted for no operation at all, he would remain at 4F. He consulted Doctor Rathbun, the doctor who had brought all of the Jackson boys into the world, and the good doctor declared that Jeff did not need a hernia operation. So much for the draft.

Jeff then turned to the Marines, picturing himself resplendent in one of those smart red, white and blue uniforms. They agreed with Doctor Rathbun and required only that Jeff gain more weight to meet their stringent standards.

So he went home and left it to Mother to fatten him up. The Marines had given him two weeks to pick up the extra poundage and when he again stepped on the scales he qualified.

The new application form revealed that in that short interim he had experienced his 30th birthday which meant that he was too old now to enlist.

He then tried the Navy whose doctors also agreed with Doctor Rathbun, and he was told he'd hear from them as to a commission. While waiting for the Navy's decision, Jeff was approached by Charles F. Chapman, editor of *Motor Boating Magazine*, and a Plandome, L.I.N.Y. neighbor of the Jackson family. He was the father of Mary Chapman Mathes, my sister-in-law, and he was the author of the sailor's bible, *Piloting, Seamanship And Small Boat Handling*. Mr. Chapman had been asked by the Army to round up some small boat yachting types who could add some salt water flavor to the farm boys they had drafted for their new Engineer Amphibian Command. This latter was created because the Navy had refused to bother with any small boat fleet of boats that were not directly combined with their big ships. But the Army needed to keep the landing craft active for continual operations, and couldn't bind the landing boats with large Naval ships.

Mr. Chapman sent Jeff to Washington for an interview with the officer in charge of the program, and he and his medical staff found Jeff acceptable. He received a commission as a first lieutenant, commensurate with his age with an effective date of July 4, 1942. Actually that silver bar meant that Jeff was overqualified for the run-of-the-mill positions, and so he was primarily placed in a special slot, battalion headquarters of the 592nd Boat Regiment. In time they broke up the 592nd and divided it into three boat and shore regiments each with a boat battalion and a shore battalion. The former operated the fleet of landing craft, and the latter was to handle the beach operations, establishing supply dumps, setting up communications, and other base needs. First assigned as a liaison officer to a

Headquarters Company, Jeff ultimately ended up as a company commander.

Jeff's initial training was done on Cape Cod. The company didn't have many boats but did run a number of little cruiser-type crafts that had been contributed by patriotic citizens. They'd run mock landing missions to Martha's Vineyard from their base in Washburn Island near Falmouth. Some of the excursions involved some choppy seas, and all were conducted at night. The Regimental Commander was a veteran colonel who patterned himself after the famed General Patton. He wore two pearl-handled revolvers at all times, and toured the camp while standing up in a jeep. He was very tiny and tried to compensate by being spectacular. Jeff recalled one occasion when the company had been issued inflatable life-jackets. The colonel asked a G.I. if they worked. The young soldier said, "I don't know, sir." Whereupon the colonel promptly put one on and jumped into the water, pistols and all. It worked.

Mother visited Jeff at Camp Edwards, shortly after he started training. She watched from her hotel window and saw the tiny boats maneuvering amongst the many islands off shore until 4:00 A.M. Jeff looked fit, but with her Mother's intuition she could see the grind of training reflected in his eyes.

I had a brief visit with Jeff in a Providence hotel the week before he left for Fort Ord, California. I was but a short distance away at the Navy base in Newport at a time when Dad joined Mother for the weekend. It was short but satisfying and our parents were proud of their two sons in uniform as we moved about Providence in what turned out to be our last such meeting for the duration of the war.

On November 8, 1942 the boat battalion entrained for Fort Ord, in California. There they continued training, and once again, had almost no boats of any sort, but were kept busy with range practice, close-order drills, demolition training, etc.

On one occasion the outfit put on a full-dress review on the parade grounds. Jeff filled the position of adjutant, barking out the orders. (Battalion-n-n-n! Parade Rest!) He couldn't believe that his thin voice managed to reach far enough so that the men responded to each command.

*Ensign Richard S. Jackson, the author/editor,
pictured early in his military career.*

First Lieutenant Franklyn J. (Jeff) Jackson was the first of the Jackson boys to enlist in the military. He got his first furlough and first promotion (to captain) upon his return to the States after almost four years of combat in the Southwest Pacific Theater.

On another occasion the battalion went on a 2-day bivouac. Their campsite was in a nice little copse of scrub-oak trees, and the whole battalion came away suffering from poison-oak, with symptoms similar to poison-ivy. In those days, Jeff was immune to poison-ivy, and so escaped the itch.

We received a letter from Fort Ord on December 8, 1942. It sounded as though Jeff's outfit was preparing for a trip to the South Pacific.

Fort Ord,
California
Dec. 8, 1942
Dear Dick & Math,

High time that I wrote to you and Math, but darn it, the days do slide along somehow.

I'm glad to hear that progress is so good at your end, even though living quarters are cramped and holidays non-existent. Your program sounds plenty interesting, and I guess its refreshing to be specializing after the necessarily broad course of sprouts they put you through at Newport.

And isn't it swelligant about Math! Gosh, I sure am a lucky brother with guys like you and Ha picking such wonderful sisters for me, and now collaborating with said sis's to produce little nieces and/or nephews for me to be an uncle to. Please keep me posted on the big news, now, wherever I am, when the time comes...

...I would like some snapshots of you two, and they better arrive soon. Because I don't know at all how long we'll stay here.

Please give my best to all the gang, including, of course, the whole Mathes clan and the Dartmouh '39ers.

Lots of love to you both,
Jeff

My birthday being on December 16, I received some recognition along with gifts from my family and my in-laws. I wrote a thank-you note to Mrs. Mathes, her mother Gaga Dearborn, and her youngest daughter Fuffy.

U.S. Navy
Washington, DC
Dec. 18, 1942

Dear Mrs. M., and Gaga, and Fuffy,

Tires 'n gas 'n sugar 'n lots of other things are rationed. Now I think my own time appears to be rationed. So I hope you don't mind if I kill three cute little birds with just one stone.

Need I go into details on how delighted I was with my splendid birthday gifts. It was so great of you to think of me in such wonderful ways...

...Math made the day a very big occasion. She went out and got a little cake and fixed it with candles. She arranged my gifts neatly around the cake, and she beamed with delight while I gurgled with surprise and pleasure when each gift was opened. She is indeed a wonderful wife.

I must now work on my term paper on the 40-mm gun which, when it gets to the fleet, will be quite a gun.

Lotsa love,
Dick

1942 ended with a sobering Christmas gathering, but not as sobering as 1941, that had been hard after the treacherous Japanese attack on Pearl Harbor. That year-end saw the country confused and frightened, even though few were surprised that war was declared. But a year later the country was well into arming rapidly and building its forces almost overnight. A citizen military force was being trained and thrust into the breach as needed. Math and I spent a brief Christmas leave between her home in Greenwich, Conn., and mine in Plandome, New York. We had missed Fuffy's pre-wedding party, but we participated in her wedding ceremony at St. Bartholomew Church in New York City.

In early February some of our ordnance class were temporarily detached from our Washington classroom to go to the Anti-Aircraft Training and Test Center at Dam Neck, Virginia. It was a desolate spot on the ocean where we fired 20 millimeter AA guns at moving targets that were towed behind small planes. The pilots must have been frozen with fear.

By April 2nd we were detached from our Anacostia fire-control classroom and dispatched on a tour around the northeast to various plants that provided the equipment for the Navy's fire control systems. I joined nine other engineers in the tour. Life began to open up.

CHAPTER 4

NEW YEAR, SAME WAR

MATH'S BROTHER, Jim Mathes Jr., who had been in Agricultural School in Farmingdale, Long Island during 1942, was actively trying to join the Navy. His problem was a physical one. He had a chronic kidney condition, and was classified 4F in the draft.

Jim was an exceptionable person. A leader at college, he was voted the president of Green Key, the Junior honorary society, and the following year he was voted to lead the Dartmouth's Senior governing body. He was not a college athlete, being somewhat small of stature, though he had excelled in soccer and hockey at Phillips Exeter Academy. He was well liked, and seemed to have an interest in everyone he met. He was a superb listener, and gained wisdom from his listening.

We had grown up as close pals, living but a quarter mile apart in Plandome, Long Island. We had roomed together at college. He was an easy man to live with, if you didn't mind sharing him with his various animals including flying squirrels, a rhesus monkey, a marmoset, or a pregnant skunk who gave birth to 6 babies in our fourth floor room in Lord Hall. It was fortunate that this zoo did not share our room at the same time.

Jim had an active mind, and in the opinion of many, was destined for a position of leadership in whatever he tackled.

His father was a successful advertising executive and president of J.M. Mathes, Inc. at the time one of the country's ten largest agencies. Obviously he had a spot in the company for his only son but Jim had only briefly been folded into the organization. I think it was an attempt to please his father. His nature was softer than his dad's, but he was equally independent. He had a deep love of nature, and had momentarily opted for the life of a farmer until the war provoked his interest in the military. He had married a Plandome neighbor, Mary Chapman, who fortunately believed in him sufficiently to support his independence. In September of 1942 he had returned to his dad's agency in New York from where it was obviously easier to make the rounds in an attempt to join the Navy. He had also been taking flying lessons to earn a license which he thought might be his ticket into the nation's service. Despite his usual success in life, he could not be considered a glad-hander and it was out of character for him to use friendships or contacts for self-purpose. But in the matter of gaining entrance to the Navy, he resorted to just this, as his letters below might indicate. Following is a thank-you letter to his flying instructor:

> January 5, 1943
> Mr. Bugbee,
> Bugbee Flying Service, Inc.
> Twin-State Airport
> White River Junction, Vermont
> Dear Bug,
>   Thanks an awful lot for the prompt job you did on my log book. I am glad to have those extra hours in there. Thanks too for adding up my total. Good luck to you, Bug, in the New Year.
>   Yours,
>   Jim Mathes Jr.

He also enlisted the help of President Roosevelt's law partner, a classmate of his father's at Dartmouth, who was the president of the American Red Cross at the time.

January 26, 1942
Mr. Basil O'Connor
1220 Park Avenue
New York, NY
Dear Doc O'Connor:

Thanks so much for your typically helpful attitude. I was more than a little hesitant about calling you up because I know that you are plenty busy right at this time. However, I know that your word carries lots of weight and I am trying damn hard to convince the navy that I am perfectly fit physically.

Appreciatively,
Jim Mathes Jr.

He called upon Dartmouth's president, Ernest Martin Hopkins. Following is a letter to Al Dickerson, the Secretary of the College.

January 26, 1942
Mr. Al Dickerson, Secretary
Dartmouth College
Hanover, NH
Dear Al,

I received your note yesterday with President Hopkins recommendation attached. Many thanks for your help in this matter. I will let you know how I do.

Yours,
Jim Mathes Jr.

In time it worked! As of February 9, 1943, he accepted appointment and executed the oath of office in the Navy.

February 10, 1943
Lieutenant-Commander Boyd
Naval Aviation Cadet Selection Board
120 Broadway
New York, NY
Dear Commander Boyd,

As of yesterday I became an ensign in the Navy.

I am very happy and proud about this, and I am grateful to you

for your friendly and encouraging interview.
   I hope to be seeing something of you in the future.
   Very Sincerely yours,
   Jim Mathes Jr.

On May15, 1943, Jim went on to a Naval Flight Training course in Bloomsburg, Pennsylvania as an ensign, A-V(P) to rank as of Jan. 30, 1943. He had an almost impossible task to try and earn his wings. His classmates were all seasoned civilian pilots ticketed for training jobs in the primary Navy air programs.

*   *   *

One seasoned pilot who was an equally free spirit was named Fred Borsodi. We met Fred and his wife Marcia in Hartford, Conn. It was inevitable that we should meet because we had a mutual, very dear friend, Bill Webster. Web was a classmate of mine at Dartmouth, and he had been in flight training with Freddie, at the Naval Flight Training School in Pensacola, Florida, where they became close friends.

When we first knew Freddie, he was a test pilot for Pratt & Whitney Aircraft Corporation in East Hartford. He had served his time aboard the USS *Nevada*, and had been released from the Navy into civilian life when he had let it be known that he was married, a sin in the eyes of a young, building, Navy. But he qualified with the Army with an inactive reserve commission as a second lieutenant.

Anyone who knew Fred Borsodi thought he was a fabulous character and his fame has long out-lived him. He lived dangerously but not recklessly. He was one of those fellows who would try anything for the first time, just to have the experience. And because of a quiet, compelling, self-confidence he was generally successful at whatever he tried.

Born into a wealthy oil family in Texas, he had the financial means to exploit his burning interest in mechanical speed. He had raced his automobile in official road races in Germany and upper New York State, and had been instrumental in organizing the Yale University Flying Club. The last was featured in a *Life Magazine* article in which the contest on cutting rolls of floating toilet paper with planes was a featured, well-illustrated story.

But his interests were diverse and so too were his talents. He was an outstanding golfer with a scratch handicap, and he learned almost overnight to become an adept skiier. He shared my enthusiasm for drawing and sketching, and together we visited the Hartford Art School, one night a week, while Marcia and my wife, Math, visited at home.

After Pearl Harbor Fred was anxious to take an active part in the fighting war, but Pratt & Whitney considered his services too valuable for release. Eventually there was an ultimatum from the Army, active duty or resign his commission. He chose the former, giving up an attractive opportunity as chief test pilot to hustle into the uniform of a second lieutenant.

He became the father of a pretty little girl two weeks before he left for army training. Because he was an experienced pilot, he received only two weeks of fighter instruction with his squadron at a field in Providence, RI, before shipping out.

We learned from Marcia that his squadron was assigned to the British 8th Army. They arrived in time to start the drive against the forces of Germany's famed Field Marshall Rommel in North Africa.

In his first letter he refers to the impending happy event in my new family.

86 Fighter Sqdn., 79th Fighter Group
APO #3200 c/o P.O.New York
January 10, 1943
Western Desert
Dear Dick,

Well, Papa, I'm mighty proud of you, mighty proud indeed. A little playmate for our small moppet is on his (or her) way. You can see how pleased I am to hear from you as your letter arrived only yesterday and I'm answering already.

Marcia told me in one of her letters that you and Math were in Washington. Gad, it must be hell to be stationed in that mad house. From what I've heard you are lucky you don't have to share your room with one or two other couples.

I haven't heard from Web since I left the States, but it was good to learn from you that he is o.k. Quite often I think of all the fun we had skiing the past few winters, and I'm wondering what you and he were doing. Well, maybe those days will come back before too long. It will be quite a sight to see you streaking down some trail with your youngster right in your wake astride a couple of barrel staves.

I wish I could tell you all that has happened since we left the good old USA. It would fill a book. We are flying the P-40's (Hitler's secret weapon!) which needless to say is hardly the ideal fighter. We flew our own ships all the way across Africa—that certainly was an experience. Have seen a fair amount of action so far out here in the desert.

For amusement, I've been keeping a diary, taking pictures, and occasionally trying to draw, and finally, of all things, collecting poems and songs. You guessed it. 99% of them are filthy. We see quite a bit of the RAF pilots, and some of them know the funniest songs and poems you've ever heard. What a dirty old man I am!! But I think what fun it will be after this mess is over. You and I can retire to the study, drink brandy, and sing bawdy songs while Marsh and Math try and make the children go to bed.

This desert is hardly the spot I'd pick to live in although it is a perfect place in which to fight a war—nothing but sand to blow up. Strangely enough it gets damned cold out here, particularly at night. I sleep under four blankets regularly. Then too, this is the time of year for sandstorms. Often they last as long as two or three days, blowing like hell and so much sand you can't even see your feet. All you can do then is get under the covers and wonder why the hell we're fighting over a place like this. The native Bedouins are the dirtiest people I've ever seen. I used to think the Mexicans in West Texas were pretty bad, but no longer. These Bedouins make them look like the cleanest people in the world. They are terrific nuisances too because they will steal anything they can get their hands on. They even climb on the back of a moving truck, throw stuff off, and then jump off themselves.

It's past my bedtime. My last candle has burned down almost to the beer can so I'll have to hurry if I'm going to get undressed in the light. My flashlight is, as usual, out of whack.

Give my love to the little mother and write soon.

Ever

Freddie

Bud Brett came through with his first letter in the new year with multiple apologies for its *tardiness.* He asks more questions than he provides answers, though it is obvious the *Honolulu* has been in action.

His ship remained in the Solomons, operating in Task Force 67 in an attempt to engage the "Tokoyo Express," the line up of Japanese ships which sailed the so called waterway called "The Slot" in the heart of the Solomons to reinforce and supply their troops.

> February 1, 1943
> Dear Dick,
>   …I am just fine and in one piece, by the grace of God. One year of war is over and enough narrow ones to last ten. I hope that lady luck keeps smiling on us.
>   Did I tell you that I am now a Senior Lieutenant. I got promoted in November, or was it the first of December. I now draw $246 per month, not bad at all. And what is better, I save about $200 of it since I have no place to spend it…
>   I'm wondering where you are stationed…And where is Math? I see by the papers that the last of the Mathes girls has found her man. How are all your brothers? Do you like the Navy? Sorry to be asking so many questions but it has been so long…
>   Bud

Not long after Brother Jeff's December letter to Math and me, we received word that he had landed in the South Pacific. It was in the form of a copy of a letter received by Mother and Dad. He had departed the States on January 28, 1943. Copies were sent to us, also to Jeff's twin brother Harry, and younger brother Tom. Dad explained that henceforth, this would be the *modus operandi* for all such letters in the future. It made good sense.

In his letter he speaks of V-mail, a popular means of communication used during the war. It consisted of a form on which you wrote your letter, either by hand or typed. It was then photographed and reduced to a smaller size. This saved paper and standardized, as well as formalized the system.

At Sea

February, 1943

Dear Folks,

By now you probably realize that there has been a reason for the complete absence of mail from your Army son. We've just sighted land and I hope this letter will be on its way soon. Needless to say it has been a long, long way to travel. By the time it arrives you should long since have received my safe arrival giving my new, permanent mail address. Incidentally, you and everyone writing are to use V-mail as it takes less space and is more dependable. From now on this correspondence matter is going to be more irregular but I intend to write as often as I can, and tell as much as I can. I hope that you all will keep the letters coming because they sure do mean a lot.

Our trip was a pleasant vacation, really. Lots of lazing about under a hot sun and doing little of anything. I had a couple of busy days since I was appointed Ship's Finance Officer and had to pay off the troops on pay day. Can't tell you how much dough I handled, but can say it was so large it scared me. I ended up with an error of 42 cents in my favor.

Your son has become quite an actor. Had a part in the ceremonies when we crossed the Equator and also in a musical comedy we put on last night. Both entertainments went over successfully and did a lot to liven up the trip.

There was one disturbing factor on the trip. We just happened to cross the International Date Line on my birthday which meant that we skipped that day completely. Does that make Harry a year older now? A fine state of affairs, one twin a whole year older than the other.

I upheld the family honor by not getting sick at all, though most men did. However, the sea was pretty smooth most of the time, I'd say.

Love,

Jeff

Bud Brett, our voice from the Pacific Ocean, continued to keep up a lively correspondence. He was more interested in what I was doing, than perhaps even I was. The *Honolulu* was still operating out of Espiritu Santo, New Caledonia, and active in the Solomons.

USS *Honolulu*
c/o Fleet Post Office
San Francisco, Calif.
March 22, 1943
Dear Dick,

They have really sent you around for the training. I do wish that I could have had the opportunity because it certainly would do me a lot of good. All that you're learning is what I am dealing with all the time, except, of course, your equipment is newer.

My acquaintance with the Mark I computer has been a peek at it now and then aboard other ships. The Mark X Rangekeeper is my stand…[censor]…a bit in detail following my duties. I am 3rd Division Officer (AA division—5" 25, 20-mm & 1.1's) situated in the forward director which controls four of the 5-inch guns. At present I am fourth senior in the Gunnery Department and about tenth senior aboard. If I stay here long enough I'll soon be finding myself really holding down a big job, that of Anti-Aircraft Officer.

I'm responsible for the guns and most of the fire control equipment and I must admit that about half of the latter goes sailing over my head. But I have a pretty fair first class petty officer so I usually manage to get along.

Don't get the idea that the old chiefs are the boys to depend on, because Fire Control is relatively new and some of our best men are the young fellows. As for me, I know something about a lot but not very much about any one thing. I would like to work with the computer, but I guess I better drop this subject before I step on the censor's toes.

Well Poppa, how does it feel to know that shortly you will have a little offspring? Be sure and give my love to Math.

As Ever,
Bud

CHAPTER 5

THE THIRD SON IN

BROTHER TOM, the youngest of the four Jackson brothers, was the next in the family to go into the military. While finishing up at Rutgers University, he was already a member of the Army Enlisted Reserve Corps. Toward the last few months it was anybody's guess as to whether Tom would be graduated and receive a diploma, or whether he would enter the Army short of his immediate goal.

It was difficult for me to think of Tom as a soldier. I suffered under the conventional delusion of an elder brother, that he seemed much too young. Point of fact was, though five years my junior, he was now 21 years old. But what would the Army, with its regimentation and its mass mannerisms, do to a young thoroughbred like TCJ? It seemed to me that his nature was too fresh, vibrant and rebellious.

The answer wouldn't be long in coming. He was ordered to active duty on March 25, 1943. His first letter sheds a new light on the "Army sergeant."

> U.S. Army Reception Center
> Fort Dix, NJ
> March 22, 1943
> Dear Folks,
> I am well, healthy and uniformed. Since we are liable to be shipped out at any time I think it wise if you don't write until I get more permanently established, as I understand that frequently letters aren't forwarded. I don't want to miss anything.

My R.O.T.C. experience has helped immeasurably in marching, and we're ahead of everyone else here in that respect. It's funny how similar a reception center is to a prison. We are very restricted to one small area. Our non-com officers are like jailers, our fatigue uniforms are exactly like those worn by prisoners even to the little caps guys are issued. Everyone is pathetically eager to get shipped out, as if they were after a parole.

The sergeants are wonderful. Just like in the movies; big beefy guys who scream and swear, and make wonderfully sarcastic remarks. Of course they occasionally scare me, but generally I find them delightful.

My uniform fits fine, and I guess I look like everyone else. I find the food very nourishing and really damn good. I understand it's considered to be relatively poor considering the haste and disorder which predominates.

Love,
Tom

Fred Borsodi's next letter from North Africa brought the war considerably closer to home. He described an exciting adventure in the heart of the desert.

Tunisia
March 25, 1943
Dear Dick,

Everything is popping along fine at the moment and if all goes well there is a chance that we may be sent home for a breather following the successful conclusion of this campaign. The enemy is pretty well cornered at the moment but this fellow Rommel is really a wizard and I feel that he is still a good way from being beaten. General Montgomery is equally as clever and if we can judge from past events, he will turn the trick. It's a funny thing how your views change out here. I remember back in Hartford, when Crete and Tobruk fell to the Germans it meant hardly anything to me. But out here, your outlook certainly changes; the mere shifting of the bomb line a few miles, one way or the other, means all the difference in the world.

I wish you could have seen the last field in which we were located. It was only a short way from Tripoli and must have been quite a spot before the war. I suppose it was the Italian version of Pensacola or Randolph Field. There was a lovely swimming pool, bar, officer's club, and very snappy quarters. When we got there it was mostly in ruins, but you could see that at one time it must have been beautiful. On the field were tons of Italian and German equipment, wrecked airplanes, etc., so you can imagine what fun I had rummaging through the piles. I also had a chance to fly a captured Italian Macchi fighter. It was quite nice, and would really climb.

March 30, 1943

Hello again; now to continue the letter. Sorry for the delay but I have been very busy in the past few days. First of all I was hit by anti-aircraft fire (the ship, not I) while strafing some German and Italian troops about five miles over the lines. The darned airplane caught on fire and naturally young Borass turned for home. Before I could get to our lines the ship was burning so badly that I had to jump. The ole' shoot opened o.k. and I landed right between the two lines. I just lay flat as there was a helluva tank battle going on. Finally I was picked up by a New Zealand tank.

A funny little sergeant poked his head out and said, "You alright, Yank?"

So I scrambled in and off we went, and what a ride it was. The tank eventually broke down and we had to beat it the rest of the way on foot. One Jerry nest on a hill had spotted us and were peppering away while we beat it. I don't think Jesse Owens could have done a much better job on that first hundred yards than we did.

Eventually I was taken to the Colonel in charge of the advance units. What a cool turkey he was. He greeted me cordially and said, "You'll have to excuse us if we neglect you a bit but we're right in the midst of a battle you know."

He said I was fortunate that the wind was blowing towards our lines, as I had bailed out over the Jerry side, and the wind had blown me to the space between the two forces.

I spent the night with them in the hills and got a ride back to the landing ground the following day on a hospital plane. Needless to say it was quite an experience.

How is Math? I believe you mentioned in your last letter that the new addition was due to arrive sometime in April. Gad, that's pretty close now, isn't it? When all the excitement is over, write me all about it as I am anxious to know whether it's a boy, girl, or twins.

Gotta close now and write Marcia. Give my love to Math and write soon.

Ever,
Freddie

Tom, our latest recruit, was still too new to find fault with the Army.

Fort Dix, NJ
March 31st.
Dear Folks:

Already I feel sufficiently at home in the Army, so comfortable in fact, that I dodge KP with the best of them.

Although I had a bad cold when I came down here, I have already lost it without taking any medicine at all. This amazes me since we have to get up in the morning when it's very cold, with our collars open, etc. But I guess the army life is healthy. One thing, though, my army shoes hurt my heels terrifically. I've been trying to soften them with saddle soap.

There is an awful lot of procedure you have to go through here, such as IQ tests, aptitude tests, physicals, venereal disease tests, articles of war movies, inoculations, and vaccination, uniform fittings, etc. But so far I like the life fine. Of course it's much different here than it will be in my permanent base. It is all rather aimless as there is nothing to learn.

Love to all,
Tom

Tom has a few more words about the non-coms in his next letter.

Fort Dix, NJ
April 6, 1943
Dear Folks:

…At present I have a job working in the supply room handing out bedding. All the non-coms come in and hang around to talk, and they are all old experienced army men. Naturally they talk

about their commissioned officers, and from this talk I am getting
a definite idea of what a good officer should act like. These guys really respect and admire a good officer, and are quite contemptuous
of a bad one. If I finally get to be an officer, I know I'll be a lot better one because I came up through the ranks, and I shall be thankful that I started off as a private…

Love,
Tom

In the meantime, we received another letter from Jeff. We had
guessed that he was in Australia, but not until the following letter
arrived were we sure.

Hdq. Company—Boat Batt.
APO #301
c/o Postmaster, San Francisco, Calif.
April 11, 1943
Dear Folks,

About time I wrote in detail, telling you how things are going
with this branch of your widespread military representation.

Today is Sunday and I'm sitting at a home-made table under
the trees in front of my tent. The wind is blowing softly and the
sun is shining brightly. Black and white magpies are chattering and
once in a while a kookaburra bird gives out with that awful hyena-
like laugh. It is a mighty serene setting indeed. And serene is the
word for me and my heart, too. I certainly have little to complain
about. Almost each day brings at least one letter from you folks,
and that really is a comfort. If it meant so much to me back in the
States you can imagine what mail does for me here. I'm in the
pink, physically and mentally and am ready for anything that
might happen.

Australia is much like America, in many ways. They have rolling
plains and huge ranches on which Americanized Australian cowboys herd white-faced cattle just as they do in Wyoming. The
towns have theaters which show American movies almost exclusively. Most of the popular songs are American, although there are
some catchy Aussie tunes too. The people are quite friendly, especially the girls.

On Saturdays, in the towns, everyone goes to the race tracks.

They love horses, and everyone bets. I made a visit to a track
awhile back and picked up 2 quid ($6.50) for my day's work.

Here at camp we are quite comfortably fixed. We show movies,
(just as new as the ones in town) four times a week in an open-air
amphitheater constructed by the soldiers. Makes a pleasant setting
with stars overhead. Of course, it's a different sky, with the Southern Cross instead of the Dipper, but it still makes me feel closer to
you each time I look up because some of the stars are the same. I
figure we have those few in common anyway…

10,000 miles of love,

Jeff

Jeff's regiment had disembarked from the States on February 18 at
Brisbane and camped for four days at a racetrack outside of Brisbane. They then moved to Rockhampton, north of Brisbane where
he wrote this letter. However, in that four-day interlude, Jeff was directed to head a small group of regimental clerks from the finance
division to transport $1,000,000 in cash to a bank in Brisbane. The
regimental general had strangely brought along the money for pay-
roll purposes, and on arrival was told to get rid of it as the troops
were to be paid in Australian shillings.

Jeff had to sign for the money and get it to the Brisbane bank
pronto. He took a train with a couple of second lieutenants and the
squad of clerks armed with rifles and one "tommy" gun. These men
had not seen a rifle range in many months and Jeff was obviously
nervous.

The Australian railroad cars were like those in England and
Europe, each car compartmentalized with a door to the station
platform for each compartment. Jeff had the funds stashed in one
section, locked the doors and drew the blinds. He was a nervous
wreck until they got to Brisbane and loaded the several bundles of
bills and bags of coin into an armored car, and reached the bank.

There he was greeted by a typical British banker right out of
Savile Row. He was in a handsomely tailored Poole suit, shining
Peale shoes, a stiff white collar on an immaculate shirt and a regi-
mental-striped tie. The banker arranged for the counting, and
fortunately, it was all there. Jeff received a proper receipt which he

described as the "most beautiful piece of paper that he had ever held, except for his wedding license." He guarded it carefully until he got back with the unit in Rockhampton.

The bank president, for his part, was delighted to have all those American dollars. So everyone was happy, and the bank probably made a bundle in foreign exchange.

At Rockhampton, the regiment built an attractive chapel out of Australian ironwood, a tough, hard tree that was difficult to saw and trim. It was open on all sides, but had a thatched roof.

The delighted chaplain, a genial Catholic priest from Notre Dame, conducted a Protestant service as well as a Catholic one each Sunday. He was, according to Jeff, a wonderful guy whose hobby was collecting the names of popular songs. Needless to say, Jeff contributed to his list. He later volunteered to fill a vacancy in an infantry regiment and sustained a combat injury that earned him a Purple Heart. After the war he became Archbishop of Atlanta, but suffered a fatal illness, and died at a relatively early age. Jeff declared that he would never forget Father Paul.

The regimental commander, a graduate of West Point, called Jeff in early on at Rockhampton and ordered him to establish an Officer's club. This Jeff did, creating a gathering place using a hospital ward tent, equipped with home-made tables, a bamboo bar with bamboo stools and an enlisted man to act as barkeep and chef. Native bamboo was excessive, growing all around the area. They served Australian beer and steaks. One of the features of the club was some sort of gambling game that one officer suggested to Jeff. Soon it was apparent that "the house" was losing each time, so Jeff finally shut it down. The big winner appeared to be the sly guy who had suggested the game.

* * *

The first step of Private Tom Jackson's career became past history. He seemed to enjoy the prospects of the second phase.

708th Training Group, 73rd Training Wing
Sq. A Room 113
A.A.F.T.T.G.
Atlantic City, NJ
April 11, 1943
Dear Folks:

Excuse me for not writing for so long, but I've been rather busy. As you have no doubt noticed from the address, I am now located in Atlantic City with the technical command of the Air Force. I guess they suspect me of having hidden technical talents.

Accommodations are fine. I'm living in the luxurious Shelburn Hotel on the boardwalk. (This is, by no chance, the one we stayed in the time we saw Dick play football?) At any rate, each room has a private bath with a nice big tub which has salt water taps as well as fresh. The food is very good, much better than Dix, with plenty of fresh green vegetables. The only thing I miss so far is companionship as I have become separated from people I know, and the guys I am now with are typically dull, drab, uninteresting Jersey boys. However there are many southerners here, mostly from Tennessee and Kentucky, and they help to keep me amused.

This is where I get my basic training. I will be here from three weeks to three months. After this I will be sent to an advanced school, according to how I have been classified from my various I.Q. tests, aptitude tests, interviews, etc.

The first week we are confined to the hotel (except of course in connection with our training), and the entire seven days is given over to our getting oriented. This includes various instructional movies, lectures and the like.

Incidentally my ROTC helps me not at all since we have to learn everything all over again from the beginning.

I am impressed by the efficiency and intelligence with which this place is run. I am indeed fortunate to be picked up by such a fine organization.

You folks will be interested to know that we are *required* to sing when we march! This is hard on me, but I find myself shrieking "God Bless America," "Roll Out The Barrel," and "Over There," with the best of them.

Love,
Tom

The complicated Army personnel machinery clanks along as a company of tanks might, and Private Jackson is swept up into the line. Every man must fill his niche.

Atlantic City, NJ
April 15, 1942
Dear Folks,

   ...Saturday we find out to which part of the Air Force we have tentatively been assigned. Right now we are listed as belonging to the Signal Corps Wing, but I hope desperately to get into Air Force Intelligence. I'm very interested in this work and fairly well qualified for it. It would be a good background and training for me. Besides, I'd hate a technical job. A lot hinges on the interview, so I intend to turn on as much personality as I can muster.

   The other day I was one of a selected group who took a three hour test to see whether or not we are sent back to college for advance training. That would be alright too, but I'm not too optimistic as the test involved a lot of math and physics, and you know how I am in that stuff...

   Love,
   Tom

It's hard to imagine Tom doing the arduous task of Army KP. It just doesn't match his character. But the Army doesn't favor its privates.

Atlantic City, NJ
April 18, 1943
Dear Folks,

   I just got off KP which is a 15 hour steady job starting at 3 A.M. I don't feel much like writing.

   I'm eventually going to clerical school, as Intelligence guys have too many special qualifications that I don't have. This job of mine has both advantages and disadvantages. It sounds like a routine and boring job, and not at all soldierly, and I'd like to contribute more directly to the war. But, there is less chance of being a casualty, and I'll be getting invaluable experience and background for the future...

   ...I've had KP twice this week, which is back-breaking, and then marched and exercised strenuously. And I've seen two movies this week, which I consider important, since they offer some much needed diversion to me...I am inquiring about getting a clerk job here, and I rather think I'll be able to get it. I like Atlantic City...and it's a much better set-up than the average Army post...If I get shipped out of here to clerical school I will be sent to God knows where. This way I quietly spend the three months preliminary to my Officers Candidate School application near home and will be able to partake of the plums thereof...

Incidentally, Moth, in case you have forgotten, that translation of the New Testament was by Moffatt, and no other one will be acceptable to me. My interest in religion has not been accelerated by the war, and by approaching maturity, or by Dick's recent letters. I simply realize that the Bible occupies an important part in life and literature, and I'd like to increase my cultural capacity by becoming quite familiar with it...This methodical and self-enforced education process is what I can remember Jeff railing against. He maintained that it was bad to learn something for the express reason of improving yourself. He thought you should be naturally interested in a subject before you tried to familiarize yourself with it. Then I agreed with him just because he said it. Now I disagree violently.

Love,
Tom

CHAPTER 6

AS ORDERED, A BABY IS BORN

ON APRIL 13TH, we gathered at the General Electric plant in Schenectady, NY, the same ten men now officially under the leadership of Senior Lieutenant William F. Terry, of New Haven, Connecticut. He was our senior in age and rank.

This plant turned out the Navy's prize anti-aircraft gun, the 5-inch 38-caliber mount, the heaviest caliber cannon for aerial work. As such, the gun had to be agile in movement and elevated, depressed and trained sideways at a rapid rate, making it capable of tracking a fast enemy fighter plane.

At the plant we were placed under the tutelage of a young engineer who knew the operation of the mount backwards and forwards. After a number of classroom sessions going over the schematics and other features of the mount, we were finally introduced to the real thing. It stood alone, in a separate room, like a precious sculpture, the one dominating feature in the center of the space. We were separated into five two-man teams and each had its opportunity to work on the big gun. Our young leader would maladjust the mount, so that it worked contrary to the norm. It was the job of the two-man teams to put things to right in as short a time as possible. Each two-man team, in order, was locked into the room and told not to come out until the mount was running properly. It was a heady challenge for most of us, and certainly for me. I was, however, extremely fortunate in that my teammate was an Ensign Kay whom I considered the brightest member of our group.

Ensign Kay and I were left to our own devices in due time, and both of us went to work. The first thing I noted was that when I worked the elevation controls, the barrel of the big gun depressed.

"Simple," I said. "Why don't I take care of this. It's only a matter of switching leads isn't it?"

Kay nodded in agreement and continued with his examination of the operation of the gun. Unfortunately he happened to be working directly under the barrel of the gun when I switched the leads and tested the action of the barrel. It came down with a thud on top of Kay's head. As I looked around in dismay he crumpled silently to the floor.

"My God, I've killed him," I uttered to nobody. I rushed for the door and tried the knob. It was locked as promised. I pounded heavily. No one came. I knew that we were to be left for three-quarters of an hour, and if we hadn't done the job in that time, we were to be released, in presumed disgrace. We were only seven or eight minutes into our trick.

I checked the body. Kay was breathing, but his eyes were closed, and he was limp. I looked around for water, and spied a sink against the wall. I filled a dirty glass tucked off in a corner, and poured it over his head. His eyes popped open. He was okay, but he had a horrendous headache, and was relieved when our trial was completed, and we were released. But we'd managed to make the gun operate perfectly.

On Saturday, May 1, 1943, we were separated from the GE plant in Schenectady and ordered to report by 0800, Monday, May 3 to the GE Ordnance plant in Pittsfield, not far over the state line in Massachusetts. Here they made the directors for the AA batteries, the units that controlled a battery of guns from a central source high in a ship's superstructure. We traveled between stations in three private cars, one of which was my black Ford. We pooled the gas coupons that each man held, which were sufficient to get us to our destinations.

I was concerned about my wife Math. According to the doctor, she had been due on April 26 for the birth of our first child, and I was a nervous father-to-be. I screwed up my courage and made a trip on Saturday, May 1, into the Pittsfield plant where I was to report on Monday, and requested an interview with the Captain, USN, in charge of the operation.

"Captain, I live in Greenwich, Connecticut, only about a two and a half to three hour drive from here. My wife is scheduled to have a baby shortly. I wondered if it would be possible to take an emergency leave if the baby is born?"

He looked up from the pile of papers that he had been glancing at as I talked, and without the slightest understanding twinkle in his eye, he said, "I suggest you tell your wife to have her baby on Sunday."

Math was accommodating. She had our first born, Richard Seymour Jackson Jr. on the very next day, a Sunday, May 2. I had driven to Greenwich late Saturday afternoon. By 2:30 A.M. Sunday, pains were such that we went off to the hospital. Nurse Effie Hubbard, a reliable friend of the family, and Math giggled and laughed happily between pains in anticipation of the arrival. In time she was taken to the labor room and I was banished to the downstairs waiting room where expectant fathers pace.

Well after daylight, Effie appeared and announced for all to hear, "It's a boy!"

After ascertaining that mother and son were *just fine*, I followed her upstairs, and waited briefly until she came out from the nursery with my son. He was swathed in blankets, red, wrinkled, his brow folded down over the top of his nose, his head misshapen, and two small feet sticking out from under the package. Strange, but he looked absolutely splendid to me.

I made a phone call to Pittsfield and secured a one-day liberty on Monday because of the event. Could it have been approved because I noted that my wife had followed the captain's orders to deliver on Sunday? Whatever the reason, it made little difference in my training. Indeed, in Pittsfield, we learned absolutely nothing about the gun directors they manufactured, or anything else. We sat around in the lobby waiting room in the plant playing games, such as *Battleship*, and *checkers*. We were bored. It was the only plant in which our time was wasted.

*   *   *

As I recalled my happy days in Hartford, I had played softball on Chet Loomis's team. It was a good team, and we used to beat some of the top industrial league winners about town.

We met Chet through his wife Jean, who had gone to college with our Plandome friend, Mary Chapman, who had in time married Jim Mathes. Chet and Jean were a fine couple and their son, Teddy, I recall, was the first baby in whom I took an active interest. We were his first *sitter,* when we offered to keep an eye on him one night during a command night out by Chet and Jean.

Chet joined the Army just a few weeks after I entered the Navy. He took his preliminary training in Florida, and was successfully graduated from OCS as a second lieutenant.

I saw Chet for the last time during the war in Washington, DC. Only a few weeks later we learned that he had embarked for Africa. He was with the Air Transport Command, and he wrote shortly after he had landed.

Hdqts. AMEW
PO 625
Miami, Florida
May 1, 1943
Dear Math and Dick,

...We had a good trip over without incident...Life here isn't bad but there are a few things we miss, especially home-cooked food, a hot shower, a cold glass of American beer and a little diversification from the nightly movies which is the only thing to do in the evening. There is however, a marvelous beach and wonderful surf. It is great fun to ride the waves on surf boards but Sunday afternoon is about the only chance we have to take advantage of it as we work 6 days a week.

This afternoon there are horse races downtown. They have them every Saturday and it is practically a holiday with everything in the town closed up tighter than a drum. The jockeys are natives and they run around the track clockwise and the favorite always wins, which means you're lucky to get your money back.

It doesn't look as if I shall be able to get home for a good while, possibly not until after the war is over... Teddy probably will be in

Yale and taking me to the Yale-Dartmouth football game when I
see him next…I imagine Math is about due. Write me with the
details.

Every precaution is taken against getting malaria which is quite
easy to pick up, but the Army has done a marvelous job in the control of it, and the number of cases is small. There are more damn
bugs and insects of all kinds, sizes, shapes and colors and we have
to sleep under a very fine mosquito net. It reminds me of my days
at camp.

I must get dressed for dinner which means taking off my short
pants and pith helmet and putting on long pants, high mosquito
boots which look like the kind the cowboys wear, and a necktie.
This is considered formal dress. In the day we go around practically
naked.

Let me know of the progress of your family

Best,

Chet

In the meantime, Brother Jeff sent Mother's Day Greetings home
to Plandome from the South Pacific. We always called our Mother,
Moth, pronounced "Muth" by simply dropping the "er."

Australia

May 9, 1943

Dear Moth,

Today I visited our little chapel and sent up a prayer for you. To
me, it was the only proper way to recognize Mothers' Day. It would
have been nice to send a wire or a phone call, but it's so impractical
to try such things. A wire might take 4 to 10 days, and must be in
stock wording; the same message for everyone. A phone call is handled indirectly. I call the censor and he calls you. I'm hoping you're
tuning in on my thought-waves, though, because I surely am
thinking of my Mom, and not only on Mothers' Day.

I'm sitting in the new Regimental Officer's Club. It is only a
tent but serves well enough as a place where the officers can go for
a nibble or a nip. The Colonel put me in charge of it and so I'm
struggling along with one more duty. We built a fine grill and serve
steak sandwiches at a shilling a throw (16 cents). I got my men to

cut some bamboo and built a fancy bar. We have tables and chairs made of boxes and so far the joint seems popular.

Nothing new at this end. Things appear to be going along smoothly, as before. I'm still well and happy, though every once in while I get to wishing this thing was over and that I was on my way home. Then I realize that what the heck, so far I've been lucky, and the main thing is to finish the job at hand.

Thanks for all your fine letters.

Love to all,

Jeff

On May 8 our ten-man team learning about fire control left Pittsfield to report to the Ford Instrument Company in Long Island City on 0800 May 10th. I was to learn about computers at Ford Instrument, and stable elements in the Arma plant in Brooklyn. We reported early each morning at the plants, but had our weekends free. We were not due until July 12, to leave the area and journey to the York Safe & Lock Company in York, Pennsylvania. This gave me some time to get to know my new son. The weekend that Richard Seymour Jackson Jr. smiled was a banner day. By now, the fold over his nose, the misshapen head and the red, wrinkled skin had been fashioned into a handsome face.

By July 19th we had completed our training in York, Pennsylvania where they made the 40-mm Bofors gun mounts. We were billeted at the YMCA in York, and spent but seven days digesting a three-week course on the intricacies of the gun mount. We received instruction in the operation, maintenance and repair of the hydraulic portion of the York power drive unit as well as the electrical portion of the drive. I managed to pass the final qualifying test, in good shape. My head was buzzing with information from many sources, and scads of notes which I was allowed to take from station to station.

I was quite anxious, after ten long months of study, to receive an assignment that might take me to some outpost of the active war where I might be of immediate value. It had been rumored that we would each be sent to a repair ship, and for some time I had been busy preparing myself mentally for such duty afloat. It would be terribly wrong to give the impression that I was not concerned about leaving my family. But it had always seemed to me that a fellow should be ready and willing to sacrifice the pleasures of home and family, if he honestly feels he might be of more value elsewhere. The Navy doesn't leave such decisions to its personnel; nevertheless, I felt it was important to prepare oneself for whatever might lie ahead.

I received my orders in York assigning me to the Boston Naval Yard. I immediately called Math and plans were formulated. We decided to drive to York Harbor, ME to her folks summer home, just an hour or so drive north of Boston, where we'd leave Dickens in good hands and scoot down to the Boston area to look for housing. We had a 9-day "delay and proceed" leave that I had been granted to accomplish this deed.

We found a delightful little house at a reasonable rental with a stone façade, off Brattle Street in Cambridge, that fit our needs neatly.

I reported for duty in Boston on July 29, 1943, my mother's birthday.

CHAPTER 7

CONGRATULATIONS

FROM THE Solomon Islands came Bud Brett's congratulations on the birth of our son.

USS *Honolulu*
c/o Fleet Post Office
San Francisco, Calif.
May 18, 1943
Dear Dick,

Congratulations to you and Math! I am so doggoned happy for you and my only regret is that I'm unable to get to Greenwich to get a look at the youngster. I take it for granted that the moniker will be RSJ Jr. I think that is fine also. Isn't it nice that mother and son came through it all so nicely and how lucky you were, Dick, to be able to get the time off to be present.

I agree with you in your remarks about the peculiar methods of the Navy in trying to fit a man for a job. For your sake I hope that you get a chance to get some sea experience, but at the same time I'm not wishing any distant outpost on you. It's much more important for you now that you have a junior that you be with your family.

Not long ago I received a peach of a letter from your mother. Wasn't she sweet to give me a thought. I will write soon, but be sure to give her my best.

Bud

From Bill Webster came congratulations, and an update on his activities. He was now a test pilot for Curtiss-Wright in Columbus, Ohio. We were aware that he had, at one point, deliberately put a new plane into a spin, then found he could not regain control. The plane plunged 10,000 feet and he climbed out of the cockpit and jumped. His parachute landed him in a field with a sprained ankle. The jump qualified him for the "Caterpillar Club" so named because parachutes at that time were all made of silk. It seems to me it could have been this parachute leap that caused Web's hip discomfort he describes below, or it could have been the pounding he took as an interscholastic and intercollegiate high hurdler.

May 24, 1943
Dear Dick,

The good news reached us just before I left for the hospital. Bunny and I were certainly thrilled at your new addition. Sorry that the small gift which was sent some time ago to your Washington address was so slow in reaching you.

Your news of Borsodi was good to hear. I have heard nothing since his letter about six weeks ago.

Since seeing you last month we have been very busy at the plant. For a while things were really humming and for the first time all of the pilots were busy. However the rush didn't last for long and with the slack period in sight, I decided to have this operation on my hip. Doc claims it is calcium on the hip and he hopes to carve it out, and relieve the situation. So here I have been for two weeks, and I'm going home tomorrow...

...After several days at home we are going to take a short trip to Kentucky for a rest and a chance to stock up on whiskey. Our liquor stores closed 2 weeks ago and will open up for rationing the first of June. We are allowed 1 pint per person per month!! Or 6 quarts a year. We all might get our health back here in Ohio.

Take good care of Dickens. Bunny joins in saying best to all.
Web

Air Cadet William O. (Web) Webster, who served aboard the USS Tenessee *as an ensign after getting his Navy wings at Pensacola Air Base. Released from the Navy because of his married state, he spent the war with Curtis-Wright as a test pilot.*

Major Frederic A. Borsodi flew fighters in the African campaign against Rommel in 1942, and led his squadron of P-40s on to Italy for further battle. Returned to the U.S. he was stationed at Wright Field and was the chief of the Fighter Branch Flight Section, Air Terminal Service Command at Wright Field. He lost his life over London on January 31, 1945, demonstrating a new Army jet to the brass.

Chester S. (Bud) Brett Jr. became an ensign when he was graduated from the first Prairie State class in New York City in 1941. He experienced the Japanese attack on Pearl Harbor as the officer of the deck on the light cruiser USS Honolulu. He was separated at war's end as a Lieutenant Commander.

Captain Chester Loomis, Army Transportation Corps, who served most of his overseas duty in Africa.

Chet Loomis received the news of Dickens' birth in Africa, and was warm in his congratulations.

May 18, 1943
Dear Dick,

I am glad to learn officially that you have at last joined the ranks of men. Anybody can have a girl but believe me, it takes a man to have a boy. I'm tickled to death to hear the good news and to know that both are doing well. It sure is a break for you to be able to live at home for weekends. It sounds too good to be true to me. I can't wait for that Yale-Dartmouth game in 1962…

…The latest excitement here is killing rats. Last night our house boy bagged seven. We ran them out of the door and he clouted them as they went past. He really is a gem, and can do anything. I wish I could bring him home with me. You should see him coming down the pike with bundles three times his size balanced on his head…

When are you going to get through going to school? From my experience with Army schools, one can't learn much practical experience out of a book. We have to start from scratch because conditions aren't the same in any two places. In the Navy, however, I suppose the technical side of things is the same wherever you are.

Haven't heard from my little spouse in several days. The darn mail is very uncertain. Some letters take two weeks and one fellow got one from Boston today in four days. They come in bunches. I got thirteen one day last week which means I had to take a day off and read them…

Jean sent me an article about Fred Borsodi which appeared in the *Hartford Courant*. He's quite a boy…

As ever,
Chet

Brother Tom reports he's off on a trip, but security limits as to exactly where he is headed. He has a promotion to report.

> En Route
> New York Central RR
> May 26, 1943
> Dear Folks,
>
> Well, I'm taking a little trip. Right now we're approaching Chicago, and will continue on, although where they won't tell us. Speculations are ripe as to where it will be, and the Dakotas, Colorado and California, are all mentioned by rumor mongers. It'll be a clerical school anyway, but whether it's a college or a regular army post we do not know.
>
> Troop trains are good fun because there's really nothing to do but sleep, talk, and read. The only trouble is that they're very crowded. Two guys sleep in the lowers which makes it quite uncomfortable...
>
> ...You folks will be interested to know that I've been promoted to a Private First Class.
>
> Love,
> Tom

Tom's trip ends in a mid-west heaven.

> Company A.
> Army Administration School
> Branch Three
> Brookings, South Dakota
> May 27, 1943
> Dear Folks,
>
> As you can see from the address, I'm in Brookings, South Dakota. It is a beautiful little town housing South Dakota State University, which has an equally attractive campus featuring fine trees, wonderfully green grass, and spacious meadows.
>
> The whole set-up seems ideal. We room in a sunny and nice dormitory, have unbelievably wonderful food, served by ladies (no K.P.) and have very fine officers although our sergeant seems unpleasant. The course will apparently not be too difficult, and I am practically a sure thing for a good non-com rating if I do okay. As a

PFC I get $54. Also Officer's Candidate School appointments
seem to be well within reach, so it will definitely behoove me to get
on the ball and create a good impression...

I'm staring at everything suspiciously around here because there
must be something wrong. No Army post could be so good.
There's even a swimming pool, and beautiful co-eds...!

Love,
Tom

Tom would get no "toy doll" at the county fair for guessing weight.
In a letter to us, he misses Dickens weight by eight pounds, which is
more than somewhat in a three-week-old infant.

Brookings, South Dakota
May 29, 1943
Dear Dick and Math,

As pleasant as it is out here, and as wonderful an opportunity as
it is, I still would like to be available for an occasional peek at Dickens—all 22 inches and 16 or so pounds of him (All measurements
approximately correct?)...

...I am just about to go into town for the first time and have the
USO people sew on my newly acquired chevron, which should be
a considerable source of satisfaction. Unfortunately I will have little
chance to do anything else but walk about and observe the 5,000
population, since I have been out of money, and will not be paid.
At least I am getting practical experience on whether or not the
best things in life are free. I have concluded that they aren't after a
rather lonely walk about. Money is still something to be treasured,
and a joy and thing of beauty forever.

It's interesting to know that South Dakota is one of the few dry
states. Nothing but 3.2 beer is sold. But as one of the officers said,
"The bootleggers are so plentiful that they have to wear buttons to
keep from selling each other."

People are very cordial to us. Maybe they are trying to treat us as
they hope their boys are being treated wherever they are.

Love,
Tom

Tom is feeling the war even in beautiful Brookings, and he is beginning to get bored with his idyllic posting.

> Brookings, South Dakota
> June, 19, 1943
> Dear Folks,
>   …I'm getting tired of this mid-western rural existence.
>   I just got an Alumni Bulletin and am quite shocked to note the "deaths in action" of guys whom I remember as being very much alive and seemingly indestructible. It's those kind of vibrant, colorful people whose death gives you such a turn because it's simply impossible to realize that they'll never laugh with you again. Their death just doesn't seem consistent or at all logical with their personality…
>   …It certainly is hot out here. The sun beats down unbelievably, and its 93 degrees in the shade…And the mosquitoes are plentiful also…But out here you get so much more an awareness of America. The people are sturdy, healthy, plain and pleasant people. There are none of the screwy, and unhealthy folks you see around New York.
>   But I'd much rather live in New York…
>   Love,
>   Tom

Jim Cooney is usually referred to as "Dinner," not because of his gigantic appetite, but because his twin sister couldn't pronounce the name, Jimmy, in her early years.

Dinner is one of those homey, close friends whom we've known all our lives. It is impossible for us not to enjoy his company. He is a good, kind and comfortable person who generally keeps us convulsed with laughter.

Being single at the time, and feeling his patriotic duty acutely, he was unhappy with his job at the Fleetwings Aircraft Corporation in Bristol, Pennsylvania. There was little room for argument that he was benefiting the country in his capacity as a leading engineer of the Fleetwings plant, but it wasn't active enough for Dinner. After months of quiet bickering with Uncle Sam and the Fleetwing's management, he was able to join the Army as a buck private in basic training as an Air cadet at Yale University, his civilian alma mater.

He managed a Sunday pass and came to Greenwich to see our new addition. He helped us make imprints of Dickens' feet in Math's Baby Book, and helped wash the sole of Dickens' feet when the process was complete. We played croquet, and we laughed over the hazards about the lawn provoked by indiscreet dogs. Here is his thank-you letter.

> Squadron G
> New Haven, Conn.
> June 22, 1943
> Dear Math and Dick,
>
> It was wonderful fun being with you all at Greenwich Sunday, and thanks loads for everything.
>
> I was glad to see your son, Dickens, looking so well. He has grown a lot since I last saw him and sure is a good little guy. Say hello to him for me and tell him if he ever needs his feet washed again to get in touch with me...
>
> The Air Corps has no croquet sets up here so you can see that it was merely a matter of being out of practice. I doubt, however, even if we did have the facilities, whether the mallets would be as carefully balanced with droppings as mine was. It was excellent fun, needless to say...
>
> Dinner

The news of Dickens' birth continues to find its way about the world. From a wind-swept battle with Rommel in the African Desert, Airman Freddie Borsodi sends congratulations. Since his last letter he has been promoted to Captain with some new responsibilities.

> Capt. F. A. Borsodi, 0420960
> 86th Fighter Squadron, 79 Group
> APO #485 c/o Postmaster, NYC
> July 9, 1943
> Dear Dick,
>
> I have been very bad about writing you and feel thoroughly ashamed. But I promise to be a better correspondent in the future.

First of all, you and Math please accept my belated congratulations on the arrival of young Richard Jr...You've probably already had him fitted out with skis for the coming winter...

...Now for a bit of news from this section. First of all I don't expect to come home for a good while—possibly not until Christmas. It's very hard being away from Marsh and the babe but frankly I'm rather glad to be out here. My feelings haven't changed since leaving home. Right now there is something big in the wind and I certainly don't want to miss the show. I feel as though I'm just beginning to learn a bit about this business and don't feel qualified to go home yet, and tell how it should be done. Incidentally, our Squadron Commanding Officer was recently released and I got the job. Naturally I was pleased to get the position but there is a good bit of responsibility and plenty of headaches connected with it, particularly out here where there is so much for the men to bitch about. At times it's the devil keeping peace in the family.

Marsh sent me the announcement drawing of young Richard in your Navy hat. It certainly was clever. I assume you must have kept up the drawing. When this mess is over, you and I will have to take up our course at the art school again.

I had a letter from Web a while ago. Apparently he is rather dissatisfied at Curtiss and is contemplating going to work for Grumman out on Long Island.

Ever,
Freddie

From the other end of the world, Brother Jeff wrote a birthday letter to his mother, trying to gauge its arrival on the right day, July 29th. There is a suggestion that he is on the move, but he seems to be enjoying it.

Australia
July 11, 1943
Dear Moth,

First of all I feel fine and happy and doing work I like. Each day brings new experiences and at present there is certainly no monotony.

But this is a birthday letter. I know it seems as if I never write unless it's someone's birthday, or Christmas or something. This is a condition I swear to correct, and immediately. While it's true that I've done my share of shifting around, that's no excuse for a guy to fail to write steadily and often to the swellest dear family in the world. Most of all, though, I want to get this particular letter off so that you'll get it at the exact right time...

...Despite the war, despite three sons in the service, despite rationing, and worry and all that, have a Happy Birthday, Moth. Forget all those troubles and unhappy things of this crazy world, if only for one day. You can't know how much I miss you and how much we all (your five men) love you! And listen, don't think for a minute that we all won't be together again, enjoying the good old days once more, before too long. Time has a way of slipping along, and no matter how measured in years and months, we'll get there somehow. Just so long as we don't lose patience...

Love to swell ol' Dad, and everyone in the clan. Especially to you, the Birthday girl!!!

Jeff

It is often difficult for the layman to follow the intricacies of the Army. Brother Tom makes a noble attempt to do just that re: the Army Air Force.

July 18, 1943

Dear Folks,

Well, I have been assigned to a tactical unit in the Air Corps.

We got assigned to various branches of the service which are attached to the Air Force. Such as Signal Corps (to whom I was previously attached), quartermaster corps, ordnance, etc. But I am in the straight Air Corps. The whole thing is called Air Force. Being assigned to a flight unit, of course, means that I am almost certainly booked to go over, but it will probably be some months from now.

I am quite delighted, as I think this is the best branch of all. If I must be a clerk, I want to be a part of a unit which really does something concrete, so that I can see myself helping in the effort, rather than some tiring desk work which some WAAC should be handling.

I've been reading a lot. Recently I've read two books by Christopher Morley, one by John DosPassos, one by J. F. Marquand and one by Somserset Maughan, a book of plays by Ibsen, and twenty other varied plays. I have also read *One World* by Willkie, and my Modern Translation Bible.

Don't write me here anymore as I believe we're due to leave here next Wednesday.

Love,

Tom

Tom went further west with his next move, and finally found his specialty.

Army Air Base

Salt Lake City, Utah

July 24, 1943

Dear Folks,

Since I am going to take a short course in cryptography (coding and de-coding), I will be here an extra two weeks or so. Consequently I will welcome letters...

This cryptography looks like a good thing. It's very interesting work, and actually good fun. It will give me some more qualifications and also a foot in the door of intelligence.

...This base is a bombardment unit, and because bombers need plenty of space they operate in this spacious western area. From here we get assigned to one of the units and will get sent abroad with the unit in from two to six months, depending on what stage of training units are in when we join them.

...Utah is pretty. We're surrounded by mountains. People only stay here a few days, just long enough to get equipment, physicals and assignments. It's sort of a big reception center. There are lots of guys here who've been overseas, with ribbons and medals.

Love

Tom

CHAPTER 8

THE NAVY YARD

ON JULY 28, 1943, I reported to the Navy Yard in Charlestown, Mass., the same yard in which the revered frigate, USS *Constitution*, lay along the docks, her work accomplished years ago. I was advised that I was to be attached to the South Boston Yard, an adjunct of the venerable Charlestown Yard. The main feature of the South Boston Yard, which was outboard of the Charlestown yard in Boston Harbor, was a huge dry dock. I learned that this was perhaps as large as dry docks go, and indeed, during my stay at the yard, it managed to house at one time or another, the French battleship *Richelieu*, the British battlewagon *Lloyd George*, and, if memory serves, the *Queen Mary*.

I joined another 5 ordnance specialists. We were now officially designated S(03), which in Navy language meant we were fire control specialists. All of the group of ten specialists with whom I traveled were ordered to a Navy yard. One of the ten, Ensign Jack Kenny, from New Haven, Conn. was now an associate in my new post. Our immediate boss was a full lieutenant, Donald Loomis, a nice man, slightly older then his charges, but who had come out of civilian life, as we all had, with one exception. He was a fellow ensign named Grimes, a career Navy man, who had been promoted to his rank from the highest enlisted rating of chief warrant officer. This suggested that he probably totaled more hours in the gunnery field than our entire complement in Boston. However, most of the equipment on which we worked was new and forever being upgraded as the war progressed, which leveled the playing field somewhat. Still our veteran was a font of knowledge. He was quiet and capable, and we became close friends, and worked many jobs together, particularly with the new Navy computers used for setting a gun on target. We learned the new trade together.

But it was rare when we had the opportunity to use our knowledge in a positive way. Our primary task was one of liaison. The "bread and butter" work, for the most part, was accomplished by the civilian yard workers who represented various trades such as mechanics, metal workers, pipe fitters, etc. The Yard's ordnance planning officers issued job orders that they fashioned from sitting down with the gunnery officer of each new arrival and discussing his ship's needs. Work orders were issued for each job. Perhaps one of the 40-mm quad mounts needed work. It was our responsibility to see that collectively the various trades properly pursued the work orders and accomplished the repair or replacement job correctly before the departure date of the ship. Because our specialty, fire control, was so intricate and frequently so new as to be beyond the average yard birds's ability to cope, we had the assistance of assigned experts from the manufacturing companies, civilian employees who provided the know-how for repairing a unit. For instance, he could be from Ford Instrument Company, which provided the computer systems. The massive computers for the most part were housed deep in the belly of a ship in a room called the plot room. It was here that information was assimilated from the gun directors, high in the ship's superstructure where sighting the target was most efficiently accomplished. Such information was immediately digested, and sent out to the big guns to automatically provide the proper aim.

Or it could be an expert from Arma Corp. of Brooklyn, NY, the provider of a ship's stable elements. These were gyroscope units tied into the fire control circuits. They provided the necessary stability for firing guns off the unstable deck of a ship diving through ocean waves. Its input was continually fed into the computers, and hence the guns kept their aim on target.

The ordnance repair officers' shifts were generally rotated. About every fourth week or so, I would spend a month or two on the night shift. This was a quieter and less active shift, and yet it burdened an officer with more personal responsibility simply because at night, he was his own boss, so to speak.

Being at the Yard at night was an experience in itself. It is possible to drum up a very romantic picture. The tall superstructures of the big ships poking up in the blackness looked just a touch like a group of ferocious hobgoblins. The occasional blue flash of welders' torches threw an eerie glow and like fireflies gleamed momentarily in front, and then flashed at ships on either side, and back again to the front. The silence of the night was split intermittently by the rat-a-tat of the chippers' hammers. And when the noise ceased, the silence could be overwhelming. On some particular nights, if you were to look sharply, you'd spot the tall outmoded towers of an old battleship, the *Nevada*, which on Dec. 7, 1941 rested at the bottom of Pearl Harbor. You'd find her on the north jetty, where the wind blows in from the ocean and bites at your face on an unseasonably brisk September night. By the signs of the activity aboard her, even in the early hours, you'd sense a struggle of old age; an effort to get her into shape for another journey, maybe just once or twice more before she groans and chugs to a final stop.

For that matter, if you were lucky, you'd see a huge black mass of steel representing our newest and largest battlewagon, the USS *Massachusetts*, sliding noiselessly from her pier and nosing out to sea. All lights extinguished, you'd guess her size only by the phosphorescent splash of the securing lines as they were tossed from the shore, and hauled aboard ship. The shrill pipe of the bos'un splits the darkness, articulating the next command, as the ship disappears into the blackness of the night.

A casual walk about the Yard, and more than likely you'd pass a Norwegian sentry standing silently at the gangway of an old US four-stacker destroyer. Now she's His Majesty's Ship... Or it could be a clumsy British Marine, standing guard at the brow of his cutter; the stock of his rifle lying flat on his shoulder, and his big boots suggesting the stolidity of England.

If you happened to be about when the big French battleship *Richelieu* was on hand, and you walked aboard her, it would be a pleasant surprise to be officially piped aboard, with the sailors lined up on either side, rifles at "present arms." It would not take long to realize that she is complete in every way, even to a well-stocked wine cellar, and the characteristic over-sized breed of French rats. Vive-la-France!

It was this ship, trapped at its port in the clutches of the invading Germans, which made a daring escape by brazenly putting to sea. Indeed it was well after the rape of France, much to the Nazi's chagrin. Her whereabouts a mystery, she was hunted by the German fleet. In time she appeared in the friendly Yard of South Boston for repairs.

It would not take long either, to spot another massive superstructure, this one belonging to the ex-luxury liner *Manhattan*, with floodlights playing on her yellow priming coat of paint down by the floating dry dock. Renamed the USS *Wakefield*, she was converted to a troop ship. She caught fire at sea, and ablaze, was towed back to Boston, a black and hollow shell.

On one morning in October, I had just completed my night shift and was preparing a brief report for the day crew. I had only one concern. My report could impair my long-standing friendship with John C., the Yard's civilian engineer from the Ford Instrument Company which manufactured fire control systems. C. had been under extreme pressure. He was trying to locate the cause of a malfunction in the controls of turret #2 of the USS *Canberra*, a newly launched heavy cruiser which had reached the Yard on October 14, 1943, and was being readied for line duty.

Each turret of this class ship contained three eight-inch guns (an 8-inch diameter measurement at the end of the barrel) protruding from the turret's slanting front. The turret's tons of weight was moved effortlessly on a circle of ball bearings at its base. The turret was trained or moved horizontally by a Waterbury Speed Gear. The guns were elevated, moved vertically, by the same power gear. The action was controlled by a rush of oil forced at extreme pressure through a tangle of copper pipes that responded to the opening and closing of valves. The valves moved in response to signals from electric generators in a gun director situated high up in the ship's super-structure. Similar synchronous motors located in the turret faithfully duplicated the directive from above. Such a system made it possible for a gunnery officer to aim or direct his ship's main battery of three turrets, with the necessary information, to hit a distant target.

The job order, which was provided by the Yard's naval planning office, was distributed to the civilian workers who were charged with completing designated work on ships in port. In this case I was responsible to the captain of the Yard for seeing that the work was completed, and completed on time. Time was one of engineer C.'s problems. The *Canberra* was behind schedule and Captain Bush, USN, the ruling officer of the Charlestown and South Boston Naval Yards, was under pressure from his superiors. They had demanded that the ship depart for line duty in twenty-four hours without fail. C. had left strict instructions for the night shift to leave turret #2 alone. He would, he said, return with a fresh look at 7 A.M. to tackle the problem for one last day and hoped he could find a solution.

I dutifully passed on C.'s words to the civilian "leading man," the boss of this particular yard crew, who was delighted to learn that another fruitless night would not be spent working amongst the pipes. It is not much fun rooting around in the bowels of the turrets. I often likened the tangled piping to how I imagined one's intestines might appear. The tangle extends up, down, and around for two decks within the turret, and even under the best of conditions the pipes perspire oil, and coat themselves and the decks below as well. A man crawling on or about the piping literally wears the oil and even a welcome shower after work doesn't relieve him of the odor and texture of the stuff. Under the best of conditions, it is warm in a turret, particularly during the summer months, and this can be brutal if one is spending the better part of a day among the pipes. But until the cause of the malfunction was found, the turret would not respond properly to its signal from above, and the *Canberra* would be at risk on the high seas.

Certainly a method for spotting the solution to such a problem came from a careful study of the schematic, a large detailed diagram exposing the intricacies of the system. Indeed, I had studied these plans, ad infinitum, as, of course, had C., each looking for a possible explanation of where the error in the piping flow might be located. A myriad of valves controlled the oil flow, and were controlled themselves by the electric impulses from the synchronous system. Only one valve in the entire complicated system was a manual valve, that could be turned off and on by hand, and this, located in the midst of the piping, was in the precise center of the piping system.

My English-major background was a subject which provided C. with many a good laugh, and I was, in his view, totally misplaced as an ordnance officer dealing with the intricacies of the engineering world.

During a lull in the activity on this particular night, I made a final study of the diagram, and wondered if the key manual valve could have been inadvertently shut. This would have nullified the entire system. Could it be possible that the solution was so ridiculously simple, and that all the hours spent on the supposition that the answer was a complicated one were needless? I convinced myself that this supposition was correct, and this was the burden of my report. But I assumed that C. would not agree, and feared that I would become the laughing stock of my colleagues and the butt of C.'s humor, should I be proved wrong. I was sorely tempted to rouse the ship's gunnery officer to allow me to put the system into operation, but this would be countermanding my orders to leave turret #2 alone.

In the dark of night, I crept into the turret, slipped down to the deck that contained the manual valve, crawled over the pipes and turned the valve. Visually it was difficult to tell if the valve was open or shut. So the burden of my report was "to try the system, and I think you will find it works beautifully."

I guessed that C. would probably not accept my premise, and feared that he would turn the valve back to its original position, so I remained at my desk and watched the day crew filter into the yard, drink quick cups of coffee, and go about their chores.

C. arrived at his office promptly at 7:00 A.M., and picked up the night report. I could see him through the glass partition of his office. He read the brief report twice, threw it on the desk, and came storming out of his office. By this time, only my immediate superior, Lieutenant Don Loomis, and I were in the office.

"Look. I told you not to touch anything in that godamned turret until I came back this morning. What's all this stuff about running the system without changing anything. By the time we set the test up half the day will be shot. What the hell are you getting at, Jackson?"

"Believe me, John. I am sure that we simply overlooked the most obvious of all things on this schematic. It's got to be that manual valve. Just give it a shot. What have you got to lose?"

C. turned to Lt. Loomis. "This godamned English major is trying to tell me how to run my business. What in the hell does he think I am? The manual valve, hell. Did you read this detailed report?" He was livid as he threw his copy on to Loomis's desk.

"Yeah. I read it. All he is saying is turn on the system and it'll work," said the Lieutenant.

"Work, hell!" said C., his voice up an octave and his face turned crimson with rage.

Loomis shrugged. "What have you got to lose, John? We're just about out of time. The Captain will have our ass if we don't correct the problem. Why not give it a shot?"

"Yeah, and it'll take half the morning to set the damn thing up."

"Well, I'm betting it'll work, and it'll save your ass, John," I said.

And it did. After another twenty minutes of storming around with Loomis, C. set up the test, and the system worked perfectly. The USS *Canberra* would leave port as scheduled. But John C. and I were never quite as close as we had been previously. His teasing had an added "zing" to it.

* * *

In the meantime a letter from Tom written in obvious haste arrived. He felt compelled to undo his previous revelation about his cryptography work.

Sub Air Base #1—43F
Salt Lake City, Utah
August 3, 1943
Dear Folks,

First of all, please forget that I'm in cryptography. It's very, very secret. We even have an armed guard outside our classroom building. So please mention it to no one and if you've already done so, try and smooth it over and say I'm still at advanced clerks school. You guys are not even supposed to know.

Another thing, I might go over sooner than I thought and possibly without a furlough.

Excuse the abbreviated length of this letter. I'm in a terrific hurry. I'm well and fairly happy. The food is good. Note the new address.

Love,
Tom

Again a few days later, Tom writes.

Salt Lake City, Utah
August 6, 1943
Dear Folks,

Things continue o.k. here. I'm surrounded, surprisingly enough, by a group of very intelligent and well-educated guys who are congenial as well. I have a fine time discussing literature with them. It's very nice.

Only a short while longer and I'll be sent to my bomb group. I hope it's a nice town like Denver or Boise, but most likely it will be in Texas or New Mexico.

Love,
Tom

A letter from Jeff arrived next. Obviously he has left Australia, but his cautious words leave us without a clue. My guess is New Guinea.

APO #503
August 10, 1943
Dear Folks,

It's been a long, long time since I last wrote. But it's been a longer time since I've heard from you folks.

The fact is that I've been on a special mission that has taken me away from my unit for a time. Until I get back, my mail can wait. Incidentally, note the new A.P.O. number...

Knowing that incoming mail would be out of the question I brought your old letters to maintain my morale this trip.

...When in Australia we built a chapel. One of the officer's designed it and the men built it. It was so attractive that even I found myself there on a Sunday. It's a speck disturbing that all the Protestant chaplains seemed to be Methodist or Presbyterian. And I must say, to one used to the Episcopal dash and color, their services seem flat by comparison. Not even the hymns were familiar. So for me, it was hard to be a conscientious church-goer. There were none of those good old rollicking alleluia jobs that really gave a lift to the good old days. At chapel, one Sunday, they issued little khaki colored New Testaments, and I treasure mine for I had neglected to bring along my own Bible.

I wish I could tell you more about where I am and what I'm seeing.

Lots of love,
Jeff

In the meantime, Tom continues with his education—about the Army and his own. Also, he's apparently due for a move shortly.

Salt Lake, Utah
August 10, 1943
Dear Folks,

...Last night I got out to see the Cole Brother's Circus, and had a fine time. A circus certainly is a marvelously contrived and complicated affair. On Sunday I investigated the Mormon Tabernacle, which I found interesting, I guess.

I don't know if you realize that the Army sponsors correspondence courses with accredited colleges. It is possible to get a degree by this method. I have been thinking that it would be a nice opportunity to get a Master's degree in English, so I have written them inquiring about it. I really can't lose by taking courses. It's a method of employing my spare time usefully. It's free, it's educational, and it certainly would be a delight to have an M.A.

I think I'll be leaving here Saturday, which is the day we conclude the course and "graduate." So you can see how badly they need us...

Love,
Tom

Chet Loomis wrote a brief letter from Africa recounting a recent visit from a touring star.

Africa
August 13, 1943
Dear Dick,

I am trying to write this while at the beach. This is the first good day for swimming we've had in ages so I thought I would knock off for a while and take advantage of the weather...

...Al Jolson was here the other night and he sure is getting along in years. He has been making a tour of Army Camps all over the world for almost one and a half years including Dutch Harbor. His first remark was that he had seen mud before in his travels but nothing like it is here...Every morning during this rainy season the roads have to be plowed as after a blizzard at home. Some places it is two feet deep. I have secured a pair of rubber boots and wear them all the time, sometimes to bed...

...Well, Richard, must knock off. I have a few more letters to write. Got a letter from a friend in Honolulu in just 12 days. How's that for speed? I guess the airplane is here to stay.

As ever,
Chet

Tom has joined an active air group, but remains in the vicinity of Salt Lake, Utah. He is soon to enjoy his first furlough.

August 19, 1943
Dear Folks,

First of all, I'll be getting home shortly. The only trouble is that it's expensive. It would alleviate matters greatly if you'd send me, via money order, about $65. I'll pay you back. You see I only get ten days, which includes travel, so I plan to fly from Salt Lake City to Chicago, and then a train from there. It costs $115 all the way by plane, so that's out of the question. I'll utilize the Red Cross for the rest of the money. So thanks, Dad.

This field is right in the Salt Flats, and is completely flat and arid with no trees or grass whatsoever. Our group is quite disorganized to date. We live in Army tents (six to a tent) and some (not mine) don't even have floors. Our mess-hall consists of a few tables outdoors, and the kitchen is a tent, but it gives the meals the aspect of a picnic. My department won't begin to function for a while, so I am going to make myself useful by helping with clerical work.

…I'll let you know more definitely about the furlough as soon as I can. Meanwhile, please send the money quickly, and don't plan anything for me when I'm home. I don't even want people to do nice things for me, or entertain me.

It certainly is interesting hanging around these big bombers. A bomber squadron is really a fascinating set-up.

Love,
Tom

A brief note from Jeff. At the time we had no indication of his location. I was convinced that he was in New Guinea. It turned out I was correct, because that's where he was headed.

August 24, 1943
Dear Folks,

I'm still on that special job and I sure do miss my mail. But when I finally catch up with it I'll have a real feast; two month's worth.

…This traveling around makes for a strange life. One moment you're dining in high style with white tablecloth and napkins and native serving boys, the next you're eating canned jungle rations and glad to get 'em.

Love,
Jeff

Brother Harry, Jeff's twin, was our only civilian. Because the twins never were lookalikes, and Harry towered over his twin, it always seemed to me that he was our senior sibling. It is said that in their early youth the twins were called Mutt and Jeff by their friends, taking a page from the famed comic strip of the day. But the assumption is that Harry was big enough to discourage the use of the term "Mutt," which he disliked. And Jeff just didn't care. Moth used to encourage her children's neatness, or whatever, with contests, providing a handsome prize as a reward for the winner. Perhaps a baseball bat, or a glove, were dangled before us as the contest commenced. Harry was the traditional winner. I can't remember when any of the other three Jackson boys made the grade. But no one resented his success. This is just the way it was.

It seemed right and proper to me that Harry should remain a civilian. But if there were to be any criticism of his status, he would be his own harshest critic. As the father of two tiny children, pretty daughter Joy, and son Jeffie, he felt his parental duty strongly. The government is willing to be the sole judge of what men it feels are essential for its service, and so far it had not considered tapping those of Harry's status. But it was no secret how Harry felt with his twin on special missions in the South Pacific.

In the following letter Ha tells Dad and Moth of his vacation in Wakefield, Mass., and of our visit in the nearby Boston Navy Yard.

Wakefield, Mass.
August 27, 1943
Dear Folks,

Vacation is just over. I'll leave here some time tomorrow, but Bets and the two tots will stay for a while longer...

Bets has told you something of what we're doing. We have stayed right here in Wakefield for the two weeks. It's a change of scene and a restful time with a wonderful chance to see much of Bets, Joy and Jeff, of whom I see all too little in the regular routine.

I had a swell day with Ensign Jackson at his South Boston Yard. I saw plenty of things that very few guys in my place would be privileged to inspect and hear explained. Nevertheless, I must confess that such information in my hands is not the least bit dangerous. Even if I had a mind to reveal what I saw and heard I couldn't do the slightest damage. It was way over my head and I'd say that Dick with his liberal arts background is as remarkable as the Navy higher-ups regard him in absorbing such complicated stuff. He took me aboard a heavy cruiser to which he is now assigned as what he calls an expediter. His job is to see that the ship is repaired as per specifications in the allotted time. Although he does very little actual work, he arranges for its accomplishment and has a bunch of underlings to manage. I felt like a big shot being associated with a man to whom workers would bow and scrape and come running with complaints.

Then we visited a destroyer and had lunch aboard her with the officers. This was all possible because an ensign aboard just happens to be a Dartmouth Beta, Class of '42…

…This morning we took Joy and Jeff to a local zoo. She loved it, especially a monkey who performed for her benefit and who fortunately acted in such discreet fashion that I don't know whether it was a little boy or girl. It was much better behaved than most humans. Joy is bigger and older-acting than ever, and Jeff no longer looks like a priest; now it's a Pope. I expect I'll see a change in them in Larchmont in a week or so.

Love,
Harry

CHAPTER 9

PICKET BOATS AND NEW GUINEA

JEFF RECOLLECTS his arrival at New Guinea. He had been given an assignment that brought him closer to the war effort on July 9, 1943. He was sent from Rockhampton on a mission to Brisbane to fetch three "picket boats." These were small cabin-cruisers to serve as command boats for the three boat battalions.

He took three boat crews, with a coxswain and engineer for each crew. They went by rail, and after an agonizingly slow preparation period, the boats were turned over to Jeff and his men. The craft and crews were put aboard the *Koondooloo*, a well-known ferry boat from Sydney harbor. She was to be used for transport around Milne Bay in New Guinea, which, by this time, was a staging area for Allied troops.

They went up the Australian coast, past the Great Barrier Reef, with two stops in Cairns in northern Australia, and Port Moresby in southern New Guinea. They had to cover some open water, and during a rainstorm encountered an angry sea that caused them to cut loose a large metal barge which had been under tow. As Jeff recalled, "That baby may still be menacing navigation in those waters."

They finally made it to Milne Bay in New Guinea, where the soldier crews and their three boats were transferred to a Dutch ship that was finishing unloading its cargo. The officers were Dutch but the crew consisted of brown-skinned, white-teethed Lascars from India.

These latter were Muslims, who took frequent breaks for prayer.

They would congregate on deck, wearing wrap-around skirts and tee-shirts, plus skull caps. They'd roll out their prayer rugs and face east and chant, while bowing down on their knees, all in unison.

"How pagan!" Jeff thought as he watched them.

These Muslims had a flock of sheep on deck, their main source of sustenance, since they could eat no meat other than that killed by some Holy Man among them.

Jeff's gang sat in Milne Bay for days waiting for a go-ahead and in the interim, Jeff ran into Heath Steele, a neighbor from Plandome who gave him two fresh eggs, which he put in charge of the ship's cook. Needless to say, there was only one egg that reached him for breakfast. He considered himself lucky.

While they sat in port, Jeff went along with a ship's officer and some of the seamen to get coconuts. The sailors were poor rowers, and were going in circles. It seemed that each man was his own cox. Finally, the officer said, "Bad row, no coconuts; good row, plenty coconuts." That did the trick. On shore, these same poor rowers were like monkeys climbing the trees.

Many air alerts were experienced during Jeff's stay in the crowded harbor of Milne Bay but nothing dropped from the sky. Jeff figures that our fighter planes must have done a great job of scrambling.

During one such alert, the bos'un said, "Many people will be killed in this war."

"Yes," Jeff said more to reassure himself than the others in the boat, "but not you; not me!"

"No," he answered. "Not you. Your God will protect you." And then he laughed uproariously, along with the crew of fellow Lascar pagans. Jeff recalled that he hadn't realized until then that there was another side to the coin.

Jeff and his crews finally got moving and eventually unloaded their boats at the new home of his unit at Buna, near Oro Bay, along the northeastern coast of Dutch New Guinea. While Jeff fidgeted in Milne Bay, his whole boat battalion had moved from Rockhampton to New Guinea.

The Japanese occupied most of the northern coast of both

British and Dutch New Guinea, and Jeff's outfit was to play an important part in winning back the territory.

On the 11th of September, one day after Jeff had arrived at Buna, Dutch New Guinea, near Oro Bay, with the three picket boats, there was an assault on Lae by the Allies. It took place on September 9, 1943. Jeff's regiment, the 542, did not take part in the successful assault, but on November 11, the 542nd moved its base from Oro Bay to Lae. This location, incidentally, was the last known stop on Amelia Earhart's fatal flight.

Jeff had written a reassuring letter of his good health.

> Hq. Boat Batt 542 Regt.
> APO 2503 c/o Postmaster
> San Francisco, California
> September 2, 1943
> Dear Folks,
>
> Once again I have a chance to mail a letter… although as yet incoming mail is out of the question. I'm looking forward to the mountain of letters that awaits me whenever we connect…
>
> …[censored] isn't bad. Of course it's hot and steamy, but I am not unduly bothered by the weather one way or the other. I feel in good shape, and am pretty well tanned though with that yellowish tinge that we all get from atabrine, the malaria pills. I'm beginning to think I'm a tough guy, it's been so long since I have had any sickness. That comes from a good sound background in childhood no doubt. Every so often I sneak a peek at your pictures, and it makes me feel good. Because in all of them you're laughing, and dammit, that's the only way I ever remember our family, always laughing.
>
> Love,
> Jeff

Tom enjoyed happy times on his furlough at home in Plandome. Dad and Moth saw him off at LaGuardia Field at the conclusion of his stay. He was off for Nebraska and tells of what he found upon arrival. Apparently he drew heavily on Dad's finances while at home, but "It was only a loan," Tom proudly states.

726 Sq. 451 Bomb Group
Fairmont, AAF
Geneva, Nebraska
Sept. 1943
Dear Folks,

They finally have me working my specialty and while its rather elementary, at least it's a starter. I work from 6 A.M. to 12 A.M., so the hours are really perfect. However, we work in rather confined quarters in the back of a big truck, and it gets to be rather a grind for six hours at a stretch. But, I do have plenty of time for sleep, movies, general relaxation and reading. I have always loved to have lots of time for myself.

Although, it's quite hot during the day, it really gets very cold at night and I shudder to think of spending the winter here. I doubt if I will, however.

This country is just like I always imagined Nebraska to be; flat fields everywhere. The facilities for amusement on the field are adequate. They have a nice movie theater, a good library, a service club with out-of-town newspapers, and Omaha, Lincoln and many small towns are handy. So I should be kept busy. Our squadron is rather comfortably set up with nice roomy barracks and a good mess hall.

Needless to say I'm quite contented with my lot...
Love,
Tom

Brother Jeff is off on another special job. Our curiosity and anxiety increased by leaps and bounds.

SWPA
September 25, 1943
Dear Folks,

Sorry for the long time between lines but darn it, I've been pretty busy lately. No sooner had I finally returned to the unit after two months, than off again for another little job.

Mighty interesting work, this present assignment. Wish I could talk about it here. Matter of fact it's tough trying to think of something I can write about...I must admit that my favorite diversion these days is dreaming of things as they will be when we finish over here…

Have some of those victory garden vegetables for me.

Love,

Jeff

Shortly after a successful assault at Finschhafen further along the Dutch New Guinea coast that did not involve Jeff's regiment, it was determined that a radar listening post was needed. Tami Island, a small atoll off the coast was the ideal site. Jeff was ordered to pick up an Australian radar team for the task. The team arrived on a ship which Jeff met with two LCM's off the town of Morobe, on the coast of New Guinea. The LCM's were new, so before Jeff could set sail, he had to "swing-ship," the term for calibrating the compasses. Through a pelorus set on a compass rose he matched the boat's compass for various headings, all the way around 360 degrees. His mission was to take the Aussie team around the southeastern tip of New Guinea to Lae, where his unit was camped. On his way to Red Beach at Lae, from the pick-up point, which was an overnight journey, they were certainly "sitting-ducks." The radar guys were far from neat and they must have been a funny sight, with a mess of poles, tarps, antenna dishes, and other equipment cluttering the usually trim crafts. The only watercraft they encountered, however, was a curious PT boat which took a quick look and went on.

Back at Lae, Jeff was named mission leader for a night-time "invasion" of Tami Island. They had about two waves, twelve LCVs and two loaded LCMs and a company of Aussie infantry.

They reached the target at daybreak on the 3rd of October, 1943, as planned. They discovered, to Jeff's dismay and horror, that, while the crescent-shaped beach was broad enough, it could be reached only through a narrow opening at the mouth of the lovely lagoon.

They had to go in single file for shore instead of six abreast, as was their usual procedure. They waited for the onslaught. It never came. The natives greeted them happily explaining that "Hapon go two moons!" But the Japanese had surely been dug in, with sturdy log machine gun emplacements along the beach. The lagoon was beautiful, lined with fantastic coral reefs and with colorful tropical fish swimming happily down below them.

They unloaded the Aussies and headed back to Red Beach, with great relief. When Jeff reported in to the Regimental Commander he was commended for a "job well done." He received a letter of commendation expressing appreciation for "excellent seamanship and wholehearted cooperation."

Jeff notes that his commander's comments on his next mission were not so pleasant. A new commander for the troops at Finschhafen was to be taken there from Lae, and Jeff was to handle the transportation. He was to take a small cabin-cruiser named *Hector* donated by an Australian civilian, which had seen action earlier in the Salomon campaign. Jeff set his usual routine, where the "charge of quarters" was to awaken him at 5 A.M., and also the three-man crew for the boat. He failed to do so, and Jeff awoke about three quarters of an hour late. He roused his coxswain, who in turn got his crew mates up and they reached the pick-up point an hour late.

"Of course there was hell to pay," said Jeff, but they finally got the general aboard, along with a couple of foot-lockers, his deputy commander, a colonel, and his aide, a captain, who was especially testy.

Once aboard, the general went below for some more shut-eye. Jeff had his boys provide some hot coffee and doughnuts for the others.

The seas were calm enough, the sun was shining, and Jeff tried to relax. But the colonel decided to disturb things by firing his 30 caliber carbine at some playful dolphins who were happily swimming along by the *Hector*. Jeff whispered to the cox to give the wheel a little jog now and then to throw off the guy's aim. It worked; at least no hits were scored on the friendly playmates.

When Jeff checked in with his colonel, late that night, he was waiting for him. He said, "When I was a lieutenant I'd have been two hours early. I'm surprised and disappointed."

Jeff answered, "Yes, sir."

* * *

Fred Borsodi writes and tells us of his latest activities. He now appears to be in Italy.

> 86 Fighter Squadron
> 79 Group
> APO #485
> c/o Postmaster, N.Y.C.
> September 21, 1943
> Dear Dick,
>
> ...We were in the Sicilian business and you can imagine where we are now. Some of the boys in our Group were sent home for a rest a couple of weeks ago and I must admit that I would like to have been with them. In two weeks we will have been away for a year. Sometimes it seems like ten. Anyway, I think I'll get home for a bit of leave sometime before Christmas. Right now, we are very active which helps as the time does pass more quickly.
>
> I had a letter from Web about the same time as yours. He enclosed a picture of young W.O.W. Jr. Don't forget to send along one of young RSJ Jr. so I can decide which I shall approve of as an escort for Miss Lindsley.
>
> There isn't a great deal to write about. Censorship rules are very strict and I'd rather say nothing than have the letter bounce back in my face. So I guess I'll just have to wait and swap all the long stories over a martini and a thick steak.
>
> Ever,
> Freddie

Tom is happy as usual. In the last paragraph of the following letter he carries on about his wishes for Christmas. He seems to burst at the seam when discussing the subject of money.

> PFC Thomas Jackson
> 726th Sqn., 451st. Bomb Grp
> Fairmont AAF
> Geneva, Nebraska
> September 26, 1943
> Dear Folks,
>
> ...With only a six-hour working day you can imagine the field

day I am having with the base library. I am averaging at least one book every day and a half, except of course, when I am brought up to a thoughtful walk by people like Proust and Freud. The library is really quite a well-rounded one; they even get "Downbeat!" (That's the dance musicians' trade magazine.) I've also been seeing more movies than you can shake a middle-sized stick at. Most of them, of course, are pretty bad, but I've always been able to enjoy a movie no matter how wretched it may be. In fact sometimes the very wretchedness of the thing perversely pleases me...The steady diet of books, movies, and sleep I get is getting a shade boring. However, I am thinking of going to Lincoln some Saturday to see Nebraska's football team in action.

Moth, as for Christmas presents, I have little or no ideas. Money, of course, is the foremost consideration of my life. However, if presents it must be, I can think of nothing save books and records. Books that I would like include all written by Sidney Perlman, and if you can find it, *Jazz-Hot and Hybrid* by Winthrop Sargent. I can't remember the publisher, unfortunately, but it is rather an obscure firm. The book may well be out of print. It costs $5.

I should prefer that you concentrate on the money angle. In fact, Dad can check off my debt to him as a present, but absolutely no fair to scratch off too large a chunk. I insist that the honor system be instituted to keep him from striking off any more than he would give me in hard cash. But please don't use all my gift money to neutralize the debt. I'll eventually pay it via the extension method. Perhaps it would be well to knock off an odd war bond for me. Incidentally, this accent on money might give you the idea that I expect tremendous packages instead. Such is honestly not the case, although I can hear you chuckling cynically at that. Really though, not too much.

Love,
Tom

The following letter to me from Tom explains his position in the Air Corps. It would appear he will be leaving shortly for overseas duty. It still seems incongruous to me that the little fellow is up to this army life.

Fairmont Army Air Base
Geneva, Nebraska
October 11, 1943
Dear Dick,

First of all let me congratulate you on the promotion to Lieutenant (jg). It must be quite a relief to get out of that over-populated ensign bracket...

Now here is the dope on my set-up. I am in a heavy bombardment squadron, which consists of 12 bombers (B-24's) and is the Air Corps counterpart of the infantry company. There are 4 of these squadrons, each consisting of somewhat less than 400 men to a group. It is as a Group that we function. Although the Squadron is a self-sufficient unit and might be separated geographically, the Group maintains administrative control over all four, comparable, I believe, to the infantry battalion. Since we operate with heavy bombers, we are comfortably settled well behind the lines. The ships are big enough for long jumps and too important to be subjected to the poundings they'd get near enemy lines. So we live comparatively safe lives, and unless something unforeseen happens, are only in danger of bombings or gas attacks. B-24's, incidentally, are so called Liberators which have been doing yeoman service...

Of course, in the war theaters all communications must be in code. There are 5 of us to a squadron and 3 men in the Group headquarters. My job consists in merely encoding and decoding these communications, as well as safe-guarding all materials used. Consequently there is little work for me here in Geneva. As a matter of fact there are only 2 of us assigned to squadrons to date. The table calls for 5 cryptographers, one to be a staff sergeant, 2 sergeants, and 2 corporals, so I am a cinch for sergeant.

OCS is out, at least apparently until we reach our destination, and then chances won't be that good. I'd like to be an officer both for purposes of prestige, and for social reasons. Conversation among the average enlisted man is really unimaginative and limited, and gets tiresome. I guess I'm kind of a snob.

I wish I could see Dickens.

Tom

From Brother Harry comes a letter with some of his sly humor. In the first paragraph he refers to the christening ceremony of his son Jeffie. Later he refers to his military status—or lack of same.

Hartford Fire Insurance Co.
Incorporated 1810
Hartford, Connecticut
October 11, 1943
Dear Math and Dick,

Here, at last, are the christening pictures…Sorry as the devil about the delay and will make no attempt at apology, reconciling myself to the fact that I'm a bad boy…

…It must be swell to be living a comparatively normal life again after so many months apart…I hope that Dick won't be assigned to night duty as he said in his letter he might. You service families have to be ready for anything, don't you?

…As a matter of fact, families in our position can be no more certain of the future—perhaps less so. How long I will be a civilian is just a guess and the uncertainty no little disturbing as you, from your past experience, can well appreciate. One day I'm in, and the next I'm not and I never really know what my status is.

Bets has been home several weeks and taken up the usual routine, which can best be described as working herself into the ground. The vigorous ball of suet with the long black hair and the mouth full of teeth, whom we call Jeff is a crawling fool with an uncanny ability at disrupting anything he comes in contact with. And his lanky sister gets around too, although in a more ladylike and genteel manner. Together, they are a handful…

Love,
Hads

CHAPTER 10

FALL LETTERS IN 1943

JEFF'S LETTER written on Columbus Day tells us a bit about life in the south Pacific area. He is just back from his Tami operation which took place earlier in the month. He includes a little-known fact to his Grandmother (Gram) in his last paragraph. Gram has worked for years in her support of the Salvation Army, and is always interested in their efforts.

FJJ
SWPA
12 October, 1943
Dear Folks,

Back home once again after another trip away from the outfit. Had an interesting job and got in on some of the excitement. The CO said I did a good job so I guess it was successful. Best of all, on returning, there was a good batch of mail from you guys...

Tom, Ha, and Dick are swell to write as often as they do. I wish I could match them letter for letter...

...Speaking of cooking, you may be interested in the food situation here. When we are at our present base the life is mighty comfortable. We eat so-called "B" rations which occasionally include fresh meat, fresh eggs and fresh fruit. We bathe daily under showers made of tin cans with holes in the bottom, or if lucky, as I am, under a small but cool waterfall. We can swim in the ocean too. At night about three times a week, we can see movies or perhaps attend a show or concert of some kind. Magazines (months old, but what's the difference?) are available and pass from hand to hand, usually in the latrine, of course.

However, things are slightly more rugged in the forward areas. The food is canned, but substantial enough when you get a chance to eat it. Entertainment is out of the question and so are magazines. A brave attempt is made to send up mail, but I always like it to be held further back as that way I'm more certain to connect with it. Bathing is a cinch if you are near a stream, no matter how shallow...

...The jungle hammock is an ingenious device, having a waterproof roof and built-in zipper-closed mosquito net. The jungle rations come in handy-sized wax-wrapped cartons and contain tasty delicacies like gum, candy, cigarettes, cocoa powder and lemon powder for drinks, as well as small cans of meat, cheese, raisins, prunes, cereal and powdered milk. They even contain a few squares of Scott tissues! Every effort is made to pack these carefully and tastefully and it does help morale.

Gram—in one of my letters I praised the good work of the Red Cross. You countered with a question about the Salvation Army. Well, at that time I hadn't seen hide nor hair of them. Now I know why. The Salvation Army are right up at the front lines. They are the only ones so far forward and always ready with coffee or a fruit drink or other refreshment. The Red Cross and YMCA are doing a swell job too, but in the bases where recreation is more practical...

Love to all,

Jeff

Tom is becoming worldly indeed. He reports his first dealings with a dentist other than our time-worn Doctor Holch of Brooklyn, NY, whom Tom refers to as "The Clinton Avenue Butcher."

Geneva, Nebraska

Oct. 17, 1943

Dear Folks,

The first casualty of World War II for the Jackson family has been suffered. I had a wisdom tooth pulled! You can well imagine how startled and completely terrified I was when the dentist told

me that it had to come out. Noting my stricken look he assured me
that it was absolutely necessary; but that hardly satisfied one whose
family, with the kindly collaboration of the Clinton Avenue Butcher, have always clung doggedly to each molar. But when the doctor
is a Captain and you are a PFC, there can be no arguing.

Now that it's over, I firmly believe that everyone should have at
least one tooth pulled because it certainly is the most unique and
amazing experience that I, at least, have ever had. First of all he
shot novocaine into my tense jaw, which commenced to feel swol-
len and numb. Then, after about 5 minutes, he came back, tilted
my head back and without further adieu, yanked the tooth. I felt
nothing, although I could hear a slight grinding, then a pop like a
cork coming out of a champagne bottle. He then dismissed me,
doing nothing else and preceded to the next man. The utter casual-
ness, and dispatch with which the operation was accomplished
makes me realize how sly the civilian dentist is, when he tinkers
about the mouth with oils, cotton, etc. and insists on another
visit…Incidentally, I don't miss the tooth at all.

Love,
Tom

Jeff wrote me shortly after the successful invasion of Tami that he
led. He reveals something of the Navy's role in the landings, and an
interesting rapport between the services.

FJJ
SWPA
20 October, 1943
Dear Math, Dick & Dickens,

Back once more to my outfit and able to get off letters again.
Before proceeding further I want to say thanks for all the many
swell pieces of mail coming this way out of Cambridge. The little
fellow is a "hot sketch" as Dad would say, and sure looks as if he
can handle himself under any circumstances.

It is now safe to report that I've had a chance to see the Navy in
action, and they do alright; plenty good. Also they are mighty swell
to everyone when it comes to sharing their many luxuries. One
time I was on an allied merchant ship lying at anchor for a few days
in a harbor. The OD of a nearby Navy ship blinkered to us and all

the ships within a goodly radius that we were invited to see their movies. They sent launches for us and in general did it up brown. The invite included seamen, engineers (I mean oilers and wipers) as well as officers. The sailors gave away valuable things like cigars and chocolate bars which they could easily have sold at exorbitant prices. This business went on every night by the way.

Another group I admire is the Air Corps. I've seen those guys go up and really bust up the Jap formations, knock those guys out of the sky and then fly low and give that good old Victory roll that looks like a frisky colt feeling his oats. Don't underestimate our flyers; they're phenomenal...

I was so glad to learn of your swell situation at Cambridge, and to hear that Dick is doing so well at the Yard. Sounds to me like a very important job. If that cruiser got out in an engagement and the big guns didn't operate she'd be in a fine fix indeed. Point is, those guns must be set up just right by an expert. Only place this can be done is at the home base and only time is at the beginning. So naturally the place for the expert is where the job is. You didn't ask to be a gunnery expert...The next time our mutual friend gets uppity bust him in the snoot for me. You're doing more for the Navy than he is, I'll guarantee that...

...Life here goes along smoothly enough. The sameness of the warm humid climate is wearying to a guy used to four seasons, and makes a fellow become listless at times. Continual dosing with ata-brine, salt tablets and shots-in-the-arm, and steady applications of insect repellent combine to make prevention of tropical diseases plenty annoying, though this annoyance is far less unpleasant than that of the disease itself... To further insure against illness the Army has given us still another pill to take daily. This time it's my old friend the Vitamin tablet. One of those all-in-one deals and of course right down my alley. Makes me laugh—the Army is miles behind our Mom when it comes to discovering new things...

Math I can't wait to get home to see you fellas, and to get to know lil ol' Toady, Dickens.

Love,
Jeff

Tom always gives a discussion of religion a peculiar twist. And yet, he seems to apologize for bringing up the subject. Funny little guy!

Geneva, Nebraska
November 8, 1943
Dear Folks,

Everything is still okay here. I just got back from a 24-hour pass to Omaha which was a pleasant outing and change. Fats Waller, the colored pianist, happened to be in town and I spent an enjoyable evening listening to him.

…The other day Gram sent me a handy little New Testament with a steel cover, apparently for my protection rather than that of the Good Book. This found me with four bibles. However, I had already planned to send the big Moffat edition home as it was too good and big to carry about with me. Anyway I wanted it only for literary reasons, and will study it after the war; preferably in my own comfortable establishment when I can revert to a tall drink with some authority when the miracles get too miraculous for even me. So I decided to give the other small edition away to somebody who might feel the need of a little enlightenment, Brother! But, (and this is the point of this paragraph) I was amazed to learn that every single guy had a bible, and in fact, 80% of them had two. They were trying to get rid of the extra one. I finally gave mine to a curious Jewish boy named Levine.

Love,
Tom

In a letter to Dad, Tom writes of a promotion.

Fairmont Army Air Base
Geneva, Nebraska
November 11, 1943
Dear Dad,

…I certainly seem to be accumulating lots of money. I hope I can keep the habit up until death.

I just heard I was to be put up for corporal next month. It's not much but at least it's a step forward, and $12 more. I was supposed to get it last month, but there was a mistake.

Please say nothing about it until it becomes official in about 20 days.

Tom

Freddie Borsodi flew home in a captured German Junker 88 early in November. A feature article in *Hartford Times*, dated November 12, recounted some of Freddie's accomplishments in over a year of the war (see facsimile on next page). We received the following postcard from Fred and Marcia Borsodi from Sea Island, Georgia. From the picture on the card, Fred was enjoying a bit of golf, a game at which he is extremely proficient.

November 22, 1943
Dear Dick and Math,
    Got back a couple of weeks ago and have been down here on leave. Hope it won't be long before we see you three—I'm anxious to meet young Dickens.
    Love to you both,
    Marcia and Freddie

Jeff had written a thoughtful note to me on my birthday but, below, he wrote again, a special note to our little family with a Christmas greeting.

December 9, 1943
Dear Sis, Broth, and Neph,
    This trying to time Christmas mail from a point 10,000 miles away is a tough job. Hope this one rings the bell.
    Sending Christmas greetings from the vicinity of the equator, with not a reindeer in sight, seems plenty unreal indeed! Yet warm as this tropical climate is it can't begin to approximate the warmth of my Christmas wish to you three. After all, there's more to the season than snow, evergreens, mistletoe and tinsel. Of course they help; they constitute the back-drop and the props. And I love and cherish every memory of them. But the big thing is, of course, the Yuletide spirit itself. And the only way for me to capture that spirit is simply to close my eyes and think of my swell family and friends. To think of the swell times we've had on previous Noels and of the even sweller Noels to come.
    So, no matter if I am a million miles from sleigh-bells and reindeer and old Mr. Red-Pants? A feller doesn't need all those things when there's a Christmas tree in his heart.

Flier Comes Home in Nazi Plane

Major Barsodi, Former Local Test Pilot, Delivers Letter to Arnold in Washington

By JOHN CLEARY

Maj. Frederick A. Barsodi came back from Europe the hard way—as the pilot of German Junker 88 transport plane.

He arrived at his home on Orchard Rd., West Hartford, last week after a side trip to Washington where he delivered a letter and a souvenir from General Carl A. Spaatz to Gen. H. H. Arnold, head of the Air Forces.

Story Attached

"There is a little story attached to that plane," he told The Times today. "Our Intelligence had wanted one of them for a long time. My squadron, the Comanches, was sent on a strafing mission against an advanced air base in Italy. There on the ground were four of them, and we got them all with fighter fire.

"As soon as I got back to our base, I sent four sergeants ahead to claim one of the Jerry planes. They went in right behind the tanks, and got one which could be patched up from spare parts captured on the field.

Champagne But No Beer

"We used it for a while as a transport plane, carrying non-flying personnel from one field to another. I had hoped to fly it out for some beer, but there was no beer around. After the invasion there was a lot of champagne for a while, but it dried up somehow.

"I have been fortunate enough to have flown several captured enemy planes. The Focke-Wulf is the best thing that Jerry has been able to throw at us, but I like the English Spitfire better."

Commands Squadron

The major, promoted early in October from captain, is commanding officer of the Comanche fighter squadron. Before going into the Army he was a test pilot for Pratt & Whitney Aircraft. He expects to spend his leave as quietly as possible with his friends and family in West Hartford. His wife is the daughter of Mr. and Mrs. Porter B. Chase of West Hartford.

"I wish that I could express how much the men of our outfit appreciated the show Jack Benny put on for us in Italy," the major said. "We had expected him in Sicily, but he finally caught up with us in Italy. Back in Sicily we prepared signs for him reading, 'Welcome Fred Allen,' but they were wasted. When he visited us in Italy, we bought a cow and all the champagne we could find, but he had to go on to another engagement. You know, he really can play the violin a lot better than he pretends. He and Larry Adler put on a musical skit, all of it ad-libbed, that had us rolling on the ground."

He was reticent about his decorations, all but one of which he does not wear, but his wife told the reporter that he has received the Distinguished Flying Cross and the Air Medal with three silver oak leaf clusters.

"You know, that means that he has been awarded the Air Medal 16 times," she said. Her husband stared shyly at his hands, obviously uncomfortable at the implied praise. Like all members of outfits with high morale, he thinks that the credit for air victories should go to the squadron as a whole, not only to individual members. He has been credited with four planes shot down in the air, not counting any destroyed on the ground.

Enjoyed Fighter Sweeps

"We enjoyed the fighter sweeps best of all. In that style of fighting, whole squadrons go out just looking for any trouble they can find. We considered ourselves lucky to find Jerry at all. He made pretty scarce once the invasion started.

The major spoke of the Germans as "Jerry" and the Italians as "the Eyeties." These are British slang terms. His group was attached to the British Eighth Army during the whole campaign. "I was a messenger for General Spaatz on the trip back to America," Major Barsodi continued. "He sent a letter and a captured German flag back to General Arnold in our German plane. I gave it to General Arnold in Washington yesterday.

"The toughest job of all is strafing ground troops," the flier remarked. "It is a nasty job, but it has to be done. It doesn't feel good to know that you are throwing bullets at men who are practically defenseless. However the sight of your fire hitting something tangible is a gratifying sensation. In the air, everything is over in a few seconds. Strafing on the desert is very tough, because Jerry can see you coming. In the hills, you can hide until you are right on top of him."

Ran For It Once

One of the major's exploits, published before, will bear mention in passing. He was shot down in Africa between the German and English lines. Picked up by a New Zealand tank, he had to sprint for cover when the tank drew German fire and was disabled. "I'd like to know my time for that 200 yards," he said. "It would make Jesse Owen look like a barge dragging its anchor."

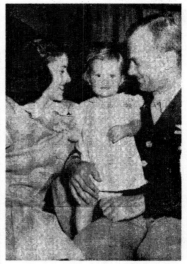

Major Barsodi, back from the battlelines, gets acquainted his family. Daughter Lindsley was a baby when the Major West Hartford for service.

The Hartford Times *reports on Fred Borsodi's homecoming.*

As for you guys: Have fun, and maybe sometime during the day you'll find a chance to join me in a quiet prayer—that sometime very soon we can look out over the world and truly find "Peace on Earth, good will toward men."

Lots of love to you all and to all the Mathes, and shucks the whole gang!

Jeff

Tom's first overseas letter lets us know of his safe arrival and reveals his location. This was a great source of satisfaction to all of us on the home front.

North Africa
December 20, 1943
Dear Folks,

I understand that none of the letters I've written have been mailed as yet, so you have probably been wondering about me, and perhaps a bit worried. First of all let me assure you that I'm in the best of health and sprits. This overseas service really is an extremely interesting and educational thing, and of course, it won't do me a bit of harm. But don't get me wrong, I'd a damn site rather be home. Since I can't be though, I consider myself lucky...

...North Africa is very interesting. My French came in very handy, and I became quite popular with the natives. The Arab kids are a great source of amusement, because they speak very good English, which is strongly flavored with profanity and soldier expressions. One even sang, "Chattanooga Choo Choo" for me. Oran is the only big city that I visited but it certainly looked interesting. As soon as I get more permanently and comfortably settled I'll write more.

Love to all,
Tom

Jeff shares his New Year's resolutions. In the last paragraph of this letter he makes two startling requests. I guess all soldiers want "Good Luck Charms" but I dare say none will have the same as Jeff.

New Guinea
APO 322
December 31, 1943
Dear Folks,

Once again we are allowed to admit that we're in New Guinea. At first we couldn't, now we can. Funny army.

On this last day of 1943, I've been taking stock of things. I've been figuring how I can make 1944 a better year than this one. A very obvious point for improvement is letters home. Heaps of correspondence in '44...

...Another point is my job here. I am going to bear down a speck harder. This is actually a selfish resolution because the better the job, the quicker the victory and the sooner the long voyage home! You'll have to excuse me from talking shop, but I've got to share my resolves with some one (to kind of make it legal) and I'd look like an ass going up to the C.O. and promising to be a good little soldier in the coming year. Yet, that is my fervent prayer, and I intend to keep ever conscious of my obligation to you and all other mothers and dads and kids everywhere.

Also, now, at year's end, I've been looking back—and feeling grateful. Grateful for all the lucky breaks I've had over the year. For the loving support of the world's most wonderful family and for the magnificent equipment and cooperation and leadership of the world's best Army. When you look back you realize that it hasn't been so bad after all. I can't help thinking of Dad's way of putting it as we pumped up to the North Hempstead Club on those cyclist delight junkets; "This hill, like anything in life seems long and steep and tough to take when you look at it from the bottom, but when viewed from the top it turns into a gentle slope, almost level." And damned if it isn't true in war. At least the war as I know it. Of course, I've been lucky. It may not hold out forever. But even if it doesn't, I have much to be thankful for now.

So Merry Christmas, you chaps. And may the New Year find things looking up!

Love,
Jeff

CHAPTER 11

SECRETS AND WELDING LINES

BY THE END OF January I had put to sea on the USS *Augusta*, an older 8-inch cruiser, that had been overhauled in the South Boston yard. The assignment lasted but five days, but it was special. It was my chore to make sure that the fire control equipment was in good order, and that the guns were on target. It was special, because the ship's work was unusual, and it harbored a top secret. It was a secret, however, that was pretty well known by all hands in the sprawling navy yard before the job was finished. Its ship's ladders, for instance, were for the most part converted to ramps, and it became obvious that some important personage was to be aboard and needed a special means for getting about the ship. And what well-known high official could it be, other than our president, Franklin Delano Roosevelt, who, we all knew, needed a wheelchair to get about. We also knew that Roosevelt was a great sailor in his younger years before being crippled by polio, and indeed loved the sea. What we didn't know, but were subsequently to learn, was that the president had arranged an ocean rendezvous with his opposite number from Britain, Sir Winston Churchill. The *Augusta* had been designated to carry Roosevelt to his meeting.

I was aboard only as far as Portland, Maine, where the ship lay in Casco Bay over a few nights, and took off each day for gunnery practice in the ocean off Portland. For the most part, we fired the AA battery, aiming at a cloth target being dragged laboriously by a small plane off our starboard bow. Our gunners were generally on target, yet I felt great sympathy for the lone pilot charged with pulling the target through the crisp New England sky. The guns worked as they should, and the fire control equipment was in good order, so I left the ship in what I considered good shape on the 31st of January. It was only later at the completion of the president's mission, that we, and the world, were to learn of his rendezvous with Churchill.

It was shortly after this sea voyage that I started another tour of duty at night at the yard. It was back to the old routine and jobs, jobs, jobs, each demanding attention, and surveillance by the responsible yard officer. I remember one such annoying incident, not at all unusual, but for some reason I had jotted the experience down in my journal. I tell it now as a means to describe some of the more mundane occurrences with which we were faced. At the time, I was a lieutenant (jg).

"Lieutenant, we can't get the welders for that job in turret #1. Will you see what you can do?"

I went to #1 turret on the USS *Baltimore*, an 8-inch cruiser. I slid down onto the shell deck, and found three machinists, all sound asleep. So I banged the hatch behind them, and all three men jumped up. "You're supposed to be working on the cut-out track," I said accusingly.

"We're waiting on the welder. He ain't showed up," one of the men said.

I noted that the cut-out track was blocked into place with a couple of chunks of wood. No point in arguing. Let's find the welder. I went into the turret officer's booth and put in a call to the welding shop. The shop leading-man, a euphemism for foreman, said, "We sent him out an hour ago."

On the way back to the shell deck, I passed a little kid, hunched over against the powder hoist, with a welding shield lying beside him. He was sound asleep.

"Hey," I said, shaking the kid awake, "what job you on?"

The kid, who looked like he should still be in grammar school, said, "I dunno. They sent me to weld in Turret #1."

So I stuck my head down into the hatch and yelled, "Hey machinists. Here's your welder. Why in the hell don't you look around, before taking your damn nap?"

But the welder slithering down the hatch and seeing all the

powder bags and shells, said, "I can't weld here with all that ammo unless I have some watches, and permission to weld from the officer of the deck."

"Okay," I said, "I'll get you some watches, and permission, but you stay right here, you hear me?"

I went to the OD who fortunately was an ensign. He responded to my request by asking me to please delay any welding until the morning. "I'm no gunnery officer, but it doesn't seem right to weld with all that ammo around."

I said, "Hell, you can weld around ammo. We've done it a million times. I have my orders and I intend to carry them out. We've got to get this job done tonight."

"I'll get the chief gunner and he'll take a look at the job and pass on it. Okay? He knows his shells and all. Do you know where compartment B-301C is?"

"Of course I don't," I said.

So the OD turned to a sailor and said, "Messenger, take this officer to compartment B-301C."

It soon became obvious to me that the messenger had no more idea where the compartment was than I. We were lost, so I went my own way, and fortunately passed the gunnery chief on the way to his breakfast.

He followed me down to the shell deck of turret #1, reviewed my request and as he stroked his chin he said, "You can weld if you have three watches on hand. One there," he pointed, "one behind the bulkhead there, and one there."

We went topside while the chief rounded up his three watches, and with the three men following, I returned to the turret. Would you believe it? My three machinists were napping again, and so too was the welder. I kicked them awake, and I said to the little welder, "Okay, son, weld."

He looked at me sheepishly and he said, "I ain't got no lines nor my torch."

"Where the hell is your torch?" I asked.

"It's up on the deck with my lines," he said weakly.

"Well, get your ass up there and get the stuff, and make it snappy,"

I said. I accompanied him through the hatch and waited on the deck for his return.

While we were gone the three sailors, who had been grumbling ever since they appeared, had disappeared. A machinist said they told him their watch had been relieved.

I was determined to get the job done, so, in a mounting rage, I went back up to the OD. With the change in the watch he was no longer the passive ensign; I was now confronted by a two-and-a-half striper, a lieutenant commander.

"Could we have three fire-watches, sir? We have a welding job to do in turret #1"

"Sure," he said. "You'll find the men under #7 quad mount over there…" Then he did a double-take. "Did you say weld? Where in turret #1 do you want to weld?"

"The shell deck, sir," I answered.

"Oh, no. Nossiree Bob," he said. "With all those shells lying around, there'll be no welding in turret #1 while I'm in charge of this ship," he said.

The sun had risen over the horizon to the east. My watch was coming to a close. I had fifteen minutes left, just about enough time to get back to the office and write my report for the morning shift. In the report I wished the next shift well with respect to the welding job. I found a cozy seat on the early train to Cambridge, and managed to doze as successfully as the little welder and the three machinists, on the way home.

* * *

The boys were not the only Jacksons contributing to the National effort. Our mother had volunteered her services. Below is a letter written by Dad to tell us of Moth's graduation exercises as a Red Cross nurse. Moth was a rare person with the necessary energy and efficiency to make a fine nurse. Nursing four boys through the knocks, cuts, and diseases that afflict growing boys, she had a sixth sense of how best each emergency should be handled. Well along in years she felt her duty so strongly that she pitched into a nursing course with girls young enough to be her daughters. And I would bet that she was the most efficient of all.

Feb. 4, 1944

Dear Ha, Bets, Jeff, Dick, Math and Tom.

I have been meaning to write ever since the big graduation exercises on which occasion Moth was capped and received her Nurses Aid pin. That was on the evening of January 25th, at the Cathedral House at Garden City. The exercises were quite impressive, and the graduating class was made up of about fifty, most of whom were young ladies with a fair quota of middle aged persons, and very few in Mother's category. In fact she is called the grandmother of the class. I missed you all very much when she mounted the platform and was handed her credentials and capped, because on such occasions our family is generally out in full force, and we could have given her the ovation that she was justly entitled to receive. However, I told her that my weak applause had in back of it the sturdy clapping of all of you. She looked sweet and charming in her spic and span uniform, and as she takes the work very seriously it all meant a lot...

...Mother is doing a fine job, having chosen the Meadowbrook Hospital as her base of operations. As you probably know that is Nassau County's charitable institution with up-to-date equipment and a very fine clinic, ambulance service and all that goes with it. As you can understand she does a fine job having a wealth of experience in nursing all of us over our respective illnesses, broken shins hit by a running sled, etc. Some of the patients have already indicated their preference, and Mae promises to be a busy person. She has already made good friends with a couple of big colored gals, who, in a desire to reciprocate, promise, when well that they will give her first call should she need help in the kitchen. In these days that is a better measure of pay than all the money in the world...

...With the splendid progress our side is making one cannot be blamed for a little enthusiasm such as I know I now have toward the possibility of a shortening of the war. You seem to be doing a good job over there and here (I mean the fellows in the service) and we civilian folks are doing our part in several ways to help things along. Let's hope before long we may all have a genuine get together and jollification, soldiers, sailors, nurses, mothers, Hartford Insurance man, the babies and the old buck.

Love,

Dad

USS Baltimore (CA-68) off the Boston Navy Yard, Massachusetts, 10 September 1943. Courtesy of the U.S. Naval Institute. Collection of James C. Fahey. U.S. Naval Historical Center photograph.

USS Augusta (CA-31) off Honolulu, Oahu, on 31 July 1933. Diamond Head is in the distance. Official U.S. Navy photograph, now in the collections of the National Archives.

Mae C. Jackson, the mother of the four Jackson boys. She served diligently during the war as a Red Cross nurses' aide, in both Meadowbrook Hospital in Mineola, NY, and Mitchell Field Military Hospital. She maintained a weekly correspondence with her four boys and kept her house in order and her husband well fed, during the entire war.

PFC Thomas C. Jackson, the youngest of the Jacksons, was a cryptographer with the 15th Army Air Force, 49th Headquarters Wing, stationed in Italy. Unable to describe his daily chores in letters, he spent his time well. He reported in his letters on his voluminous reading and his attendance at movies, shows, concerts, and operas. Promotions were slow for Tom, but he finally made sergeant by war's end.

In the meantime, North Africa must have been only a brief stop-over for Tom's bomber squadron. His second letter from overseas was postmarked from Italy.

> Italy
> APO #520
> January 3, 1944
> Dear Folks,
>
> Now I'm in Italy, a very interesting place indeed, but exactly where, I am not permitted to say. The first thing you notice about this place is hunger. The little kids, mostly barefoot (and it's quite cold), beg for scraps from the mess kits. And I understand it was much worse when the Americans first moved in. It certainly gives one quite a turn, and makes you thankful to know that America has so damn much of everything...
>
> ...We sleep in an uncompleted building that has no windows and on cold marble floors. But that part of it is only temporary I hope...
>
> Love,
> Tom

By mid-January, Tom had answered a letter from me, his first by V-mail, which was a tiny copy of an original letter sent via air on a for-mal V-mail form. Such mail was used extensively during the war, and saved valuable space in shipments of mail. Tom elaborates on his living quarters and has comments about the British tommie.

> APO 520, New York, NY
> Jan. 17, 1944
> Dear Dick and Math,
>
> Just got Dick's letter this afternoon and enjoyed it. I'm anxiously awaiting the picture of Dickens, but as you say, I wish to hell I could see him.
>
> I have discovered that the oft-mentioned "American Ingenuity" is no myth, except in my case. When we came here this place was quite a mess, but we've built a floor in our tent, have a big stone fireplace, electric lights with a switch, and built beds (two of which are double deckers). And the whole damn area (I'm swearing too

much in this letter) really is beginning to look quite nice.

Another thing which amazes me is the antipathy of American soldiers to the English. In fact everyone from the New Zealanders, Canadians, and Australians on down, dislike them. This appears to me to be because of their reserved temperament—although they make no effort to pick up hitch-hikers, and frequently act quite nasty. These are just my first impressions, however, and are always subject to change.

The weather here is much colder than I thought Italy had a right to be, but I understand that their spring will be in a few weeks. I can't stand cold and dampness. I hope you had a merry Christmas.

Love,
Tom

Tom takes time out from his own griping to express his sympathy for the doughboys. And he got his promotion.

Italy
February 7, 1944
Dear Folks,

Well, after numerous false alarms, I've finally made Corporal and I guess it's about time.

The weather around here is miserable. I certainly am surprised at so-called "sunny Italy." It's a very damp climate, but I guess it will be quite pleasant when spring finally comes. The guys I really pity are the infantry and all the boys way up at the front, where it's snowing and raining etc. People in heavy bombardment groups are very lucky (comparatively that is) because of the relatively comfortable situation we have, well back from the front lines.

This outing is undoubtedly an educational and worthwhile experience. Of course, I'd gladly pass it up to stay at home, but as long as I'm here I suppose I might as well admit it. One thing, I'm lucky to live with a guy who speaks Italian extremely fluently. He gets along with the natives so well, in fact, that he is going to be a Godfather which is a signal honor in Italy for the child is named after the Godfather.

Love,
Tom

Dinner Cooney called us in Cambridge one night, much to our surprise. We had last heard that he was in Texas. He had just been stationed at the Army Materiel Center in Boston, with his duties mainly consisting of liaison with the various private concerns that provided air force equipment in the Boston area. We saw each other frequently and had some hilarious times. One day, he asked me about an amplidyne power drive, used on some navy gun mounts. I was familiar with such a unit through my fire control work. I sent him some pamphlets and explained as much as I could about the unit. A few days later I received this formal reply.

War Department
Army Air Forces Materiel Center
Eastern Procurement District
Office of the Army Air Forces Representative

February 10, 1944
Lt. j/g Richard S. Jackson
Building 21
South Boston Dry Dock
South Boston, Mass.
Dear Dick

I have examined the Amplidyne pamphlets thoroughly and they have certainly cleared up many things for me (including my sinus trouble). I appreciate your help in clearing up these matters as I was able to telephone the gentleman at Sturtevant and explain to him exactly what an Amplidyne is. It is certainly an amazing device and Mr. Melzard of Sturtevant was extremely interested in all of the information I gave him.

One of these days I hope to go down to the South Boston Dry Dock and look things over. Maybe you will be able to show me an Amplidyne in use as I am extremely interested in these items as I explained to you over the phone.

Sincerely yours,
James S. Cooney
P.S. What the hell is an Amplidyne?

Jeff wrote this letter on his 32nd birthday. Dad added a postscript on our copies, saying, "This is something from a fellow who has had to take the nastiest of deals for over a year."

New Guinea
February 15, 1944
Dear Folks,

Right now I'm thinking of a day thirty-two years ago…And I'm thinking of what you were thinking about just then. I imagine your thoughts went something like this:

"Well it's different now, isn't it. We're no longer Mr. & Mrs. Jackson, that cute young couple in 1042 East 14th St. North. Now we're a family—the Jackson family! And you can bet your bottom dollar that we two will do everything possible to make our family a happy, peaceful, successful one. That we'll give these two little tykes all the advantages obtainable, in order that they will have a 100% chance in a mighty tough world. And we solemnly promise that these two guys will never ever have cause to complain that they were denied a square deal…to this we are dedicated, through sicknesses and in health, for richer for poorer, 'til death do us part."

Yes, I'm pretty sure that those must have been your thoughts on that day thirty-two long years ago.

And I know, too, how wonderfully well you have followed that guide. I know how you've worked and saved; how you've foregone pleasures and luxuries that you had every right to enjoy; how you've steered us along the right path by the beacon of your shining example! All this I know and feel deeply grateful. And I think Ha is one with me on this. Think? Heck, I know he is. Haven't we talked it over a million times?

All this is fact. But what about the other side? Have I carried my share of the burden, have I pulled my oar? When I contemplate that question I grow a bit afraid. Have I done my part? Have I let you down?

Gosh, I don't know. I've accomplished a few things. I have friends; I've stayed out of trouble; have respect. Yet all these things are merely the reflection of the ingredients which you two put into the mold. They're nothing I can claim credit for. You see, I'm looking for some contribution I can call my very own. As I say, I am not sure that such a contribution exists. As a matter of fact I'm not so sure that such a contribution can exist. For you two have contributed all the good things there are. There is one thing that is 100% mine though. And that's my 100% love of you. You are all that any parents could ever be. Each night I thank you for everything; and each night I thank God for choosing me to be a Jackson.

Outwardly, today is just another day, no different from yesterday or tomorrow. Cakes and candles and kisses have no place here. Inwardly, though it's a very special day. No Jap in the world can change that. And no Jap in the world can keep me from getting back to rejoin the other three members of the foursome who were in at the beginning of the G.H.Jackson Family Inc. Nor can he keep me from rejoining the ever-increasing additions to the concern. No sir. You're all too precious to me for that! Don't ever doubt that we'll all be together again soon, and don't ever doubt that I love you. God keep you and Bless you.

Love,
Jeff

Tom's letter of February 16 cautions Mother to pace herself in her nurses activity. And he refers to one of Jeff's letters in which a homecoming meal was described by Jeff calling for "Wine, let's have wine."

Italy
February 16, 1944
Dear Folks,

Everything is still running in a routine and uneventful fashion.

Moth, I think it's wonderful that you went ahead and became a nurse's aid; and I think it will be a good thing for you, because it will keep you from being lonely. But, as I understand it that job is a tough one, and knowing the vigorous way you go about a job, I hope to hell you don't overdo it, and wear yourself out. You can do plenty without tiring yourself so please don't.

I just read Jeff's letter requesting "wine—let's have wine" for his homecoming meal. Well, if no one minds I'll skip that and concentrate on "scotch—let's have scotch." Wine is the same as water around here and I'm quite fed up with it.

Dad, I hope the optimism that you mention in the States is the right dope. But from what I've heard here, these Germans will take an awful lot of beating.

Love,

Tom

A March letter from Tom cautions against too much optimism concerning the end of the war. It was always foremost in our minds that the big break would come and the war would be over. We kept hoping…

Italy

March 30, 1944

Dear Folks,

Things remain ok here. I'm still in very good health, and looking forward to warm weather. (Will it ever come?)

Don't you people be too optimistic—it seems to me that that's dangerous because it tends to make people let down. I can tell you one thing, the guys that fly the bombers over here aren't noticing any signs of weakness in the Germans. And undoubtedly that goes for the guys in foxholes at the front, particularly at Cassino. Personally, I think it's going to take a great while longer to beat the Germans.

I've been seeing a lot of movies lately. They're certainly a blessing, because there's really not much else to do around here during nights.

Moth, please remember not to work yourself to death in that hospital. First thing you know you'll get sick and then another nurse's aid will have to help *you*. So take it easy.

Love,

Tom

April reports from Tom herald the advent of warm weather. He also takes his father to task having apparently received congratulations from Dad for his promotion to corporal. Mother had asked why service men grew beards and mustaches and Tom has the answers.

Italy
April 15, 1944
Dear Folks,

Sorry I haven't written lately, but we've moved our area again, and the movement, plus the time it takes to tear the camp down, and set it up again, have kept us busy.

The weather has finally become wonderful. It's very sunny and warm. This place is really pretty. It's rolling, green, meadowy country, and in a little valley nearby there's even a winding river in which we can swim, if we don't swallow the water. You'd be surprised how much more pleasant life is when it's warm and with pretty surroundings. And we even had a fresh vegetable today— nice, crisp, green lettuce. God, it was wonderful.

Tomorrow we are having coca cola in our PX. It will be the first we've had since being overseas!

Dad, the army is composed of human beings and therefore is subject to human frailties. I've often noticed your awe and wonder at its workings, but although it's amazingly competent and efficient it's still very fallible. I didn't get my extra stripe through merit. I got it because of the system, and because I had to be compensated for other promotions. Incidentally, Dad, forget the ROTC. That never did anything for me. If I get another stripe, and chances are I won't, it will not be due to merit. I've kept my nose clean and managed to keep from irritating anyone. If this is cynical, check with anyone in a position to observe. Still it's a marvelous army, but you can keep armies as far as I am concerned.

Moth, the reason the soldiers and sailors have long beards is boredom. There's nobody there to look pretty for, and growing a mustache or beard, or shaving your head breaks up the monotony and gives a guy something to watch day by day. If they retain these hirsute features upon once more attaining civilization, it means they are rather proud and fascinated by it; or simply that they have spent so much time and trouble growing the beards, etc. that they are reluctant to shave them off.

Love,
Tom

CHAPTER 12

FROM THE CHANNEL TO THE SOUTHWEST PACIFIC

DICKENS HAD his first birthday party on May 2nd in our house in Cambridge. There were snappers, candy baskets, favors and a colorful birthday cake. I was there. It had been almost a year since I reported for work at the South Boston Navy Yard and started a new type of life to which I managed to adapt. It was technical work for my liberal background, and I struggled to measure up to the job. Thanks to the ten months of Navy schooling and the force-feeding of daily experience I was led deep into the job's intricacies.

The hours were long and consistent, so much so that I rarely managed to have a free Sunday, and many times worked almost 'round the clock. Sometimes the job made great demands. There was one period of two months, for instance, when I only saw son Dickens in a wakeful state on two occasions, though we shared the same roof. There were two-month stretches on the night shift when Math and Dickens stayed alone all night, and I came home in the morning to sleep. And there had been times when I stayed on the job at the yard until the wee hours of the morning after a long day. It was not easy on my wife, but she provided the necessary understanding, patience and competence in her job. Math was a good mother, and a good wife.

There were exciting moments at the yard. I remember the thrilling arrival of the destroyer *Hobson*, her depth charge racks empty, and five Nazi prisoners from the victim submarine aboard. They were just young fellows, these prisoners, fourteen or fifteen years old, and the skipper was twenty-one. The tale of the gunnery officer explaining the kill was engrossing.

As the war heated up, the entire country sensed that there was to be a crossing of the English channel and an attack on the French mainland. But no one knew when it would take place. It was obvious also, that the Germans knew the attack was imminent, and the chances were that they were quite ready.

*   *   *

Since May 15, 1943, my brother-in-law, Jim Mathes, had been struggling with his aviation course at Bloomsburg, Penn. It was a course for seasoned civilian pilots who were learning the Navy's ways in the air, and these pilots were ticketed to provide primary flying lessons to embryo pilots in training planes, preliminary to said pilots passing on to be trained as Navy fighters and bombers. Jim probably had less air time than any of his classmates, and nervously watched man after man wash out of the program as the weeks wore on.

His wife, Mary Chapman Mathes, used to visit him every weekend. She would take a train from Penn Station, New York, on Friday and go to Wilkes-Barre, Penn. From there she caught a bus and rode some 75 miles to Bloomsburg. The bus was usually crowded and she would sit on her suitcase in the aisle for most of her trips. Then on Monday she'd make the trek back to New York City where she'd purchase her ticket for the following Friday. One such Monday, she waited in line about a half hour to get to the ticket counter and when the agent handed her the ticket she was embarrassed to find that she didn't have enough cash to pay the fare. A man waiting in line heard her state her problem and stepped up and offered to give her some cash with which to pay for the ticket. When she asked if he would take a check, the man said promptly, "Sure." So she got her ticket. Strange things happen in war time.

Toward the end of the program at Bloomsburg it was suddenly discontinued, and some 80% of the class were released, which included Jim. On September 6th he was detached from Naval Aviation Cadets and assigned with a different designation, D(V)S to rank from 10 August, 1943. He was ordered for training to Naval

Indoctrination at Fort Schuyler, Bronx, NY. Given a choice for subsequent duty, he picked motor torpedo boats (PT) because they seemed more individual, and the nearest to flying that he could get. The new wooden PT boats carried torpedoes as major offensive weapons, and twenty-mm guns for surface or AA use. These craft were very fast, small, and maneuverable. As one might imagine, they would pound dreadfully in open water. This factor alone should have suggested to Jim that with his innate kidney problems he would not be a good candidate for such service. However, it was an exciting branch of the service and this is what Jim aimed for. He had help in landing his position in the PT program through his father-in-law, Mr. Charles F. Chapman, the same man who had solicited Brother Jeff to go to Washington to join the Army Engineer Amphibian Command. As the editor of *Motor Boating Magazine*, and the author of the famed book entitled *Piloting, Seamanship, and Small Boat Handling*, the nautical "bible" still used extensively by the Navy and around the world, Mr. Chapman knew most of the Navy high brass, and was able to aid Jim in getting into training at Melville, Rhode Island, the base of the PT operations.

On January 21, he was detached from Fort Schuyler and ordered to Melville, RI, to the Motor Torpedo Boat Training Center for temporary duty under instruction pending further assignment for duty afloat. Two and a half months later, Jim was graduated high in his class. During those trying months of training he and Chap spent a few weekends with us in Cambridge. They had been living in a hotel in Newport. On April 17 he received orders to join Squadron #34 in England, as an auxiliary officer to make up its final complement. In early May, he was aboard a ship bound for the British Isles. Following is his first letter to his wife, Mary Chap. It is in the form of a report, written while en route to England. Jim wrote vividly of his experiences from the time he left the States, and because he felt that it might be more efficient to direct his letters to one source, he passed on word to Chap to forward copies to the family. It was a good scheme and paralleled the plan that my Dad had adopted earlier for letters from Jeff and Tom. All Jim's letters were written in report form. He added bits and pieces as the day or days went along, and generally enclosed them as one letter. They made good reading.

The Atlantic
May 5, 1944
Dear Chap,

The number of land birds on this ship, now several hundred miles off land, is an odd, sad sight. I just got some food for them—and a catbird landed within three feet of me. They're all in pairs, too. A pair of catbirds, a pair of thrushes, a pair of sparrows and a land bird unknown to me, are with us.

The seas are calm with only gentle swells to rock us to sleep. We're well protected with ample escort and plenty of ships ahead, astern and on each beam. It's bed time. Our first night out. This convoy is a well organized thing and we're in close contact constantly...[censored]

...The land birds left sometime in the night, as the old timers said they would. I imagine they made shore ok. We're pitching a bit tonight. Have put our bow under a couple of times.

For supper tonight we had chicken noodle soup, steak, corn on the cob, and mashed potatoes; coffee, tea or cocoa to drink; canned peaches, cookies for dessert. Plenty of pickles, olives and meat sauce always on the table. Could have had thirds if we wanted them. Arthur's getting fat...

I had a two hour nap this P.M. It's a nuisance to have to keep turning our watches ahead. It cheats us out of our sleep.

The day is spent mighty leisurely. So far we have no duties. We check on our course for our own satisfaction, watch the communication in the convoy.

It's been warm weather so far, so we've sat in the sun, out of the wind in sheltered spots. The men on board have traveled a lot. It's interesting to listen to them talk of their reactions to India, Scotland, etc. Guess the Dutch colonies are the neatest and most attractive. The British evidently have done little to raise the standard of living in their colonies.

Evidently our escort made contact. Depth charges were dropped. All ended well. No harm done; the convoy plunged slowly along. The day has been overcast. The wind came up tonight. Portuguese men-of-war floated by us. Saw a school of blackfish. They are little whales, but resemble big porpoises.

I'm getting to know the men better. One man, an electrician on board, has been to sea since 1912. They've seen the world, and their comments indicate that most of them have learned something from their travels. The chief engineer spoke of Europeans tonight.

"They'll always follow a leader," he said. "They don't think for themselves, but follow the strongest leader around."

I've heard some very intelligent men say this of the German people, and it does apply to the rest, perhaps…

Stayed in the sack 'til 11:30 today. Had a good lunch. Moseyed around this P.M. Have no jobs on board so the time drags. Practiced a little blinker and semaphore, then read the rest of Reader's Digest. Played some checkers with our Army Sergeant roommate in which he beat the deuce out of me. After a tasty supper, Art and I walked around some more, watched the convoy, practiced some communications. Guess we'll be halfway over soon. Have been feeling fine and eating a lot of good food.

A plane met us this morning, much to my surprise. Looks as if we have air cover over most of the ocean. Very comforting. Guess this country and England have really done an amazingly fine job at stopping those U boats, and they sure had the upper hand too.

This ocean air really makes you go "Blah" as Mothers Mathes and Jackson would say. All we do on board is eat, sleep, and take a few short strolls. I feel pleasantly drugged most of the time. Poker is a favorite pastime among the merchantmen. We ensigns haven't even got enough energy to play poker.

…Washed my wool socks out in coolish warm water, left some soap in them. Am drying them on a towel, as I've seen you do. Every once in a while I go down and stretch them out a bit. Ah, the sun's real warm for a while. Wish we could get into shorts, but too cold for that.

Had a long talk with our Sergeant roommate tonight after a delicious supper. He was a court clerk in the Bronx. I asked him about Boss Ed Flynn. Sarg said he was a crooked bum. Asked him about a lot of other men. Now, Sarg is a Democrat. He has no use for Roosevelt and it looks like a lot of other Democrats feel the same way. To my surprise, Sarg spoke highly of Governor Dewey.

The skipper is a good man. Very Swedish, with long, wavy blond hair, very quiet, very attentive to his job. Has a happy little twinkle in his eye.

Saw seven tern-like sea birds this P.M. Needless to say, they were damn welcome. Guess we have another 5 full days, but "we be get-tin' there." It'll be darn interesting to look this new country over, speak to these people and learn their way of life.

...Slept 'til 11:30 again. The old ship rolled and my body was well rolled too. Mom could lose weight on this sort of sea. Have been feeling fine myself, by the way. So none of your Bermuda-trip-with-a-seasick-husband in the future, lady. The rest of the P.M. was spent walking around for exercise, sitting in the sun, and gabbing.

...Up at seven. Breakfast at 8, then ambitiously went to sleep until noon. Spent most of this P.M. talking to the first engineer. He's from Plymouth, NH; Mom, Dad, and Gaga would like to know. From four to five we had a catch. The Navy issues two gloves and several balls to the armed guard on board. Gosh, what beauti-ful gloves. They're more beautiful than any I ever had. Must have cost at least $15 before the war. It was fun playing, for our arms had to be good. A missed ball came pretty close to going over-board.

...Don't care for this defensive position we're in. I much prefer an offensive operation, like the work I've chosen. Things may get hot, but at least you're the perpetrator, not on the receiving end...

[Mary Chap's note in this letter guesses that a submarine was sunk during this interlude as the letter is all chopped up by a censor]

...I'm frank to say I don't like this business one bit. I'd take it in preference to armed guard any day. Don't like playing target, espe-cially out in this ocean—it's too damn big and lonely. Depth charges were going off all over the place and it was a rude awaken-ing to hear and feel a big explosion every once in a while. It brought us to our feet in a hurry! We saw lots of fish. Here's hoping we sleep peacefully 'til 8 A.M.

Gosh, what wouldn't I give to be in our house on Flagler Drive. Oh, to be bored by commuting again.

...A dreary day with low clouds and intermittent rain from dark scudding nimbus only a few feet above the water. But it's a merciful

sky, for it protects us from air attack and it's more disagreeable
for the hunting subs than it is for us. They haven't bothered us
all day. Have just started *A Tree Grows in Brooklyn.* Tell Gaga I can
see why she liked it so. It is warm, human, and full of understanding.

...It's been wash day today and underwear, hankerchiefs, paja-
ma, etc. hang from lines that criss-cross our room. Find that wash-
ing isn't an impossible job for a male, but guess you wouldn't ap-
prove the results highly. It's been a restful day. Feel mighty rested,
but after the first few days, I've not been able to appreciate this
good food. Too little exercise. Had prime ribs of beef for lunch.
Good, too, but only hungry enough for one helping.

Art, Paul and the Sarg are fine. We've all been good sailors.
Terra Firma will feel funny to our "roll and pitch accustomed legs."
It will be a good funny feeling though. The coat you gave me has
been swell. Many of these days have been cold and raw and even
the good days have been followed by cool nights. I've worn your
coat almost constantly since the day we cleared the U.S. to my
comfort and the jealousy of my roommates.

We're getting the biggest swells we've had since we started; huge
long swells that measure 100 yards from one crest to the next.
Luckily for our cargo they have smooth crests, and we roll harm-
lessly over them with only an occasional deck awash. At times we
heel over to a 20 degree angle. How many creaks and groans and
vibrations there are on this ship. Can think of better things to do
than count them, but I'll bet there are a good 20 different ship's
voices we hear at night. Another few days and we should be there.
I'll cable you the instant we hit ground. It'll be the first thing I do.

A lovely sunny day, but the air is cold. Many gulls now, but they
don't have the old York Harbor gull accent to which I am used.
These make meek, soft sounds. These look small, thinner. Even the
birds are rationed I guess.

It's a rugged, mountainous coastline that we now see, with little
islands broken off from the main coast line. The land, though it
looks rough and mountainous, seems to have a smoothness about
it. All the peaks are rounded. It's a fine clear day to sight land on.
Can't wait to see these people. Hope I get some leave time. I can
get a jeep or such to get up into Ireland and Scotland. The point
we're passing reminds me of the Nubble.

Our duty is darn interesting, especially when I compare it to this armed guard. I'm doing what I should in being here, and things could be much, much worse. Got to be over here anyway. Might as well see the good in it. I can see stone walls in the green fields. By gosh, land looks good. As we pass by more of this barren pictur-esque land, I'm more impressed with its beauty.

Seems so funny to have light enough for a good ball game at 11 P.M. Kind of hard to hit the hay. Midnight and still the sun glows below the horizon; glows so that only the brightest stars are visible in the clear cold twilight sky. We'll be in, wherever we dock, in a few hours. Can hear what sounds like big guns in the distance. See planes at night very often. All ours, I guess, so far.

Jim

Jeff's letter in early May gave us news of another landing in which he took part. Of course, we had presumed that he was actively fighting the Japanese, but his references in his letters gave us quite a turn none-the-less. If the Tami invasion had been his regiment's smallest, this one was its biggest. The staging and rehearsals for the landing at Tamahmera Bay/Hollandia were so extensive that it was divided into two areas, on both Goodenough Island where Jeff's outfit staged and at Finschhafen.

The G.I.'s, in traditional fashion, used to demean the "big shots," and referred to General Douglas MacArthur, the supreme commander, as "Dug-out Doug." However, Jeff says he will always revere him as a military genius who consistently outwitted the ene-my and conducted an exemplary campaign. In Tamahmera Bay, outside of Hollandia, Dutch New Guinea, an operation in which Jeff took part, MacArthur came ashore on D-Day, and was certain-ly not hunkered down in any dugout.

This was a classic MacArthur strike, bypassing the Wewak-Hanna Bay area where the Japanese were feverishly working to be ready to meet the Allies. The leap-frog movement caught the ene-my unawares. The Allied forces found warm bowls of rice sitting on tables, so complete was the surprise, as the Japanese troops left the beaches and rushed for the rear.

As usual the LCV's and LCM's were taken aboard the ships

which transported the infantry, in place of the Navy's small boats that usually hung from the davits. LCV stands for "Landing Craft Vehicle" but the primary load was personnel. The hull was of wood, and the armament, a 30-caliber machine gun. Unlike the LCP, "Landing Craft Personnel," they had a bow ramp. The LCM (Landing Craft Materiel) were somewhat larger, being 56 feet long and were made of steel.

For this mission, Jeff's outfit was on an Aussie attack ship, as they were called, which was a delight as the British Naval ships all boasted a "wet mess," meaning alcohol was served.

Once the armada arrived at the target, boats were lowered, and Jeff's outfit went to work, first taking the troops, in waves of six or seven boats spaced five minutes apart. Then they unloaded supplies, once the beachhead was secure. On this occasion, as on so many others, there was no immediate opposition, because the Japanese had fled inland with the Allies' arrival. The beach became organized with several well-planned supply dumps, all under the control of Jeff's shore battalion.

By nightfall, the Naval ships withdrew, leaving Jeff's outfit and their small boats at the beach to support the advance of the infantry. There being no roads in the jungle, the troops had to be supplied by boat, as they moved ahead.

On one such visit Jeff ran into a snag. When they got to the appointed spot, he flashed the shore party with the questioning code word. They were to return it with the answering one. However, what came back was the code for yesterday! Suspecting an enemy trap, Jeff tried it again with the same result.

Fortunately they had an alternate code, which Jeff asked for, and the response was positive, so in they went. It turned out that the infantry guy had been confused with his dates, and all was well. They unloaded supplies and some fresh troops and took on a couple of wounded, and returned to base. Jeff speaks of his latest action in the following letter.

APO 322

6 May, 1944

Dear Moth and Dad,

Another operation completed, and again a chance to do normal things like writing home. Sorry about the drought of letters lately but from now on, for a while at least, I'll be able to write faithfully.

This last landing, a big one, found me emerging as always, without my hair mussed. No sir, you need never worry about skinny old me. I was born under a lucky star…

…The situation out here seems to be progressing favorably enough and for the time being anyway, the little Nips are on the run. Those we see don't appear to be too full of fight. We're not underestimating them however.

I'm enclosing a couple of pieces of Japanese invasion money for use in occupied countries. At the same time I am enclosing a label from a Jap beer bottle. The invaders are now the invaded, and besides losing face they've lost their beer. It was good too!

Actually, though, I'm a lousy souvenir hunter. It seems too pointless picking up and lugging around a lot of crap that you wouldn't know what to do with. If I thought otherwise I would long since have sent all kinds of tokens to you. Hope you agree with my views on this.

I know that so far I've missed Joy's birthday, Gram's birthday, and after tomorrow, Dad's birthday. I'm also pretty sure that a couple of days ago I missed Dickens first anniversary. All these omissions tend to make me mighty sad indeed, for I certainly hate to miss a chance to tell each and every one of you how much I love you, and am thinking of you…

Lots of love,

Jeff

From Bill Webster we learn of Fred Borsodi's latest duty. Web speaks also of the future meeting of Dickens and Billy Jr. It will be fun.

Curtiss-Wright Corporation
May 9, 1944
Dear Dick,

...I have been down here in Maryland for the past ten days and expect to be here another month or two. I brought down an experimental ship, a seaplane called XSC-1, since we had no facilities to handle a seaplane in Columbus. I started flying this machine the middle of February (made the first flight on it) and we spent several months in Columbus ironing out the bugs in the land plane. It's a nice little ship, a single seater with a turbo supercharger. It's not a fighter but scoots along pretty well and climbs like the proverbial homesick angel. This flying off of water is a nice change of scenery now that I am used to it again.

I can answer your questions on old Borsodi because Bunny and I went over to Dayton and spent the week-end with Fred and Marcia the week before I came away. He is assigned to the fighter branch at Wright Field and likes it quite a bit. He's the same old Borsodi with more stories than ever now. He seems a bit nervous after his experience. He can't sit down for long and when he does he must have something in his hands. I think he is honestly looking forward to going back into action. Since he has been at Wright Field he has been all over the country flying different types of planes, such as the jet propelled jobs.

We are at the Patuxent River N.A.S. I am fortunate to be staying at the BOQ #1. Is there any chance of your ever coming down here on a trip?

My correspondence has dropped off in the last year or so. I have to watch myself to keep from talking about my son in my letters. These kids sure are a lot of fun, eh, Dick. We will have to get our boys together at the earliest opportunity...

Gotta beat it now. My ship is ready.

Best of luck,
Web

Following is a letter from James M. Mathes Sr., to his son Jim, the first letter he'd written since Jim Jr's departure.

May 9, 1944
Dear Jim:

I haven't written you before this because I imagine that many letters mailed now will probably be received at your destination before you arrive. I noticed, however, that your good wife had already written you each day—so I guess she plans that you should have a stack of letters on hand when you get there. Her good example made me a bit concerned that possibly a letter from me might be late.

In the first place, Jim, you were one swell egg and extremely thoughtful in the way which you said good-bye to me on that Tuesday morning. I considered it as kind and thoughtful of you to come down to breakfast with me—but I did not realize that it would be our last little visit together for a while. When you walked out in the hall, as I left for the train, I did notice some of your paraphernalia, your clothes, bundles, etc., lying on the floor by the foot of the stairs. Even then I didn't get the full significance of the fact that it might be your final trip with your belongings. Previously you had taken in your trunk, and the casual manner in which that had been handled I thought indicated you'd probably be home all right for dinner that evening. Then again I felt pretty sure that you would telephone me from wherever you might be if your departure was imminent.

However, the manner of the parting I think was quite satisfactory. You know, I am sure, that my love and my prayers go with you at all times during this great adventure. I smiled at Bill Watson the other day when he had said to me that your trip would be in the nature of a paid excursion, plus a sightseeing trip to the Mediterranean. I guess that is about as sensible a way to look at it as is possible—but I am frank to admit that I don't always feel that way about it…

…Love to you Jimmy, and may everything work out as you would like to have it. It would seem to me that this war in Europe would be over before Fall. I don't see how the Germans can stand this pounding much longer.

Love to you,
Dad

Jeff is apparently enjoying a breathing spell though the formation of a new outfit sounds foreboding.

Co. C, 542 Reg't
APO 322 c/o Postmaster
San Francisco, CA
11 May, 1944
Dear Mother & Dad,

The big news this time is my transfer to Company C. (My original outfit used to be called Company I, remember?) The reason is not mysterious: simply that there was no further necessity for the old job. My work there was done. No complaints with my service so far as I know.

…This old war seems to be leveling off into a steady siege of ground gaining. I'm proud to report that our outfit is doing it's job well enough to draw constant praise from the higher-ups. Makes a guy feel pretty good to know he is contributing…

…I'd like to see the Victory Garden about now. Must be a mouth-watering sight.

My letter writing recently has been confined to these last two to you. Please explain to all that I'll broaden out as soon as possible. I sure do owe a lot of letters! Once more I can't help observing how struck I am with all the folks who have been so good about writing to me.

Take it easy. Don't work too hard on the garden, in the office, or in the hospital.

Lots of love,
Jeff

CHAPTER 13

GETTING READY

SOMETIME AFTER the Tamahmera/Hollandia operation, during a lull in the battle activity Brother Jeff was named as defense counsel for a court-martial involving a soldier who had refused an order on D-Day. But his client was in custody and unavailable to Jeff, his "lawyer," until 15 minutes before the trial. And this was a general court martial with a possible death sentence, as a refusal of orders in combat was a serious offense.

Once the trial began, Jeff requested a delay so he could converse with the lad, and prepare some sort of defense. It was denied, and he continued with a claim of "double-jeopardy" (this as the defendant had been banished to a small off-shore island on D-Day, without a rifle. This island could have been full of Japanese).

The president of the court, Jeff's regimental commander, a West Point graduate, abruptly ordered a ten-minute recess and called Jeff before the court. The commander ordered him to get on with the trial without further complaints. Jeff replied that under the circumstances, he felt that he was not qualified to proceed.

The colonel's reply was, "If you're not qualified to continue, you're not qualified to be an officer." So the court was re-opened, and Jeff had to acquiesce to the court's decision. The prisoner was sentenced to 15 years in Leavenworth and a dishonorable discharge—all of which Jeff comments, he deserved.

In the Army, every officer is subject to assignment on a court-martial, either as a member of the court, a defense counsel, or trial judge advocate (prosecutor). Jeff served in all three capacities, and, after a couple of wins, he became sought after by GI's to handle their defense.

Jeff follows his recollections with a "naughty word" report in one of his recollections. (1) "One day our walkie-talkie radio conversation was interrupted by the following, 'Herro, Charwie. Wanna soot the sit? Wanna soot the sit?' We simply switched to the previously designated alternate channel and shut out the intruder. He was smart to find our frequency, but stupid to reveal that he knew it." (2) "On one of our unopposed landings, a sand bar caused us to drop the ramp a couple of feet short of the beach. One GI, as he stepped into ankle-deep water, turned around and, looking directly at me, said, 'You ain't worth a fuck; no shit, not a fuck!' I had to laugh."

* * *

In the meantime, Jim Mathes made the coast of England safely, but only in this letter did he disclose the identity of the dangerous cargo aboard his ship. His letter, as usual, reflects his thoughts and impressions. But as the tension built about the "big push" due with the channel crossing there was more concern on the home front for Jim's impending role in the action. Apparently he was too busy to worry.

England
May 14, 1944
Dear Chap,

We're safely on land, but our first night in port didn't lack for excitement. At 2:45 A.M. general alarm sounded. Air raid! Only a couple of planes were over, but with searchlights hunting them out and rocket guns and AA fire going off all around us, those few were plenty. Flares came down and so did a couple of bombs.

One burst a few miles off and seemed very near. We were on a tanker full of 100 octane gas, you see. If we'd been hit, we'd have stood a very good chance of personally tangling with those planes.

…I didn't want you to know our ship cargo 'til we were across.

…I had a few sub scares, and our DE's got one. In a convoy if you are on a 100 octane job, a ramming from another ship is about as much to be feared as torpedoes. One foggy night the guy behind us plowed by us within 15 feet, when we were dead in the water with engine trouble. Those awake were scared.

…Our train today took us by a crater left by last night's plane…

…The country we ride through is as lovely in a farming, rolling, lush way as any I have ever seen. Full of stock; healthy sheep and beef and dairy cattle. The animals make me think of home. A darn nice English gentleman who rode with us for several hours spoke ardently of his bees—his hobby. Made me think of mine.

I've rarely had so enjoyable a trip. This country is lovely, the people darn interesting and so very nice.

…I can't tell you where we are going. I don't even know yet for that matter. But I really think it's alright to tell you that we've traveled all day and that I'm loving it. These English are so wonderful. One man we rode with this A.M. told us with a modest gaiety of his having been bombed more than once, of having five neighbors in the house next door buried alive. He dug them out, and all were unharmed. The bricks from the splattered house flew into his kitchen through an open door. He and his wife were under the kitchen table.

…It's an old country alright! Hear tales of old Roman roads but have yet to pass on them. The essence of this antiquity is best expressed, I think, in the old station urinal, just comfortably visited by me…

…Everything is so lush and green. I can't get over the pastoral peaceful beauty here off the beaten track. The big industrial towns are dirty, but England is not made of all towns, I'm finding to my joy.

I hope I can get to know some of these people. For no matter how lovely a land is, you continue to look at it as an outsider until you get a key to let you in. Acquaintanceship with the native inhabitants is the only key worth using. I hope I can meet a nice family who'll take me in occasionally and make me feel at home. I'm eager to know these people and their country. I've met some awfully fine men already; I hope some such will be near-by at our destination. Our folks should take visiting British and Australian officers in. I'd love so to have someone like your folks or mine do this for me here, and I've only been in this land for the daylight of one day.

Love,
Jim

Jim has moved to a castle in Scotland, which seems a strange place for a PT boat officer. He continues to give us a typically accurate and detailed account of his experiences, flavored as always, with his burning enthusiasm.

Scotland
May 18, 1944
Dear Chap,

10:15 P.M. and I just got in from a walk. The southern slopes still getting the sun. This country is very mountainous and very beautiful. It rains in weeping fogs, but it doesn't get me down. If I stand under a tree, it's clear a few minutes later. This land is all so new to me that I walk about as if in a dream.

On the castle estate in which we are temporarily billeted the planting surpasses anything I've ever seen. It's something like Otto Kahn's and that huge estate over in Westbury we used to walk over. But that planting, though beautiful in a grand way, only goes back a generation or two. Here you see trees planted in terms of centuries. Beeches, with holly trees in between them, line the mile drives. Rhododendrons in huge clusters, flowering trees and shrubs are scattered here and there. Everything is in grand style, even to the fields, for to the visitor they seem very large. Birds are everywhere and lovely singers. They should be singing for the banks are bonnie and the high hills off in the distance guide the fogs that strike their sides into a lovely lake.

…These letters we censor are an interesting reflection of the lives of our men. So far, about one letter in five reflects a happy useful married life, or family life. Some of the letters, though written by men or boys with a limited education are full of goodness. Others are sort of in between. They have their standards and values, but the standard is apt to be a bit surprising. For instance, a fellow who wrote home an endearing letter to his girl. He kept her picture over his bed. A fellow sailor made remarks in a mixed tone of compliment and jokery every time he passed the picture. The proud owner was offended. As he said in his letter, "I told the guy, honey, that if he didn't cut out the kidding, I'd kick his ass."

We plan to take a bicycle ride up into a scenic section this P.M. Five of us will rent bikes in a town across the way. If the weather will only favor us, we'll have a fine afternoon.

...Paul got a flat tire a half-mile out of town, and we all turned back. It was raining at the time and continued to rain all afternoon, so the flat was a lucky occurrence. I had tea, bread and jam, cake and biscuits instead. Became quite full.

...We're eating royally here. They wait on us hand and foot. We have linen table cloths and linen napkins. Tonight the boys ate ice cream and steak! Went to the movies with Art and two other officers I met.

Walked home. It's now about 10:30 P.M. Twilight and rain have combined to make it a lovely evening. The birds—and there are many of them—sing beautifully. The air is heavy with the scent of flowers, wet grass, and country dust freshened by the rain. It's very lovely, very peaceful. They have a thrush over here, and this bird can sing sweetly and with great variety.

Tell Mom and Dad that their home is built much after the "Cotswold Hills" type of architecture. It's something quite special in England, set aside as a definite type of structure, lines, and general appearance. We rode in the train by some of these houses.

I'm fascinated with this new land, the people and their ways. Even the air raid, now the damn thing is over, was fun. It was a spectacle full of impressiveness.

I heard a story, from one officer removed from the foreign correspondent who witnessed it. The place: Russia. The scene: a truck run off the road, broken down. A driver. A military guard. The conversation "Who carelessly allowed this truck to go off the road? Who is the driver of this truck? I am the driver." A shot.

Thus our allies, the Russians, punish possible carelessness of a man toward a vehicle. The end means everything to these people. The means employed to enforcement of this desired end is unimportant. American intellectual communists should get more of these facts.

From the bluebells here in Scotland to Russian communism. A far cry.

Love,
Jim

In the meantime, Brother Tom is getting on with the job of reading, in his spare moments. The war in Italy is not all work.

Italy
May 21, 1944
Dear Folks,

There's not a damn thing new with me. I am still in the bombing business and all that kind of stuff. Certainly glad to see that Italian drive get started. It's a step in the right direction.

I'm very embarrassed at my monumental blunder in failing to consult my birthday scorecard. I note that the birthdays of Dad, Gram, Uncle Tom, and Dickens have all passed unnoticed. There is really nothing I can say except that there is no legitimate excuse and I'm sorry.

I'm still reading a terrifically wide selection of stuff. The only common denominator is whether or not it can hold my interest. This is at least one good thing resulting from my Italian visit. I have ample opportunity to read good books. Reading, of course, is the greatest force in education, and after all what is college, academically speaking, but books. The Professors are the road signs to direct you down the short cuts of life.

This is your old crackerbox philosopher signing off.

Love,
Tom

The world knew that it was only a matter of time before the big invasion of France would occur. General Eisenhower was to make the call, and with each passing day it seemed more imminent. This letter from Jim held that promise

May 24, 1944
Dear Chap,

We're off again. This has been a lovely day. I spent all of it outdoors most the afternoon on a bicycle. I've rented one three different days now. This last afternoon the town had a parade. Although there were some men in it, most of the marchers were women—RAF girls in gray; Navy girls (Wrens) in dark blue; Army girls in khaki. Then there were kilted men with bagpipes. Also lots of young boys and girls. This country is really in uniform. Boys and girls and women are working. Women, wives included, are compelled to take a job. I suppose if a man has a family she can make that her job.

Funny how I feel about leaving this country. It has been so beautiful, the people so friendly that I feel almost a homesickness for it. I'd love to bring you here some day.

...This current move should bring us to our final base, wherever that is. I know it'll be very unlike the lovely spot we left, but I'm hoping for the best.

Guess the character I got to know the best was the town blacksmith, Mr. Campbell. He also runs a bicycle rental, plus a general baby carriage, lawn mower, etc. repair shop. His place of work is like a junk shop, but not his home. The brass door knobs gleam, the front steps are scrubbed clean. Even dirty Mr. Campbell appears well dressed, neat and clean when he is at home.

Funny—the parade ended in the town square. The music has been playing since before the parade. I'll be darned if when I rode by I didn't hear "Home On The Range." The parade culminated a War Bond Week. The little town collected over a quarter of a million dollars.

One city in which I spent most of my time in a restaurant wash room cleaning up, was as dirty, poor and disappointing as the area which we had recently left was fresh, clean, thrifty and pleasant. I guess you've seen more of the city than I, but I've seen enough to satisfy me. True, one of the squares, a palace and some of the architecturally admirable cathedrals were of interest. The strong clear church bells sounded good, and near one cathedral I stood to hear an organ play and voices sing. I wish I could have gone to church and counteract the impression I now have of a very dirty city. Even the best of architecture is at a disadvantage when covered with sooty blackness.

...Out in the rural districts again. Just saw some lilacs near the little station where we last stopped. This is pretty country. I hope it is like this from now on.

...We've settled again and quite comfortably. Saw Lou Young of Dartmouth last night. It seemed so good to see an old friend.

...Mail came last night. Some stuff from Fuff, Dick, Mom, and Nene. None from you. But the letters I got were numbered and there were great gaps, so I know your letters will be here soon. Dick told an amusing story on Math. You must make him repeat it.

...At last your letters arrived, and in wonderful quantity. The letters make it in about ten days! Hope the wonderful luck continues.

I'm writing everyone through you and I hope it doesn't offend them, but I'd rather write you a reasonably decent letter and write only you, than to write off a million little notes to everyone.

...I've been assigned a boat and am being kept busy and quite happy. It's 10:30 P.M. and bedtime. So long for now.

Love,

Jim

CHAPTER 14

D-DAY

ON JUNE 6, 1944 the radio blared forth history-making news. The massive Allied Invasion of France had begun. Word was spread world-wide. Thousands of landing boats and huge Naval combat ships plowed the English Channel. Countless airplanes, bombers, fighters, planes towing gliders filled with men, flew overhead. In the States we had been waiting patiently for many months for this invasion. We'd seen countless pictures of all the equipment stowed in neat lines on the British countryside; we'd heard tales from returning soldiers and sailors about the exciting build-up, the preparation. Daily, the papers had reminded us of the imminent operation, and we realized how very much it would mean. For many months we'd watched the newspapers religiously, and noted the conquest of North Africa, the American landing coinciding with the British drive that started from the doors of Cairo, Egypt. We read of the invasion of Sicily, of Sardinia, of the southern portion of Italy. Many ships had entered the Yard in Boston, fresh from the battle area, and I had seen gaping holes, and indications of shrapnel along their sides. I listened intently to the officers' and men's accounts of the action, and I sensed the rhythm of battle.

But it was the invasion of France which was the emphasis of the moment. Maybe it was because we expected so much; because the coast of France seemed close to Germany to us; because France was the conquest the Germans had undertaken successfully before the United States had declared war; and most probably because we still remembered the last war with its emphasis on France, and the trench warfare so fiercely fought.

Even a greater aspect to the thrill of the great invasion was the fact that Jim Mathes most certainly would be taking part in the action. His PT unit was the only squadron of PT's to be assigned to the European theater of war. This brought the invasion even closer.

It was too early to know how successful the Allies would be. But at last, we were started and that in itself was great cause for rejoicing. Naturally, though, it provoked a great anxiety for all those young American guys who were waging the battle—classmates, friends, and all those nice young gunnery officers whom I had come to know from their visits in the Navy Yard.

Jim Mathes Sr. was in the bath tub when he got the word. He took the time to post this letter to his son on that very day.

June 6, 1944
Dear Jim,

Usually I have the radio turned on for the early morning news—every morning. I guess one of the reasons I wake up early since you have been gone is that I am anxious to have the very latest dope over the air—just as soon as I awake. The stations, as a rule do not come on until seven o'clock—as you probably know.

This morning, it was just my luck that I was in the bath at about 7:05 to 7:10 A.M. All of a sudden, the telephone rang. Mom answered and it was your aunt, Nene, saying that the invasion was on. Boy, oh boy, what excitement. Of course I put the radio on immediately and sure enough, we had plenty of news.

Apparently the people in London did not know about what was taking place any earlier than we here in America. All of which, I think, is swell. And, of course, I smile when I realize that President Roosevelt was on the air last evening for half an hour or so, talking about the invasion in Rome. He accomplished one thing for sure—he kept the Germans up and awake so that they must have been tucked in bed and fast asleep when our invasion started. Clever stunt, I'll say.

A little while ago Miss Johnson was talking with Mom. She told her that she heard a commentator on the air say that he had been over and just returned in a PT boat, and he told what the PT boats were doing. Believe me, Jimmy, it means you are right in the thick of it. I know it is exactly what you want—and I do hope and pray that you will not take any unnecessary chances.

Optimism over the success of the invasion runs high in this country. We are all so much concerned, however, about the number of our boys who will pay the supreme sacrifice—before we are far enough along to deliver the Germans the licking they deserve. I don't know that there is much else that can be done about it, but I hope and pray it will not take long. If the underground comes to the surface as rapidly and as forcefully as many of us hope, I see no reason why the Germans shouldn't realize what they are up against within three weeks or a month. They should sue for peace on any basis…Love to you with the best of luck,

Dad

Brother Tom continues to write faithfully. He is a far cry from the excitement along the English Channel and though he alludes to the invasion, he appears to be little moved by the action at this point.

Corporal Thomas C. Jackson
49th Wing Hdqs. (H)
APO 520, c/o PM NYC
June 9, 1944
Dear Folks,

Nothing new here. Just sitting around drowsily reading and thinking how horrible the army is, and what a large void it's making in my life…

…Maybe this invasion will mean we'll get home sooner than I think…

…I am quite discouraged at Willkie's withdrawal. The prospect of Roosevelt, Dewey, Bricker et al is enough to make me vomit.

…Life flows along like muddy rainwater in the gutter. Last night I saw a fairly good USO show, and a miserable movie, which did, however, allow me to once more be thrilled and amazed at the odd formation of Chester Morris' face. He looks like a Dick Tracy character.

I have a new address as you can see above. I have been here on detached service, which means I am still a member of the 726th, but eat, sleep, live and work here. It's like being lent…

…Just arrived this afternoon, but the set-up seems fine. It's a lot more comfortable than the squadron, but not as pretty. However, I think I'll have more opportunity for advancement and for work than before. A wing is completely administrative—sort of like a branch office you might say—coordinating various bomb groups…

Love,

Tom

The invasion came to life with the first letter from Jim Jr. following the June 6th D-Day. It was, as usual, in the form of a report to Chap.

June 12, 1994

Dear Chap,

June 6, 1944—Everything OK. Will write more when I can grab more time.

June 7, 1944—The war has suddenly become very real. We've been in on history and man has a damn fool way of making history.

We patrol "somewhere in the English Channel." This morning we played crash boat—the plane, a paratrooper job—(Thousands have been going over and coming back about 100 feet or so over our heads) went down just as we got to the scene, but all the crew were safe in their rubber boat. We took them aboard. I treated a slight arm wound on one. Then we transferred them to a larger naval vessel. They were so grateful. They tried to give us whatever they had.

We left station again to go alongside a "sweep" (minesweeper), which had just hit a mine. She was a mess of tangled wreckage, broken in two and barely hanging together. She was burning and sank 10 minutes after we left her. We took off 42 men in various wounded stages. We picked several men out of the water first. I went over the side to get one of them. We boarded the sweep and carried a good third of the 42 men we took aboard off. (42 must have been about half the crew—another ship got the rest). A couple I saw weren't worth bothering with. We gave morphine. I bandaged and sprinkled sulfa—and Chap, there were some awful holes

I sprinkled. We got them all onto a hospital ship—skippered by a Dartmouth man, and the Navy Doctor aboard, Doc Lynch, was even a Dartmouth classmate.

Those sights didn't bother me a bit—to my utter amazement. Putting my hands in those bloody holes—to get the sulfa in properly—didn't bother me. This is my first real touch of war, and I'm so surprised at my own objectivity. This business won't change me in the least. Already, today is a dream, an unpleasant war movie. Reality is home and you and our friends.

I'm quite contented. I'm grateful that we saved men today instead of killing men, I even got the ship's cat off safely—poor dazed, wet thing. She just had a little cut in her neck. This war must accomplish a great deal to compensate for the suffering I've seen this day. I don't think it can counterbalance the evil within it. But my place is here, and I'd be miserable as a 4-F'er back home. Frankly, for me, the worst part of the war occurred a few days back when we were regaining our sea legs, and I was busy draining my stomach. I feel so wonderfully now, but felt horrible then.

Please, Chap, believe me when I say we are very safe. Mines don't bother us. We don't set them off with our shallow draft. No one wastes a shell on us. There are too many real targets to shoot at. None of us has been even slightly damaged and records show that these PTs will come easily through.

I have a beard. I haven't washed in three days. We have a ring-side seat on this damn fool, stimulating-from-a-distance, awful and saddening-at-a-close-range show.

June 10, 1944: We are still on duty over here, and I am actually conforming to this new, dream-like environment. Generally speaking, most striking about this war is the contrast between violence and serenity. The little white house on the hill looks quietly out on the bay. Trees rise from the rolling fields—then a shell bursts. When the dust settled, a shattered skeleton of the house remains.

The Bay is smooth. Only little waves with white caps give it the look of life. A DE slides smoothly through the water, only a mile or so off shore. Whoom! The DE is lost in a geyser tinted brown with flying oil. The geyser subsides. The DE, a mass of twisted wreckage, settles lower in the water, lists to port. A mine!

June 12, 1944: My beard can no longer possibly be mistaken for a 5 o'clock shadow. I wash in a bucket of sea water, from over the side. We sleep in snatches, when we get a chance.

But we play the part of observers, not participators. We are all safe. We eat well, and lately, sleep well. The first few days of sea sickness have gone. We have our sea legs, and far more important, our sea stomachs.

None of our stuff has been damaged. You see destruction would be unduly costly. We are small stuff, lucky small stuff.

I would give much to read the papers at home. Wonder what they say about what's going on right here.

Tell your Dad that I'm learning a bit about piloting. His book is on the shelf beside my chart house table.

June 14, 1944: All goes well. My beard begins to itch. I've learned to wash with salt water. But I'm still subjected to a terrific shock when I see the color of my pillow. Why don't they have brown sheets for such occasions as these. Received your letter of May 29th, today... We're well and healthy. That underwear suit is a blessing these nights, and sometimes days too, are cold. Mom's navy vest is also darn handy.

June 14, 1944 : Back again—safe and sound. Please give my love to all.

Jim

Tom has just moved permanently from his Bomber Squadron station to the bomber wing, where he says he has more work, although it is more exacting than before. Nonetheless it appears to please him.

Cpl T. C. Jackson
HQ SQ 49th Bomb Wing
APO 520 c/o Postmaster NYC
6/18/1944
Dear Folks,

I am quite relieved to hear that a letter has finally been received from Jeff.

...I've been here two days now and to date it seems ok. The work is more plentiful, more complicated, and more exacting—but it's also more interesting. I live in a room in a sort of tower affair—which I enter by a 25 foot ladder. This isn't too rough however, since it's exclusive, and cool, a distinct advantage in this weather.

Although at first I thought the food was wonderful, it now appears to be about the same as at the Squadron. One unpleasant feature is the strict insistence of the CO upon saluting all officers, wearing hats, and the proper uniform. Another rub is the exorbitant bar prices at the club. But on the credit side, it's closer to town, and there's a fairly nice little library. The latter has some surprising books for overseas, including three play anthologies, the works of Lewis Carroll, Bartlett's *Quotations* and Volume I and II of Hayes' *Political and Social History of Europe*.

To our mutual advantage, a typewriter is now available.

I understand that I can now write of the places I've seen and as a consequence, I'll do so, as you might conceivably be interested. Frankly I am not in the least impressed by them, except as to how badly they smell.

As I wrote before, Oran was the only place I saw in Africa, and I didn't get much of a look at it. Like most towns I've run across, it was completely dominated by soldiers. But it was more modern than I'd expected a North African town to be.

While here I've had occasion to visit Naples, certainly the most metropolitan city I've seen yet in my travels.

I've also seen Bari, a fairly pretty town if you don't have to smell it, or get in it. Also I have seen Lecce, Foggia, and Arignola, and numerous other small towns.

Despite Vesuvius and the Isle of Capri, and the war, my most exciting sight to date has been a 15 piece colored band—one of those typically brassy and vigorous, happy Negro outfits, complete with enthusiasms and showmanship. Although I favor small band jazz, there is no sight to compare with a 15 piece boogie orchestra…

To clear up what seems to be muddled in your minds, I will now attempt to explain the nature of heavy bomb groups. First of all heavy bombers are used strategically, instead of tactically. In the latter classification come the medium bombers, (B-25s, B-26s, A-20s) bombing and strafing around the front lines, and maintaining air supremacy. But the heavy bombers have no concern with the battle on the ground, and invasion advances really don't mean a damn thing in their daily routine. Their job is to strike deep in the internal section of Germany, Austria, etc., in order to weaken their production, and consequently slow down and cripple their efforts on the front. Hence the tactical part of the Air Force directly aid the front, while the heavies indirectly aid it. Since the heavies must be big planes, in order to drop enough bombs to make the long trips worth while, they have a large range, and so, for safety's sake, they are based well behind the front lines. Thus they can go about their aloof job without the regular inconveniences of the front lines. Now, I hope you will see that I am, therefore, perfectly safe, and my job continues the same as ever, come Italian offensive or invasion. All we do is keep the planes flying, and maintain the squadron so it can keep them up there. In other words, members of the Air Corps can not be, strictly speaking, soldiers, since all ground crew members are specializing and do little or no soldiering…

Love,

Tom

Jeff writes from the Pacific about the latest action of his landing boats which entailed the invasion of Hollandia, at Tamahmera Bay. A tough one, he says. He mentions Dad's victory garden, which is not extensive. Dad is not alone in planting a vegetable garden. It is a war effort that many in the country adopted enthusiastically and nurtured regularly.

FJJ

SWPA

18 June 1944

Dear Folks,

Been busy as heck these past few weeks—that's why no mail. Everything's going along in good shape—no cause for worry.

This last deal has been a rough one, with lots of action. Kept old Jeff skipping some to keep free from holes. About now, after a year in New Guinea, I've got to admit I'm ready to go home. There's something about this climate, and this life that slows a guy down. You get to a point where you just don't give a wind-break whether school keeps or not. Of course, this frame of mind doesn't effect your work, because that's automatic. And when you realize that there are plenty of guys in a worse plight (eg: the poor old infantry) you forget about being down in the dumps and take on a new life.

I seem to detect in your steady, welcome letters bright hopes for a quick home-coming on my part. Wish I had your optimism. We here all look at the "Rotation Plan" as a snare and a delusion. Doesn't promise a thing, really, and hasn't yet affected this theater.

So let's just forget about any imminent return and adopt Dad's philosophy of expecting the worst; then when my break does come it will be a pleasant surprise. Meanwhile, don't worry over my morale. It is still sound and I'm good for many more months of combat.

The new job is interesting and active. Constitutes a pleasant change from the paper-ridden staff job.

Moth, can't you take it easier in that Hospital work? I'm worried about you. You go at things so energetically. The same with both of you and the Victory garden. Don't be too vigorous. Sit on the porch and read the papers.

My best to all…

Love,

Jeff

Dad responded to a Father's Day letter from me in his typically proud manner. With pen in hand he scratched out a note that almost took a cryptographer, such as Brother Tom, to decode or decipher. But it was worth it to me to take the time to read it. I shall spare you, good reader, by transposing it to type.

One Ten Fulton Street
New York, NY
June 21, 1944
Dickster,

It was fine of you to have written that Father's Day letter and I certainly appreciated it. I guess you understand that Moth and my ambitions from away back to the very beginnings were to have you fellows develop into good healthy he-men, and as time goes along we realize more and more how we exceeded our fondest dreams; because after all there just couldn't be four finer specimens. You represent a high intelligence, good physiques, a sense of honor far beyond the average. You have demonstrated the fact that you all appreciate our efforts in many ways.

Frankly it does an old fellow a lot of good to be told he is appreciated once in a while. To receive such a letter on the day the shirt and garter manufacturer's set aside for fathers is not only appropriate, but allows for a little sentiment which is good. So I'll leave it that I might be "all right" but you are a specially swell guy.

Love,
Dad

Tom attempts to "straighten" out his Dad on the matter of the war. Dad sometimes tries to will the end of the war, and it doesn't always work.

June 26, 1944
Dear Folks,

...Dad you seem to be laboring under the delusion of staggering proportions. Your ideas on the Italian campaign justify my remarkably low opinion of your news sources—those ill-informed, fact-misconstruing, sickeningly-unctuous newscasters.

The Italian campaign is by no means soft. The guys at the front have had an incredibly rugged time—and are still having troubles. By no stretch of the wildest imagination can anyone deny that they are engaged in a terrible struggle. The Germans have most assuredly *not* run, but are fighting a dogged, determined, and it must be admitted, courageous and excellent fight—we have to battle for every inch.

In the air, too, the heavy bombers are operating in the toughest air league of all. But as for the ground crews, and rear echelons, we are leading a soft life. I hope my recent letter attempting to explain a heavy bombardment group's divorce from the fighting will make you see how this is possible...

Love,
Tom

Although Jim Jr. had arranged to write only Chap to pass on the word, he nonetheless penned other letters directly to the recipient. In the cases below he wrote Gaga Dearborn, his grandmother, a very touching letter shortly after D-Day. Mercifully, he did not go into detail about his battle actions.

June 25, 1944

Dear Gaga,

Chap sent me some snapshots yesterday. The wonderful girl has been such a swell correspondent. I get more letters than any other guy in the squadron thanks to my wonderful big clan of a family— Mom and Chap especially.

...I guess you enjoyed Dickens. You spoil them, in my opinion, but I must admit that you give all children something of yourself which so adds to their life that you could spoil hell out of them and still be blessing them with your presence. Gosh what a serious paragraph...

...As I've truthfully told the rest, ours seems more the role of spectator than participant, in this war, and we are very safe and sound...

...It seems unbelievable that we have only been gone from home for a little over one month at this writing. So many things, new and different have happened since I sadly kissed dear Chapper goodbye in downtown NYC, wishfully thinking that we would see each other in a day or so, that we weren't really going to push off.

But truthfully though, too, all has not been sad and lonely since I left. I've missed you all and our life, but so many new things have been laid before me, inviting investigation, that in many respects has been so far, a fascinating new venture.

These people are different. It's all so stimulating...

...I'm in excellent physical condition—hungry as a wolf, get a good 8 to 10 hours of sleep a day. I am bumping into Dartmouth and Exeter friends at the rate of one or two a week on an average. It's always such a wonderfully pleasant surprise.

Please tell Mom I got her V mails #43 and #44, one dated June 8th. I love her letters and she is very good to write so often and so faithfully. Loved Mom's verbal picture of little Fuffy, when they left her at Boston's South Station. I can picture her, "checked gingham dress, no hat, socks and Spauldings, suit case in one hand, box of cold lobster and bunch of six pansies in the other." For God's sake, don't show Fuf this.

Right now, I'm sitting stripped to the waist in the sun, smoking a pipe, and gazing fondly at a beautiful orange just beside me. It's going down my gullet *very* shortly.

Love you,

Jim

In a letter to me, a few days later, Jim is a bit more explicit about his battle experiences.

30 days hath September—June
Dear Dick,

...I've tacked several of those pictures of you, Math, and Dickens on my stateroom wall. Need my thanks be more obvious?

I'd love to have shared those happy, lazy moments-on-leave with you all in Greenwich. And yet there's a devil—and he is that—in me which would have made it hard for me to lay back with you and love it all to its full deserving worth. I'd have itched—that's what I often have—a damned internal itch. Though while out on a farm, or in the woods, or listening to music, I never get it. Being in Dad's house, but no—I get it in my own house, too—maybe it's my dissatisfaction with my job in the Agency—for I never used to have that damned internal itch.

I'm glad, though not surprised, that Dickens behaved so admirably at the christening, and at the social gathering of our wonderful clans...

...Yes, our assignment provided a front row seat to the invasion...We escorted the sweeps (minesweepers) in on D-Minus-One-Day. Came within less than a mile of the French Coast. It was amazingly quiet. We returned to UK to refuel, and came back to the same general location on D-Day. Lines of amphibious craft stretched ant-like over the horizon. Planes skimmed low over head by the thousands. They were mostly transports with paratroopers and often towing gliders. A constant air shuttle. Some of the planes returning waist high, had trouble. Luckily, they float for some time. We went to several of them, and picked up one entire crew.

The inshore waters were mine infested. We did a good bit of rescue, first aid, and carrying to hospital ships...Our crew behaved beautifully. My own objectivity toward sights I once would have found sickening, really amazes me. We treated some gory cases. My hands were very bloody before we were through on D-Day, or was it D-Plus-One-Day? Your stuff, Dick, was all around us. Did well too, but some won't be bothering you folks any more.

D-Day was a comparatively pleasant surprise, I guess. But yesterday at this time I was hanging over the side, hoping the guy who held my ankles wouldn't let go. I was cutting the ID tag from a boy

who had been in the water for a good three weeks…Again I am
surprised at how like some other strange guy one calmly does such
things. This body was pretty badly decomposed, poor kid. Casualties are wonderfully low, but then, there are quite a few of these
poor dead or thereabouts boys floating in this vicinity.

Lately we've been nothing more but motored dinghies, hanging
astern of the big ships, taking the big men here and there. Nothing
to worry about but fenders and lines in the right place. These hulls
of ours are so damned sensitive. Just a Higgins landing craft alongside in a small chop is enough to worry hell out of us.

I went ashore on the French Coast one day for just a few minutes. The Sea Bees were hard at work. I found an anchor for our
boat, and had picked it up and was lugging it toward a line of busy
ducks, from one of whom I hoped to bum a ride back. A Sea Bee
on a bulldozer gave me a lift. It was a bumpy ride, but it was interesting to talk to this Sea Bee. He'd set four landmines off, he said.
When he had a load of dirt he hardly felt the explosion. When
empty, he took a jolt and got tossed right off once.

Fighting goes on within 25 miles of us. The chimes of Big Ben
vie with fighters for radio communication. This war is no quick,
decisive storm of death, but a queer mixture of surges and ebbs intermittently. So full of paradox, war has surprised me.

Last night I got 2 hours sleep; the night before 4, but previously
I had more than enough. So I feel rested…

Off to the sack. I eat well. Live well, but home will be very beautiful! I miss Chapper very much. She has been such a wonderful
correspondent.

Love to you all,
Jim

CHAPTER 15

THE FOURTH SON IN

IN BOLD HEADLINES our newspapers told of internal chaos in Germany and Japan;

ATTEMPTED ASSASSINATION OF HITLER!!
GERMAN MILITARIST CLIQUE GUILTY!!
HUNDREDS OF ARMY GENERALS EXECUTED!!

There are even gentle hints of imminent surrender. In Japan, Premier Tojo was ousted as leader of the Nippon Armies. Discontent in Japan appears to be multiplying. At the Boston Navy Yard, fellow officers talk of the end of the war, and peacetime jobs.

Coincidental with the news from Germany, a large transport loaded with German prisoners slipped into the Boston Harbor. Many of the prisoners were marched through the Navy Yard to a delousing station in the large Army base adjacent to the Yard. I watched a group of 500 slog along in silence. Only the thud of their hobnailed boots was audible. They were tired. You could see that. And they were ragged in over-sized uniforms of many shades and descriptions—khaki, green, gray, royal blue and black. I was surprised at their small stature, at the many runt-sized men who struggled in the hot sun, carrying their gear, and the burden of their "great coats." There seemed to be a scarcity of men between the ages of 20 and 30. There were many young faces—teen-aged boys—and many old faces—gray-haired and bald. But on the whole they didn't present too somber a picture, perhaps comparable to our own lads in similar circumstances, as far as looks went. I heard that there were a few women in the ranks, not as nurses or auxiliaries, but as regular line soldiers. One of my men asked an MP, as the women marched by, to make sure that his eyes were not deceiving him. The MP substantiated his guess.

Dad wrote Brother Jeff that his twin, Harry, was on the very eve of his enlistment in the Navy, and I got a copy of the letter.

> July 7, 1944
> Dear Jeff,
> ...I guess you know by now that Ha can't enjoy any peace of mind, and so he has stuck his neck out having some two weeks ago submitted his application, undergone an examination, and followed through on all necessary preliminaries. By presenting himself in Washington, he has probably shortened the time when his answer will come back so he is on the anxious seat awaiting a commission as Lt. (j.g.) in the Navy. With mostly all good fellows in the services I think he has done well in so deciding...
> Love,
> Dad

Brother Tom's next letter came with an enviable schedule of amusements to keep any corporal happy as a clam.

> July 9, 1944
> Dear Folks,
> As usual, I've been having a pretty good time lately with lots of varied amusements. The other night I heard Jascha Heifetz, and very fine he was too. The thing that tickled me was that a large part of the audience, inevitably, consisted of young Jewish intellectuals eagerly and loudly talking in New Yorkese, and dogmatically saying, "You know, I'll bet that 98% of these fellas never even hoid Heifetz in person before!" The bulk of the audience, though, was far superior to the ordinary Professional music-lover, because they had a fresh, unselfconscious approach about the music. They were open-minded, eager, delighted to be able to have the privilege, and

were able to judge the program on the merits alone. I think everyone enjoyed it.

The other night I saw the original stage show of "This Is The
Army" which was really wonderful. One of the featured comics was
none other than an ex-Burlesque comedian favorite of mine, Hank
Henry, who was terrific. It was amazingly well done.

They also had a real rodeo in town, which I also managed to see.
It was completely authentic, even down to the appearance of the
contestants (all GI's and ex-rodeo performers), who looked typical,
being lean, tanned, bowlegged, and with a limp. The Red Cross,
who are an amazingly well-regulated outfit this war (I understand
the Army now audits their books) produced the show masterfully,
and even furnished real hot dogs and rolls with mustard. Some
Army!

I've also been seeing some movies recently, two of which are at
least worth mention. *What a Woman*, with Rosalind Russell, who
really is a fine comedienne. On second thought, that is the only
one worth mention.

Also have continued my mad pace in reading, although I must
knock off books for today in order to finish the three copies of
Time and *Life* that have piled up. It's a rough war for me, all right.

Coming up in the reasonably near future is a trip of a week to a
rest camp, whose location I'd better not mention, but which is famous as a really fabulously beautiful and wonderful place. I think
there will also be a Mediterranean Theatre Swimming Championship that I intend to enter. And tonight there's a USO show...

Love,
Tom

The next installment of Jim Jr.'s reports, arrived in early July, and
covered from June 16 to July 8.

Dear Chap,

I sit here in the U.K. quietly waiting for a haircut. Scissors snip-
snip, a radio drones, cut hair clutters the linoleum floor. Barber
shops are much the same anywhere, it seems, for which I am most
grateful...

...I took a long walk after supper last night. These day-like
evenings make it possible to enjoy the countryside until nearly

midnight, if one wishes. It seemed wonderfully peaceful and quietly full of life—to see flowers grow, to watch the swallows fly about, to hear children laugh at play. The sea is an interesting enough place, but it is the land that lives and breathes for me. Curious, I strolled into a country church. I was surprised to find its interior dusty, with hinges rusted, pew doors hanging in tired disarray. Various plaques spotted the walls. The church was founded in 1760. Edward Penn, grandson of William Penn, gave toward the church and King George III gave 500 lbs.

I'm not supposed to disclose our position. I don't have to. The news commentators have done it for me. They seem to have told the story for us in a most exaggerated style. None of us is hurt a bit, so don't let the tellers of tales worry you. Tell Dad, that commentator, Stanley Richardson, rode with us on Art's boat.

Thank you Mr. Chapman for *Time*. All on board are enjoying it. We just got the invasion issue two days ago. They certainly are a wide awake outfit...

...I have been writing you every day when my letters could get to you, but while off at sea I've kept pretty busy doing things of unmentionable unimportance. Our lives are comparatively chopped up into little pieces, speaking temporally of course. Instead of being conscious about 16 hours at a stretch, we're more or less awake at stretches of from 4 to 8 hours on and off. While off, we're asleep most of the time.

Today was a wonderful day. I received the June issue of *Motor Boating*. Our skipper is an avid *Motor Boating* fan, and so too is one of our motor macs. Most of the others know the magazine and like it of course, so your generous Dad has made this boat very happy. Also received the June 19th issue of *Time*. It's interesting and fun to read of places and occurrences we have so intimately witnessed. But most important of all, I received five wonderful letters from you, which makes the whole boat envious of me; and three swell letters from Mom and one very nice one from Aunt Clara.

I've been ashore, and will later tell a few tales of interest. It makes me mad to read in *Time* what we are forbidden to write. I saw some friends on a large vessel, for whom we did tender duty. They were swell to see, and very helpful as a crate of fresh eggs, (first since the USA) crate of oranges, 50 lbs of beef, etc. bear vivid testimony.

I'm third officer on the 509 boat, named the "Sassy Sue" after the skipper's little daughter…

This life I lead consists of a few days on base, then some time at sea, then back to base for a few days once more. Base time is devoted to repairs, refitting, and most important, baths, shaves, sleep and food. However, we're quite comfortable when at sea. The stretches are a bit long for a PT, though, and I think they'll be whittled down soon. We sleep aboard at all times. While in base we eat ashore. I am writing this note from the chart house, using a copy of your Dad's book for a letter rest.

I just had four eggs for breakfast. Boy, did they taste good. Also had fresh orange juice. So you see we're living like kings right now. The boys on the big ships, like the fellows mentioned earlier, live very comfortably all the time, and complain of the humdrum lot. As we roll from deck to bulkhead, and as the cook clings madly to his pots and pans trying to keep them over the range, and as we wash in cold salt water, and watch the dirt stains on our pillows grow darker—we envy them. But I would not swap a good 6 to 8 months of this duty for anything else in the Navy. After those 8 months—we'll see. Here's hoping the war will be over by then.

Received with joy your snaps of Mr. Jackson and little Dickens, who looks definitely like a Jackson now. Very cute picture of the two. Please do give Dick and Math and all the Jacksons my love.

I now sit quietly in the stateroom I share with the 2nd officer, John Pavlis. I've had a nice nap this P.M., and am smoking my pipe and contentedly listening to steaks sizzling on the stove. The seas are being good to us, so all is most comfortable. Sleep in a very comfortable upper bunk, which I rigged myself—simply a piece of canvas, about 3 feet by 6 feet, made fast to the bulkhead on one side, secured around a pole on the other. As long as I keep out of it when the water's really rough, and we're speeding over it, all goes well…

One of the officers went ashore the other day and got much further inland than I did. He brought back some interesting observations, one a magazine written in French, but German controlled. What a propaganda picture of American life it gave those people. It showed photographs of strikes. Down with Hooverism appeared on the placards, showing our country disunited. It featured a cultist family living in a tree depicting Americans forced from their bombed homes, feeding on nuts, fruits, and vegetables. It showed a wedding conducted on surf boards (a typical Miami publicity stunt à la Steve Hannigan). Thus do these crazy Americans live. In other words these editors have picked veritable episodes but they've picked the unique and portrayed it as the usual. So you see, lots of these folks in occupied territory have some mighty distorted conceptions of the USA.

This Normandy section of France has been comparatively un-molested by the Germans. I guess there's a lot of agriculture here, and I understand, via *Time*, as well as this officer, that the country's now very lovely and apparently very prosperous in an agricultural sort of a way. It has fertile fields, and sleek cattle, etc.

Our duty is the safest kind. Gosh, I'll even be getting bored if I don't look out. Actually I'm keeping reasonably busy with piloting, my charts, etc. Until recently there hasn't been much extra time on our hands. When there was such a thing, we used it to catch up on our sleep.

Like you, Chapper, we now wait for the news broadcasts to get the latest dope, even though it may be happening within 30 miles of us, and we eagerly tire our eyes out on the latest pony edition of *Time*.

I tried to whip up an eggnog tonight, with a mixture of pow-dered milk, sugar, and that necessary raw egg. Tasted terribly. I'd had your wonderful eggnogs in mind. Anyway, I satisfied that pregnant woman-like-urge one gets for a thing every once in a while. I won't bother with the damn mixture again.

I'm going to get a breath of pleasant air, to do a bit of rope work. I'm having a great time learning how to splice, whip, tie various knots, etc. This whole PT experience will really be a peace time yachting help, but it won't help my sailing any. I am still learning a lot of constructive, interesting things about boats and the water and of course the newness of this whole environment we live in is still present. So I am quite happy, though that's hardly the right word. Interested would be more apt. And of course, that's a healthy mental condition. Physically I'm in good shape...

...Yesterday was another red letter day. We're out on station, but the mail is coming through nicely...

...Another night with little sleep. We seem to live a life of ex-tremes. For some time, we had a very easy time of it. Lately, they've kept us fairly busy. I'm having a lot of fun at my piloting. I hit an objective pretty well last night about 25 miles off, involving starting from an E.P. (Estimated Position), changing courses three times, bucking a fairly decent cross current. It'll be fun piloting on L.I. Sound after this war is over.

I finished my 6 to 10 stretch a while ago, and got into bed and read a bit of a book called *Life Class*. It described the early years of a young Bavarian, the author, in America. He was a bus boy at the time. He wrote so vividly of the food that I became so damn hungry I couldn't sleep. I'm back in bed again, having fried myself three eggs. I'm on from 6-10 A.M. & P.M. and lately haven't gone to bed until between 2 and 4 in the morning. These late hours should become less frequent. I'm getting plenty of time in bed, but—poor Dick Jax on the night shift in Boston—day sleep is a most inadequate substitute…

…Things are quiet with us. We go on patrols, but they are defensive ones. Our boat has quite a record. We have been in almost continuous operations since D-Day. I took a shower today, on one of the larger naval vessels and it was the first one in weeks.

…Once more we lie in millpond-like stillness. Rain patters on the deck. One is seldom without it here in the U.K. The water laps the hull. I'm on duty tonight. Ralph and John are ashore. I'm sharpening up a German bayonet I picked up. It makes a beautiful knife, and it will be fun to show it to you folks one of these days…

…I'm sitting on a hillside overlooking the water, back in the U.K. Pardon the realistic touch but when I began to write I was sitting on an ant hill, and had not the dampness of the ground made me move, I daresay I would have had ants in my pants, and would still be on the move. It's wonderful to be able to chew a grass stem when you wish, to hear the birds sing again. The ocean is a happy place to be near, to be on for short stretches, but I am a land lover, though not a land lubber, I hope. Seems good to smell the beach, to hear the waves, Maine fashion, break on the shore…

…I bought a motorcycle last night. I drove, spat, jerked, and stalled out into the country. I saw something of England's quaint lanes, because only off the highway could I swear, as I sweated and tried to start the damn thing, for stalls were common last night. I did meet a good many people, to be sure, helpful meaning folk who suggested I push this button, and then that switch. And I had a good many laughs at myself. I stalled on many a hill, and invariably in front of a bunch of GI's. It took me four hours to master the intricacies of the spark, fuel mixture, idling screws, and oil pump. By then my peaceful evening in the country was over. Actually, the thing, like a balky horse, didn't really run until I neared home. Now that I've begun to master the beast, it's time to shove off again and I'll probably not be back for weeks.

Last night though I did see a bit of England I've heard and read about. Country lanes, rambling roses and clinging ivy, quiet streams, old green trees, clean, small stone cottages with thatched roofs...To an outsider looking in, they have all the charm I had expected...

We just filled in our voting cards today. A surprising number of non-Roosevelt men on board in the crew. Many of them are southerners...

Must eat now. Wish I could put you on the back of my motorcycle, though I'm not at all sure you'd join me in my wish.

Love,
Jim

Tom writes a birthday letter to his mother. He also talks of his busy life in Italy, and the up-coming swimming race that he has entered.

Monday, July 10, 1944
Dear Moth,

This letter is especially addressed to you because it's primarily designed to serve as a birthday letter, however poor it may be in that respect. Thanks for making possible a wonderful life to date, filled with laughs and many other wonderful things. I will dispense with any further sentiment, but if I ever become famous, intelligent, and dogged enough to write an autobiography I will make an earnest attempt to knock out the fitting eulogy that you deserve.

Whenever I stop and wonder about my being over here taking part in a war, I invariably think of the World's Fair at Flushing. You may remember that I was singularly unimpressed by industries' smug and sickening display of their accomplishments, a feeling which I inherited from a talk I'd heard by Spencer Brown, a Loomis English Master, who was a truly wonderful teacher. He was a forthright, keen, and entertaining guy. From him, I got the idea that the Fair was a sort of gigantic hoax, trying to seduce us all into believing that man was really doing one hell of a fine job, that the world was our nutshell, and that General Motors was omnipotent. In fact you may recall that I was roundly scolded by the family for my sourpuss outlook on the great show. Years later, though, I am of the same opinion, only more so, and I'm genuinely proud of my previous contempt for the Fair. Because, by now, it's perfectly obvious that the world is still in a hell of a state even though Dupont can make girdles out of soybeans or something, or that Heinz could put up a tasty can of beans.

I have just entered the 100 meter backstroke event in the coming Allied Mediterranean Theatre Swimming Championships. It should be quite a bit of fun, but I am not too optimistic, as (1) I haven't much confidence in my speed, with good reason, and (2) I haven't been swimming at all, and (3) I'm in wretched shape. However, the last two reasons hold for everyone else too, so I might be able to at least qualify, anyway. The trials aren't for a few weeks yet, so I might be able to get in a little practice.

Just read *Long, Long, Ago*, by the late Alexander Woollcott... I also read the recently popular *Tree Grows in Brooklyn*, and thought it was only fair. And I saw for the third time, *The Fallen Sparrow*, featuring Maureen O'Hara, who to my mind is the most classically beautiful woman in Hollywood, and practically anywhere else, although Ingrid Bergman is the most wonderful looking. Yet, I'm still a Katie Hepburn guy, though.

Love,
Tom

A few days later Tom recounted a reluctant vote in the presidential race unfolding in the States.

July 15, 1944
Dear Folks,

I recently got a nice letter from Jeff.

I've just decided to cast my vote for Dewey. This hurts because I don't think he's so hot, but I think Roosevelt's been in there long enough. I think whoever is elected we lose anyway. I wish Wendell (Willkie) was in there.

I continue to read and see movies like mad. I haven't had such a good brand of books lately, except for J. C. Marquand's wonderful *Late George Apley* which I've knocked off for the second time.

The war news certainly does look better doesn't it. Maybe this means only about a year and a half more over here for me.

Love,
Tom

Jeff came through with a July letter from the South Pacific. He also threw in a brief caution to his Mother, suggesting that she take advantage of a furlough in her nursing career.

APO 920
24 July 1944
Dear Mother & Dad—,

High time for an "OK, FJ" from this department. Everything is going along smoothly, with the work less exciting right now, but nonetheless plentiful and exhausting. I am now acting as executive officer of the company and that takes up most of the day. It is interesting enough.

By now I am well settled in company C, and am delighted with my situation. The officers and men are fine fellows and good to work with. Being in a company has one great advantage over a staff job—you feel as though you're in a private little club. There's far more camaraderie and conviviality because it's a separate group.

I'm lucky to have seen both sides. I believe I'm a better soldier because of it…

…Moth, you ask if that little girl Sonja still figures in my correspondence. No, she stopped writing a while back and I'm relieved because it was kind of a strain keeping it up. My mail is pretty dominantly male anyway, so far as outsiders go, and I suppose I'm the only guy in the services who has neither a "girl" or a wife to exchange sugar reports with. Yet, what the hell good are postal romances? And anyway, I get all the mail a fellow could ever desire from my wonderful family…

…By all means, Moth, take advantage of that furlough from the nurse's aid in August. You must be plenty tuckered by now and see if you can't persuade Dad to knock off for a spell then too. How about a trip to Spring Lake to go Blah?

As for all of these hopes and hunches you fellows have been entertaining with a reference to my imminent return, I can only say that they have no basis in fact. We're a good outfit. They need us, and there's a good part of the road still to travel.

Love,
Jeff

CHAPTER 16

MOTORCYCLES AND SWIMMING RACES

UNDER DATE of July 23rd, Jim Mathes Jr. recounts another motorcycle trip through England. He wrote the latter part of this letter from a harbor on the French coast where his PT squadron was apparently stationed.

Dear Chap,

We're back on the deep, and once again I must get used to this rolling. Having been out about 8 hours, now, my sea legs are returning…

…I went out on my motorcycle last night. It worked very well and I saw a good bit of England's countryside. I had a fairly good conception of its country villages, I find. I had always wondered if it wasn't so over populated that large tracts of agricultural or wooded land just didn't exist. I was quite wrong. My motorcycle permitted me to go down any country lane or path I spied. How these people love flowers; their walls are matted with rambler roses, red, yellow, and many a shade in between. The houses have a way of nestling into the countryside and looking part of it. Maybe it is time that permits this; perhaps its the nearby stone and thatch. Grain fields, oats, rye, wheat and hay fields of grass and clover rolled quilt-like over the land. I rode down one lane and this sort of land, broken here and there by clumps of trees, stretched on for miles. One field, high on a hill that overlooked the water, was oddly marked. Upon it, in giant Indian mound fashion, lay undisturbed hillocks. I wondered why the land owners hadn't leveled them off. A soldier I picked up told me they were Roman grave mounds…This area was green and lush, the horses and beef cattle sleek and fat. Happy colts and docile calves romped on wobbly legs. Yes, it is a lovely place.

I just showed off my German souvenirs and I don't believe I've listed them for you. I've sent a few odds and ends back in letters to you. These things were all picked up in a recent shore excursion. The Germans had surrendered these places we entered and many of the rooms, with cards on the tables, bread and sardines, glasses half full of water, looked recently inhabited. I now have (1) back pack, swell for skiing, (1) German bayonet which makes a swell sheath knife, (2) German "overseas" caps, (2) handy gun cleaning kits, (1) pocket knife and a wooden nosed bullet of which the Germans seem to use quite a few.

I played cribbage last night with a Navy technician, a Packard representative, who is on board for the present. Hell of a nice guy. We played 'til 12:30 A.M., and were then called on patrol, and I wasn't abed until 3:30 A.M. Sleepy this P.M., but it's so nice and warm—a rare treat here—that I've put off going below until about 4 P.M. We dined today aboard a destroyer. The food was delicious. I ate like a pig, and the clean silver, table cloths, and generally elegant setting, compared to our own way of living, was such a welcome change.

Our life is very quiet, save for occasional action of one sort or another. Yesterday one of our planes jettisoned two bombs which landed near enough to throw spray on our decks. One of our boys, seated on a coil of line in the logarette, was knocked off his perch.

I was in the sack, and soon fell asleep again. I just thought at the time that it was another mine going off at some safe distance.

Let me picture this boat and us who live upon it for this last hour. Those not on watch, sleep, play cards, listen to a battery radio set on board, read, or sit topside. We lay at anchor. Of those on watch, an officer stands by in the chart house. The men are stationed topside. The wind is light and off the shore, and we are within two miles of the land. A small chop laps at the hull. We roll easily, only slightly, as we lay here. Though late in the evening, it is light, for twilight lasts long here. An enlisted man dressed casually in blue jeans, heavy marine boots in which he has cut perforations for air and his corns, in a heavy windbreaker jacket now well salted and creased, a cap askew on his head, lolls against the cockpit, dreamily playing his harmonica. I sit aft by the engine room hatch, talking to an engineer from South Dakota, about his pre-navy life as a gas station operator. The quartermaster on the duty section, walks by, a big boy, long legs which he throws out at 45 degree angles to keep his footing. It's an habitual stride on these boats, I notice. This quartermaster, in true Navy fashion, wonders why the boats are lined up so closely. If they were further apart, he'd question that, claiming they should be closer together.

Night comes on. I'm off watch, so I go below to write you. In my stateroom, which I share with John Pavlis, now on watch, and who has just poked his head in to say with a grin, "about ten minutes more." I knew John was coming because he has a sinus condition, and sniffs every few seconds. I heard him sniffing down from the chart house to our stateroom. He means that battle lights go on in ten minutes. They are dim and red, safe from detection, damned unpleasant for reading and writing...

...War is only fire-cracker real. Colorful ack-ack lights up the sky ten to twenty miles away. During the day an occasional burst of dusty, billowing smoke over the land tells us another land mine has gone off. Friendly planes shuttle overhead. We lay at anchor, we patrol, we eat, we sleep, we're bored often, excited rarely. How we all look forward to going home, and how often we talk about chances for an early return. But I realize that were I at home, I'd feel I should be here—so it is as it should be.

We lay in one of France's big harbors today. It seemed good to have shelter. Around us the buildings and the country looked quiet, uninhabited. Occasionally a dark cloud of smoke would rush upward and outward. A dull boom would follow. Land mines still going off. Here and there buildings were in rubble, or only bare walls would stand skeleton-like, with great gaping holes. All this is seen at a safe distance, at least three quarters of a mile.

I am perched now, atop the bridge of Frank Robey's boat, nested alongside. Just visited with Art. It was so good to see him again. We old friends, of six months standing, haven't been able to group together for a month. Art has been in London. Those "whiz bombs" are pretty ugly things. He had one land within two blocks of him, and another hit the hotel which he had occupied three days earlier. I don't plan to spend my leave in London.

We lay in a very sheltered anchorage. The French countryside is within a stone's throw, but the enemy have left this area. Only an occasional land mine is exploded to remind us of the Germans. The Sea Bees are, as usual, living up to their well chosen jobs. An air field, shrouded in dust, is being cleared by giant bulldozers. Two mustang P 51's treated us to a show an hour ago. They dove toward the field, pulled up into graceful slow rolls. A broken flying fortress is within sight—made a forced landing a few days ago, on this field, I am told.

In contrast, one has just to turn his head to see fertile green fields, separated by hedges and trees. Cows graze peacefully. Stone villages, each with a steeple or two, dot the rolling hills and valleys. But these villages look quiet and vacant. Jeeps and trucks have just lately begun to scurry over the roads.

I went ashore this P.M. for three hours. I had a wonderful time seeing this country and its people—so new and different to me. I tried my French, and found it terribly rusty, but great fun and fairly sufficient. I went with Frank, John and three of the men. Frank spoke a little French, the others none, so I was quite happy acting as interpreter—and quite safe, since the others knew so little. And Frank was too polite to comment. It was Bastille Day, and the people were well dressed. They are friendly, poor folks. Much of this big city (Cherbourg) is in ruins.

I expect we'll be stationed in France one of these days. Then we'll be closer to our patrol areas, and we'll spend more time ashore and have more time to ourselves. It should be a far more pleasant life…

…Any little change is greatly welcome. A trip ashore, a shower and shave with hot water and faucets which run without being pumped and petted, a meal on another boat, an alongside visit. Even sleeping and eating are entertainment. Small jobs to be done are a big help and make the time more interesting, and much shorter.

Transport planes still drone over now and then. Convoys dot the horizon. But these war reminders are quite beside the point. Our main source of amusement is the latest misfortune of some other PT in the area. Right now one of our brethren has dragged anchor until he is over a mile out of position. As the lead boat tells him to correct his sad state, we chortle with glee, make outlandish cracks about his seamanship, etc. Tomorrow, the nautical faux pas may be ours, but today we are right and he is wrong—so we giggle conceitedly...

...Some of the fellows got some fresh vegetables on the French shore yesterday, and we have carrots and radishes to look forward to tonight. Right now we're on flare duty—when a flare is dropped by enemy planes, we extinguish it with close gun fire. Safe and easy, because few flares fall.

The waves slap, slap the hull. We roll a bit. Fourth of July stuff lights up the distant horizon now and then. The sun went down, big and red as it sank, and it laid a path of gold upon the water. Perhaps a nice day tomorrow. Bye for now.

Love,

Jim

Following is an acknowledgment to a letter Mother wrote to the hospital asking for August off. She had been at it daily for over a year. Nurses aides were entitled to a month furlough each year.

Meadowbrook Hospital
PO Box 108
Hempstead, NY
August 1, 1944

Mrs. G. Harry Jackson
24 South Drive
Plandome, NY
Dear Mrs. Jackson,

During the recent catastrophic shortage of nurses your faithful services made it possible for our patients to receive the daily care so necessary to their recovery. Your contribution to the community welfare was of considerable value.

In light of the difficulties that we know exist in the planning of your home routine, and your transportation problems to the hospital we grant you a month's leave. The patients and the hospital personnel gratefully acknowledge the assistance you have given them.

As the need for your services is as urgent as ever, we hope that we can count on your continued cooperation next month.

Sincerely yours,
Lulu B. Payne, R.N.
Superintendent of Nurses

Tom's private war continues apace. In this letter he is contemplating qualifying for the swimming championship, while at the Army Rest Camp.

August 2, 1944
Dear Folks,

Here I am on a five day pass in order to enter that swimming meet. I rather think I'll be able to qualify, which means I'll get a two week trip (for training purposes) to the big, important city. This is a wonderful break. I swim this afternoon, and the vision of the two weeks should really spur me on.

The pool is quite a miserable one with pipes at either end, making it very tough to turn. And it's squarely in the center of the 8th Army Rest Camp, which is of course populated by Englishmen who yell things like—"Nicely swum, Yank." They nickname tall guys "Lofty"; no "slim" as we are apt to do. Frankly, although most GI's seem to dislike them, (and they are generally irritating as hell when drunk) I'm inclined to like most of them. Maybe this is because they amuse me so.

Love,
Tom

Eight days later Tom writes with the results of his swimming race

August 10, 1944
Dear Folks,

I'm afraid that I've been neglecting you recently. One reason is that I've had a terrible head cold, although it's gone now. Funny, I live in the rainiest, coldest weather imaginable, in mud up to my knees, and remain healthy. Then when I move into a comfortable building, with the sun shining all the time, I get a cold.

Did I tell you that I came in 4th in the swimming meet? I think this ends all chance of going to the finals, but there's still a possibility. Anyway, I at least got into the regional finals.

I just heard, via a returned letter, that a good friend from Rutgers was killed in the invasion. This is the closest the war has come to me yet. Although I've seen plenty of guys I know fail to return in the bombers, or get scraped out of a plane. That's different because

I've only known them in the Army, and my Army life is so much of a dream that their deaths don't seem real.

Love,
Tom

Tom keeps the letters coming back to the States. He continues to report on his voluminous reading, movie viewing, and on the various and sundry shows he sees. One should not perhaps be lulled by Tom's continuing cultural activity and spectating. As a cryptographer, he performed daily watches, decoding vital messages that came to his Wing, and passing along equally important messages to the squadrons. Obviously, because of security, there was no way that he could write to his parents, or indeed to anyone, about the work he was doing. Hence, all that was left to him to relate by letter was his off duty activity. To his credit, he used his time effectively, reading all manner of books, and attending various and sundry concerts, ballets, shows, and scheduled events to keep amused. Dr. Fifield, mentioned below, was the rector of Plymouth Church, in Brooklyn.

August 15, 1944
Dear Folks,

Little is happening as usual. I just read two of Dr. Fifield's sermons which Gram sent me. Pretty good, but on several points I disagree with him strongly. Especially when he says that there is such a thing as being "too late for God." His God must be a petty vengeful one. Mine's not. It's never too late for Him.

By the way, I'd certainly appreciate something definite concerning Ha's Naval peccadilloes. A few vague words trickle through to me, but are so sparse as to excite my curiosity...

Last week I journeyed into town to see Joe Louis perform, plus other boxing bouts. Joe sparred with some guys who were woefully out of his class but it was good to see him just the same. Another member of his troupe was California Jackie Wilson, a good welterweight. It's amazing how much better a real craftsman is than an ordinary guy. He makes it look so easy and natural. It's the same in everything, boxing, painting, etc.

...I continue to read a lot, and have read some good stuff

recently. *Candide*, by Voltaire, which is very funny, cynical, and bitter; some wonderful Ogden Nash poems; an anthology of light verse collected by FPA, and very good too; and some marvelous short stories by Max Beerbohm, whom I consider probably the most graceful and (though the word embarrasses me) charming writer in the business. I am about to read again W. H. Hudson's fine *Green Mansions.*

Movies seen recently were all horrible save *Double Indemnity* with Fred McMurray, Edward G. Robinson, and Barbara Stanwyck. This is a good movie from a good book.

Dad—Maybe you're right about my changing my mind about the Army. But I bet most would agree, unless of course, they were engaged in buoying up morale on the home front. One phase of this is apparently to let the folks back home know how rough and dangerous it is over here, as you wallow in your sack gulping Ruperts beer, and munching Hershey bars. Whether it is for the best or not, it nevertheless is an incontrovertible fact that at the age of twenty-three, I've arrived at the end of being a gelatinous mass of adolescence, and am solidifying into the mold that I will remain in for the rest of my days. So my opinions will remain more constant from now on, whether right or wrong. I bow of course, to your defensively conceived idol—experience. It's wonderful, Brother!

Love,
Tom

CHAPTER 17

A TELEGRAM IN LATE AUGUST

EARLY IN AUGUST, I was alone, sitting in the ordnance office at the Yard, flicking through the various job orders that had just been placed on my desk for the morrow. It was approximately 4:45 in the afternoon. The phone at my elbow rang impatiently. I grabbed it.

"Ordnance office," I said.

"Are you the ordnance officer in this yard?"

"You must want Lieutenant Loomis, Sir?"

"I want an ordnance officer, and I want him quick!"

"Yessir. I'm an ordnance officer. What can I do for you, sir?"

"You better get your ass down to the bottom of the dry dock. You got some sailors with blowtorches burning on a target barge full of live ammunition. They could blow up this whole damned yard. Get your ass down there quick."

"Well, this office has nothing to do with ammunition. We just fix the guns. You'll need to contact the..."

The caller cut in, "I don't give a damn what the hell you do. Get your ass down there! And that's an order." The phone clicked before I could respond.

I had no idea who the caller might be, but he sounded as if he was a man of authority, a ruling factor to anyone in the military. At about that time Loomis strolled into the office, and I explained the phone call.

"You know," I said, "we've been welding around live ammunition in turrets ever since I've been here. The word is that a flame is not going to set off live ammo."

Loomis shrugged. "Better do as the guy said. Go on down and give it a look, before you go home, and do whatever you think is best. But be careful."

I hurried toward the dry dock which was but a stone's throw from our office building. It was empty except for the target barge, a nondescript raft that seemed lost at the bottom of the vast chasm that formed the dock. This was the only such dock on the northeast that could take the large ships, and I recalled some of the big ships that I'd seen folded into the massive arms of the dock.

I called down toward the target barge, where sailors were leisurely applying their blowtorches to the sodden planks that formed the raft. Even at the considerable distance I could see the metal from some good-sized shells reflected in the late afternoon sun. So deep was the bottom of the dry dock that my voice would not carry to its floor. So I started down the cement side of the dock, which was in the form of stairs with very deep risers. It was slow going, and it occurred to me that I might be on my final mission, as I watched the flames below searing the huge projectiles that I now recognized as from the Navy's 5-inch 38-mm anti-aircraft batteries. I was all too aware that each shell carried explosives capable of blowing up the better part of the structure, if not the buildings that surrounded it. My common sense suggested there was nothing to worry about, but the voice of authority over the phone still rang in my ears and gave me considerable pause.

Once down on the dock floor, I approached the sailors.

"Yo! You guys. Knock off the blowtorches."

"What? You mean quit the work?" asked the nearest sailor who appeared to be in charge of the crew.

"That's just what I mean," I said. "You're working on live ammo, and it could blow up with that hot fire on it."

The sailors looked at one another. Two of the men smiled, and one said, "Well, if you say so, sir." They gathered in a group and sat on one of the lower steps.

The lead sailor said, "Who do we say gave us quitting orders?"

"You say Lieutenant Jackson gave you the orders."

"What should we do, sir?"

I had no idea what they should do. I said, "Well, don't do any more burning, but stick around here until you get further word on this operation."

"You got it, sir. Can we smoke?"

"Yeah. You can smoke, but do your smoking a safe distance from this barge. You got it?"

"Yessir."

I began the slow climb up the side of the precipitous steps of the dock, mentally cursing as I proceeded. Although I was in reasonably good physical shape, I was a tired man when I reached the top of the dock. I debated starting for home, since my shift was over, but decided I'd better stop in at the office and pass the ammo problem along to Lieutenant Loomis.

When I reached the office, it was empty. Loomis was apparently out in the yard. I started to write a note, but as I wrote the lieutenant returned, and at the same time the phone jangled. Loomis picked it up.

"Yes sir," he said quietly. He listened briefly, then held his hand over the phone mouth piece and said, "Jeez. It's the captain of the yard and he wants Lieutenant Jackson, and he wants him right now! He's tear-ass."

"Yessir," I said. I was suddenly sweating, and fearful.

"Jackson?" rasped the voice on the phone.

"Yessir."

"This is your captain. Are you the one who knocked my men off that target barge?

"Yessir, I..." There was not time to finish my thought.

"What in the hell do you think you're doing? A damned j.g. telling me how to run my business? We need that barge and we need it pronto. Understand that? Now you get on down to that barge and get those men back to work. You understand me? *Now!* Get going. *Now!*"

"Sir, they were using blowtorches on live ammo and…"

"I know what they were doing, dammit. They were following my orders."

"Yes, but…"

"No buts, Lieutenant! Get down there and *on the double! Coutermand your order! Do you hear me! on the double!*" The phone clicked.

I looked at Loomis and said, "Jeez. I guess they refused to go back to work unless I gave the order."

"Not even for the captain?" said Loomis.

I shrugged and said, "I guess I'd better go back down there, but don't blame me if the whole damn yard blows up. I'm still not at all sure that it's safe to apply heat on live ammo, and you have to assume those projectiles are still live. What do you think?"

Loomis shrugged. "How the hell do I know? But no matter what, you'd better get down there and get those guys back to work."

I made the arduous trip down the side of the dock and got the men back to work. The yard didn't blow up, and I felt just a bit more important realizing that my orders were just as powerful as the orders of the four-striped captain of the yard.

* * *

It never seemed quite right to be in the Navy and not serve at sea. I had tried to join the deck force, early in my career, but apparently, in the eyes of the Navy personnel, my civilian status as an executive in a fire insurance company ordained the pursuit of fire control in the Navy. One day at the South Boston Navy Yard I ran into an old acquaintance, Lt.(jg) Alex Holliday. He had a friend at the Bureau of Personnel in Washington and was willing to write a letter in my behalf relative to arranging sea duty. Following is a copy of Holliday's letter.

Lt/(jg) Aleaxander R. Holliday
19 Farwell Place
Cambridge 38, Massachusetts
9 August 1944

Lt. Charles E. Ducommun,
BuOrd Personnel Section
BuPers as liason to BuOrd.
Washinton DC
Dear B:

One of the O-V(S) jg's at the US Naval Dry Dock, South Boston, wanted to talk to somebody in the Bureau about his future in the Navy. He's been to several fire-control schools, and apparently is quite good at that sort of thing.

There is a good deal of talk floating around that all officers under 30 at shore bases within the continent are to be shipped out. This fellow was wondering if that were true, and in the event it were, in his case at least, if there was any chance of his getting a job suited to his qualifications. He plans to drop in Monday, August 14, and I took the liberty of suggesting your name to him. His name is Richard Jackson, Dartmouth graduate, and a good "joe"…

My best,
Alex

On the same subject I had written Lt. Bill Fox, a classmate of mine from Newport training days. He was serving with the Bureau of Ordnance in Washington and was somewhat knowledgeable about the personnel picture. He responded to my letter of inquiry.

Aug. 10, 1944
Dear Dick,

I enjoyed your letter of the 7th very much and will try to relay to you the little information I could get my fingers on.

The personnel section of the Bureau stated that the entire program of the Navy is much confused at the present time. They have suddenly decided that for the first time they have enough officer personnel and it seems that the Pacific area is flooded with actually more than they can use. Therefore it is going to be difficult for anyone now ashore to get a sea or an advance base billet. They assured me, however, that because of your experience (and no doubt your great knowledge) of fire control that if you were sent to sea, it would be on a combatant ship of good size. The amphibious program is completely filled up as is the advance base program.

In view of the above I would advise not coming to Washington even though we would be delighted to see you and show off our fine daughter.

I will keep an ear to the ground and advise you of any news I pick up...

We often think of you and Math and wish we could get together...

Sincerely

Bill

I was to subsequently write Lt. Ducommun advising that I could not make my scheduled trip to Washington on August 14. I cannot recall whether this was my inability to "get away" or whether I was following the advice of Bill Fox.

Brother Harry was embroiled in all the nasty little growing pains of moving from civilian life to the military. He had a million questions for me, now the "old hand" in the Navy.

Hartford Fire Insurance Company
Hartford, Connecticut
H.R. Jackson, Special Agent
175 Main St., White Plains, NY
August 23, 1944

Dear Dick,

As you know I was sworn in 8/14 and am to report at Princeton 9/12 provided I can get through that second physical next Monday. News travels fast, and quite a few folk have been advised of my appointment even though I'd just as soon wait until after Monday to air the news.

The old choppers aren't all they could be and I was honestly surprised that the Wave dental inspector in Washington considered them up to standard. I had visions of being told to have the infected wisdom tooth yanked and indeed, won't be surprised to hear that order come this next examination.

Meanwhile, of course, I have all kinds of forms, reading matter, orders, etc.—all very confusing. You can help me a lot with it. For example, they recommend I obtain a duffel bag or a small wooden box the size of a steamer trunk that can be broken down and disposed of. What is a duffel bag? Is it anything like those khaki ones we had at scout camp? If that's it, I can't believe such a piece of luggage would be at all serviceable.

What's the dope on uniforms? Princeton sent me instructions listing minimum requirements which don't coincide with those on the list that I was given in NY. They say white shirts, plain. That must mean with collars detached. Can I use some I have or is there an official Navy shirt? How about gray gloves? I have an Easter Parade pair. Will they do? No mention of underwear. How about that and can I continue to go without tops? Also what do you think of the paper disposable collars? Where would you go, keeping in mind that I'd be delighted to stay as close to my $250 allowance as possible.

I'm told that it's smart to get only bare necessities and to augment the wardrobe at Princeton where stuff will be available at cost. If there's anything to this, why do they submit such lists as these I have before me, pray tell?

Have been on a merry-go-round for over a month now with this matter, the house problem, and general every day job of living. We've finally bought a house a few blocks from here and it's going to be a mad scramble to get into it before I proceed.

Now I must write Jeff and Tom whom I have been neglecting something terrible. And to think that for awhile I was writing them, and two other also forgotten guys, at least once a week.

I will much appreciate the value of your wisdom and experience.

Love to all from all of us.

Hads

The telegram arrived in York Harbor, Maine on Thursday, August 25th. Under the circumstances, it was what you might expect from the Navy Department. "*We regret to inform…Ensign James M. Mathes Jr. missing in action…from August 9, 1944.*"

It was an incredible shock. Jimmy…missing!

Ensign James M. Mathes Jr., an officer on PT-509, who was listed as "missing in action" in an engagement in the English Channel in August 1944. He wrote often and at length about his experiences in England and through D-Day.

Lt. (jg) Harry R. Jackson, twin of Jeff Jackson; as the father of two young-sters, he came late to the military. He was an armed guard officer who made trips aboard the cargo ship Anniston City *to South America and Norway. Of the Jacksons, he was the last one "in" and the last one "out" of active duty in the military.*

Math called me at the navy yard from York, Maine, and I don't think I said much of anything. She was crying softly into the phone.

I went to York as soon as I could get away the following Sunday, though I couldn't leave until 4:00 P.M. It was a sad, but courageous family that greeted me. Only Dickens and his cousin Rocky Rohde, were cheerful. Neither of them could be expected to comprehend the gravity of the news. It was well for the family that the two youngsters couldn't sense the sadness. Their spirits, happy antics, and continual demand for daily care, were a steadying influence that kept the spinning wheel of normalcy from tumbling into space and utter despair.

The first reports received were indecisive. The 509 was hit by German shell fire and three men were saved…There was no report of other boats hit, and then, three or four days later a confirmed report from official sources said an accompanying PT boat was destroyed, and all hands were lost. But it was not identified as the 509. Indeed, the 509 had just dropped out of sight. Off the Isle of Jersey, one of the Channel Islands, some ten miles west of Cherbourg, and under German control, was the location of the action.

Hopes soared because it felt right to hope. It was likely, we reasoned, that Jim was taken a prisoner, and will be returned to us when the war with Germany is terminated.

Mary Chap was brave, but frightened. Mr. & Mrs. Mathes were shocked to a point of almost numbness, less capable at their age to fight back against such powerful forces. Math, as usual, bore the burden of keeping the family on a normal schedule, always comforting, always lending a strong, guiding hand, always praying.

On this day the headlines were hailing new Allied successes. The invading forces of Normandy burst out of their hard-won beachheads, overran Brittany, stormed toward Paris and around it, and then on to Belgium, Holland, and the outskirts of Germany itself. A new invasion in Southern France gushed up the Rhone River Valley to cut off German forces in western France. There were daily reports of German capitulation, and certainly it could be only a matter of days. That was the thinking of the day.

On Friday, the 11 of August, a German communiqué was printed in the *New York Times* which included this comment,

> Vessels escorting a German Convoy sank two American E-boats south of Jersey Island, one by ramming in close quarter fighting.

Mary Chap had immediately gone to work and started the queries. Her first move was to write a goodly number of Jim's fellow officers in M.T.B.Squadron #34.

She received letters expressing their personal sympathies and recounting the details of the action, as they knew it. Following are excerpts from a number of these letters.

From Art Kuesel, dated September 2, 1944:

> Yesterday, my boat (now the 501) came in from a ten day mission and your letter was waiting.
>
> I know what a shock it must have been to you to receive that telegram. It certainly was to me the morning Jim's boat did not return as I considered him one of my best friends. I can't give you much information about the action as it was foggy and none of the boats could see what did happen but it is my firm belief, as well as most of the other officers, that at least most of the crew of the 509, with the exception of one man who was found dead, are prisoners of war or might possibly be on the Island of Jersey, being hidden by the French. This last I doubt.
>
> Getting back to the night of the action—the 509 was followed by the 508. The Skipper of the 508 says there was gun fire but he heard no explosion or saw any fire although he was out of visual contact with the 509 due to the fog. The next day a plane was sent out but found no trace of the boat or crew except an enlisted man who was dead but who had not a scratch on him. He was floating in his life jacket. Several days later, the Germans claimed to have destroyed one of our boats by ramming on that night. If that was the 509, it might explain only one man being found. The others were probably taken prisoner.
>
> In the history of PT boats, no boat has ever been known to have gone down with all of the crew. In this case, they were within a mile or so of Jersey Island and with a life jacket that is an easy swim

if they weren't picked up by the enemy. To be exact, just south of St. Helier.

From Ensign Frank Koenen dated Sept 3, 1944:

I will try to give you as many facts of the action as possible for I know that these are what you want and not the rumors that invariably come out. The action took place on August 9th about 6:30 in the morning. There were two divisions of PTs on patrol. I was in one division and Jimmy was in the other. A German convoy was sighted and each division made separate torpedo attacks. Visibility was very poor, about 200 feet and the 508 that was in Jimmy's division lost contact with the 509 and had to make a separate retreat.

When we came back to our rendezvous point the 509 did not return. Immediately our boat, the 503 and 507 started out in search. We advanced within two miles of the shore when we ran into two large German Minesweepers and because of heavy gunfire from them and from shore batteries, we had to leave the area. In this action we lost two men on our boat and eleven out of sixteen on board were hit by shrapnel. One German ship was destroyed and the other damaged.

Air reconnaissance was immediately requested but because of the weather it had to be held up twenty-four hours. The aircraft found one boy and he had no sign of being hit and undoubtedly fell overboard. The plot from the vectoring ship shows a target, believably the 509, heading for shore. If this target was the 509 and I personally believe it was, there is a very good chance that the crew and officers are being held captives on German soil. A German Communiqué was quoted as saying that one American E boat (PT) was sunk by ramming. If this is true it happened very close to shore and there is a good possibility that some would reach shore and others would be picked up...

It is the general opinion of most of the officers here that at least some of the personnel are being held as prisoners of war. Art and I believe this and will continue to do so until more definite information is obtainable. It will probably not be until the island is captured by us that more information can be had.

From Ensign Buell T. Heminway, dated September 7th:

> ...However, several days later remains of the 509 were found, and
> she obviously had been quickly sunk by heavy guns, May we fur-
> ther hope that they were blown clear and rescued for it is all we can
> hope...
>   ...I have respected and like Jim immensely since I first met him
> in England. He and I traveled over the whole British Isles looking
> for our squadron and had great times together.

From Lt.(jg) Frank Robey, dated September 8th:

> ...I personally am very optimistic over Jim's chances of survival, for
> it is my belief that he was picked up and captured after the action
> in which the 509 was engaged. There is no evidence for me to be-
> lieve anything to the contrary and since the disappearance of the
> 509, only one man was found, he being an enlisted man. No doubt
> the coming weeks will unveil the mystery surrounding the entire
> action. Should Jim be captured, it is the policy of the Navy Depart-
> ment to notify you immediately after we make such a report to
> them. If this is the case, there should be no need for you to worry
> about him for the Germans adhere strictly to the provisions of the
> Geneva Conference relating to prisoners of war, just as we do, de-
> spite reports to the contrary...
>   ...I "palled around" with Jim quite frequently once we joined
> the Squadron and I must say that I really admired his loyalty and
> devotion to you—something that one does not find too often these
> days when young men are away from home and the ones they love.
> But Jim seemed to be different and it was because of this one fact,
> more than any other, that I admired him most...

Two other Squadron #34 officers wrote similar versions of the attack. Under date of September 15, Bill Godfrey wrote the wife of
509's executive officer, John Pavlis and stated that the 509 found itself amidst three heavily armed German minesweepers. His dis-
couraging report ran as follows:

> When the fog lifted, an intense search was made for the boat and

crew resulting in the finding of two (possibly three) of the crew dead. About a week and a half later my boat located a large portion of the hull of 509. After examining this hulk, I feel certain that the 100 octane gas exploded and that the boat blew up so completely that no one aboard at the time could have survived.

On the other hand, Russ Hadley Jr. comments about the large piece of the 509 that was found afloat after the action in a letter dated September 22nd.

> Chap, I don't know whether you are familiar with a PT boat or not. The wreckage we found was the bilge of the crew's quarters forward and a small portion of the galley. Other than the fact that it was undoubtedly a portion of the 509, I found nothing aboard that could be used as evidence in coming to any definite conclusion as to what happened…The wreckage we found was of such a nature that it would have been impossible for an explosion alone to have done it. The boat was greatly weakened structurally before the explosion occurred.

Letters began to come in from various sources, some knowledgeable, some consoling. Bill Minot, a friend of the Mathes family from Greenwich, Connecticut serving with the Army in France, having heard from his wife about Jim, wrote Mr. & Mrs. Mathes. Whereas his letter of October 5th was one of condolence, he nonetheless quotes facts that were misleading. He said, "I wrote a friend in Cherbourg who got me the facts on the matter. Jimmy was on PT 509, which was engaged by shore batteries off the Channel Islands…Not a chance for any survivors but it was later learned that there might be some survivors since intelligence reports that came in indicated that there were nine American prisoners taken during the engagement."

Army Air Force Captain Harry Bonneau, a Plandome boy serving with the 381st Bombardment Group in France wrote Mr. Chapman, who had actively put his good contacts to work in pursuit of information about Jim. On November 9 Bonneau wrote: "…I did check carefully the entire Army and Navy casualty lists and was fortunate in being able to also check all records covering German broadcasts since August 6th. I had been especially hopeful about the latter since news of our men is often broadcast in an effort to get listeners long before the information is received through the International Red Cross. There was nothing of any interest to you and Mary Chap."

A letter from Washington, DC dated October 10 from Navy lieutenant Dave Hedges, a family friend, in response to a query from Mr. Mathes, said the following:

> …Some more information which you might already have. This comes from *the* most reliable source though so I'm sending it along.
>
> The German hospital ship *Bordeaux* captured by the British produced 2 prisoners of war who claimed to know of the PT 509. They claimed the PT rammed a German "Varposten" ship, an escort type and a lively fight ensued. The PT was draped across the Germans' bow and the firing was at very close quarters. The Americans, outgunned and out-numbered put up their hands and surrendered. Just then, the PT 509 slid back into the water and the fight began again. The 509 was already holed below the water line and was sinking so the remaining Americans were overpowered. The P/W's disagreed on how many prisoners were taken but agreed that at least one slightly wounded one was taken to St. Helier, the German hospital. They did not know his name.
>
> Remember that this is the testimony of German prisoners who are inclined to the "we-killed-them-all" type of narration when recounting their own prowess. Neither of these men had actually been present at the fight.…

I received a V-mail letter from Lieutenant J.J. Daniel, the very same Jacquelin Daniel who had helped me gain my Navy commission, and who was my old football teammate at secondary school. Jack, it turns out, was the executive officer of PT Squadron #34.

20 November 1944
Dear Dick,
      Thank you for your letter of October 31 received yesterday. I realize your anxiety in wanting additional information about Jim and

I know how unsatisfactory letters are on the subject. I hope to be in New York before Christmas and believe it would be more satisfactory if I got hold of you then and gave you all the dope. I can speak more frankly and fully than I can in a letter. I also expect to call on Mr. Mathes. But in response to your specific question no more bodies, other than the one (1) you mentioned, were recovered.

Also we have not been able to get more dope from prisoners. I know you are interested in a full chronicle of events that happened that evening and morning. I was out there in it and will give you all details upon my return. I believe this is better as I couldn't write as much in a letter. I'll contact you upon my arrival.

Best Regards,
Jack

Of course Lieutenant H. J. Sherertz, the Commanding officer of Squadron #34 had written Chap and other relatives of those lost on the 509, but his letters added nothing new to what had already been written by his officers.

Basil O'Connor and his Red Cross were active through the International Red Cross in trying to dig out information on this particular battle. The World Alliance of YMCA sent a note in October saying they were informed that German prisoners on Jersey were immediately taken to German prison camps. In a postscript it said "I have just learned there were 16 on September first."

Chap received a sad note from a T.L. Bryant dated November 6. It came through her Dad's contact with a Mr. Jack Shillan, the managing director of the "British Motor Boat Manufacturing Co., Ltd," who was extremely helpful with Isle of Jersey contacts. Miss Bryant's father was a retired man of the cloth who had served many years on the Island of Jersey. Said Miss Bryant: "My fiancée is still in Jersey. We were within weeks of getting married when the occupation took place. Which as you can imagine was very big blow for me. Up until now I have heard through the Red Cross about every five months, but now it is impossible to get any news through and the Islands are cut off from us, and also more or less from Germany as we hold all the French Coast."

Indeed they were cut off. In a subsequent letter from Miss Bryant, she quotes from a newspaper article of November 12th.

> Although our victorious army on the coast of France is only twenty miles away from the islands, British people are still prisoners of the Germans on islands that are virtually cut off from the world. And the Germans themselves are our prisoners. They cannot escape; yet the heavily-defended islands could only be captured from them at a huge cost in lives. Knowing this the Nazi garrison has abandoned the civil population to its fate.

Despite Miss Bryant's endeavors, she could not be of a very positive assistance under the circumstances, nor could her Dad, the Reverend.

Mr. Chapman tried another angle. He had heard that a Red Cross ship was sailing from Lisbon, Spain, with food supplies for the starving population on the Channel Islands. He detailed the 509's battle and requested their specific attention to Ensign James M. Mathes Jr., a possible prisoner. His letter was written just before Christmas on December 18th, 1944.

We received a letter from my college classmate, Bill Webster. He was still in the vicinity of Washington, DC testing and demonstrating another new plane for the Navy. He had heard the news about Jim. Simply and sincerely he has added his prayers to ours.

Curtiss-Wright Corporation
Airplane Division
Sept 8, 1994
Dear Math and Dick,

We read the news about Jim in the New York papers. I can't tell you how sorry we were to see this, but we're hoping and praying that you'll receive good news very shortly.

I expect to be here another month at least. The work is progressing satisfactorily but rather slowly. Without Bunny and Billy down here, the time kind of drags.

I guess you knew that Freddie (Major F. A. Borsodi) had to

make another (parachute) jump a month or so ago. He was doing some spin tests and drew a lemon. We always use spin chutes (8-inch chutes installed at the tail of ship which when opened will help bring a plane out of an uncontrolled spin), but his failed to open. That makes two for him. A good man!

I too have had a little excitement and had to resort to pulling the spin chute. But I was luckier and mine opened.

We are still conducting spin tests. So far I have made over 75 spins and feel pretty wound up. Don't know what you've heard about the XSC-1 but it ought to be good....One of the new cruisers has one on board and advance reports are quite favorable.

Best,
Web

A short note from Jeff in the Pacific also acknowledges Jim's loss.

13 September, 1944
Dear Moth & Dad,

That was tough news about Jim. I share your optimism toward his safe deliverance. That's the only way it could turn out.

Letters of condolence by soldiers over here are rigidly regulated. Have to go through channels, unsealed. I don't think I'll send any, therefore. It's not a public matter from my angle...

Got to go—so long
Love,
Jeff

CHAPTER 18

BEHIND ENEMY LINES

MARY CHAP, Mr. Mathes, and Mr. Chapman were feverishly running down every single piece of information, every rumor, trying to unlock the mystery of the 509 and its crew. At the same time that the family was trying to come to grips with the possibility of death, Math introduced a story of life. Our doctor had proclaimed that she was pregnant. A brother or sister to Dickens was due in late April or May.

In the meantime, in France, after the major break-through of the Allied forces the wheels of victory had slowed down to a grinding, crunching pace of months instead of miles. More costly in materiel and personnel, and more rugged, the tempo of battle had increased proportionately to the decrease in territory exchanged.

In the Pacific war the Americans were moving relentlessly forward through one jungle island after another. Headlines had proclaimed the invasion of the Philippines. From letters we received from Brother Jeff, we learned only that he is well, and that he is in the front lines. And we wonder if he is in the Philippine campaign.

On the home front on Nov. 7, the United States had a war-time election. For some time, the campaign issues had been hotly debated. It was a question of whether we should "stand pat" with President Roosevelt or opt for New York's Governor Dewey. It was a battle of age and experience against youth and energy. Math and I chose the latter.

Mr. Roosevelt had been in office for 12 long years. A victory for him meant another 4, a total of 16 years as our president. It seemed

to us that such a long tenure was not in keeping with the democra-
cy of our country. No one man should be considered essential. Our
country thrives on difference of opinion, on new ways of doing
things. Never before had we doubted that other great American
leaders could carry on the job. Indeed, Governor Dewey put it simply. "It's time for a change." The people did not agree.

A few nights after Roosevelt's re-election an old friend came to
dinner. His name was Nelson Campbell. I hadn't seen him since we
both left the Aetna in August of 1942. He was one of the youngest
in our Aetna group, a shy, quiet, well-ordered young fellow. He
looked fine in his Army Air Force uniform, his silver wings, his ribbons, and his military bearing.

He was delighted to be introduced to son Dickens, and his
friendly approach had the latter sitting in his lap turning the pages
of "The Little Engine That Could." He rolled on the floor and
laughed at the same things as Dickens. At bed-time while we thrust
a thermometer into Dickens to check the severity of his latest cold,
Nelson beat the drum, and shook the rattles providing necessary
entertainment to soothe the procedure.

After supper, he told us his story. As a bombardier in a B-17 he
had left Presque Isle, Maine, for the European Theater. After a three
day stop in Newfoundland, he landed in Wales. There was schooling in England, and the forming of the squadron and then, finally,
the first mission.

Nelson said that his plane flew on the wing of a general who was
leading a vast armada of 500 planes, the famous assault (an infamous one to some), to bomb Bremen. He thought that being so
close to the leading general might mean that he was in a safe position, but he learned differently. Scheduled to pick up a fighter escort of American P-38's they ran into a squadron of German
fighters, ME 109's. And suddenly there was an enemy fighter roar-
ing directly at their plane. Nelson said that he was scared—so very,
very scared, and so amazed. It suddenly seemed incredible that he
could be faced by a German fighter intent on the kill. He said he
fired his 50 caliber guns, but so excited, so bewildered, and so
frightened, that they missed their mark. Fortunately the German

also missed, and in a flash, dropped behind to attack the planes in the rear.

There was another tense moment over the target when flak burst around the big plane. Nelson said he looked out at the tiny black puffs and felt so very helpless. "There is no way of fighting back. It is terrifying to ride through a sea of flak."

There were six other missions for Nelson. Upon the return of each, bomber crews housed in his barracks failed to return, one by one, and he felt a jinx closing in. On his seventh mission it happened. A ME 109 intercepted their flight to Mannheim, roundly whacked his big ship, and sent her scudding toward the Belgian earth. Two crew members were killed outright, and two more were seriously wounded. It was these two men who absorbed Nelson's attention so extensively that he was hardly aware of the descent of the plane. He said that the blood splattered about the plane seemed so unreal, so unnatural. He could never remember seeing another man so badly hurt, so gory.

At this point in the story, Nelson explained that he was not yet at liberty to divulge the details of his actions, even though the territory has since been recovered by our ground forces. But a few things he could tell, and the rest we tried hard to imagine.

Down in Belgium, the vast underground, staunch supporters of the Allies, rushed the crew members to cover as they hit the ground before the Germans could locate them. Apparently the two wounded men were turned over to the Germans because there could be no place for them to make their way in enemy territory. Later word received from an amazingly well-informed underground enabled Nelson and his crewmates to learn of the death of one of the two wounded, and the name of the camp to which the other was taken. Here Nelson paused to emphasize again, the unbelievable accuracy and complete accounting of the enemy's movements through the underground system.

Nelson and his companions, who were not necessarily always his fellow crew members, were located in Brussels at one point. In civilian clothes, they went out into the open only at night, stayed well hidden in friendly homes during the day.

On one occasion he did venture forth into the daylight, and then to go to a department store, where he boldly had his picture taken in a photo machine booth, and this for purposes of a faked passport.

The day after receiving his faked papers when on the move at night, he was stopped by a German patrol. Fortunately the Germans felt his papers were in order, and there was no necessity of speaking a foreign language, whether Flemish, French or German.

Moving only when the underground gave the word, Nelson and companions made their way to Paris. Here he did some sight-seeing with the 28-year-old daughter of the family with which he was housed, a family incidentally, who were very active in the French black market. On one occasion, when Nelson, taking a tour on his own, went to see the Arc de Triomphe, it almost ended in disaster. The strain of rubbing elbows with the German officers who were stationed about the arch was so intense that upon his return to his home base as he threw open the door to his apartment, he discovered to his dismay that it was the wrong apartment.

"Qu'est-que-c'est?" came the question from the occupant.

Not chancing his French, Nelson glared at the questioner, and strode boldly to the street. He even managed a dance in Paris, but nothing really gay or outlandish. He was too cautious for that.

Finally, after the fifth month he crossed the border to Spain. He spared us the detail of the hardships of his long, frightening walk, and it was a walk, through Europe, and then over the mountains to Spain. That is where he had his papers cleared by the American Embassy, and then went to Gibraltar, England and the USA.

In the meantime Brother Tom was fighting his own war in Italy.

September 23, 1944
Dear Folks,
    Nothing really new to report as life staggerrs on with lagging footsteps. Books, and movies remain my only general diversions.
    ...Last night, however, I had the very good fortune to see *The*

Barretts of Winpole Street, with Catherine Cornell. Since it was the first time I'd seen her, it was quite a thrill. She certainly is a terrific actress. She had a wonderful cast too, including Brian Ahearne, Brenda Forbes, Margalo Gilmore, McKay Morris, and many other red hot performers. The crowd was very appreciative, not because it thought it should be, like a Broadway audience, but rather because it actually enjoyed the play...

Love,
Tom

Following is the first of a number of letters from Lieut. (jg) Harry Jackson, describing in the detail that is so much his style, his first experiences in Naval training. They are directed to his wife, Betty, who extracted from them and passed the results around to the family. Harry is very correct with most of the nautical terms he has been told to adapt.

Batt. 2, Co. G Bks. 12-4
N.T. School
Camp McDonough
Plattsburgh, NY
3 Oct. 1944

It's 2:30 A.M. and here I am in the Quartermaster's Room on what is known as the security watch...It's a 2½ hour trick and I prowled the first hour, and am now sitting here comfortably by the phone with no calls coming through, of course, at this ungodly hour.

I had a little trouble sleeping on the trip up which is unusual for me who has never had a particular difficulty in sleepers. I was thinking that I hadn't been in a berth since our marriage...and I may have lost the knack for it.

I awoke at six without having to be called and caught the 7 o'clock train out of Albany easily. There were quite a few of us all with bright braid and hats at jaunty angles. We arrived on time which was 12:53, piled our luggage in a corner of the RR Station at the instruction from a Shore Patrolman (equivalent to an army MP.) who chose me and a rusty-haired lawyer from Belmont and Harvard to line up the men by fours and march them behind the truck to the camp. He selected us because we happened to be the nearest lts. (jg) to him as he spoke. Incidentally most of us are ensigns and all, almost without exception, were originally assigned to Princeton…All are somewhat unhappy about our location because it's practically impossible to get home due to poor train service. They're here from Portland, Oregon, San Francisco, Tulsa, Kansas City, Florida, etc. We are a small class of 380, instead of the regular 1000.

On arrival we went through a lot of paper work with Waves typing forms to be signed, etc. We took all afternoon and we had lunch midway through. We eat cafeteria style with food dished on to six compartment aluminum trays. For lunch we had Virginia Ham, f.f. potatoes, stewed corn, spaghetti, b & b, peach halves, coffee.

By four we were finished and assigned to barracks with this student officer drawing a top berth which has to be made just so. We have lockers and what they call foot lockers, small wooden trunks at the foot of beds for stowage. We had to unpack, put our suitcases in the attic, don grays, and march to chow where we had frankfurters, mashed potatoes with tomato sauce, Harvard beets, stewed corn again, rolls, jam, cocoa. There are four companies and our company eats last, so our stuff is inclined to be a little cool and we are always late for what follows meals.

After dinner we had a company meeting in the hold (basement to normal folk) listening to our commanding officer, a swell guy who is also a jg himself, give us a quick resume of what to expect. We will be going every minute, said he. After that, we went to the clinic for examination of a certain part of us to make sure that we're healthy there, then to the barracks for a lesson on how to make up a sack (bed). It must be taut said the C.O. My assignment to this security watch from 12:45 to 3:15 is just because my bed happened to be where it was. Here come two more suckers to relieve us and we will go back to bed.

Harry's next letters were written in short order, 10/6, 10/7, 10/10, and 10/14. We shall take the liberty of excerpting the excerpts only because we feel there is something of a "deja-vu" in the naval training about which the reader is already familiar.

10/6/44

...We started classes Wednesday. We have four of them every morning: Fundamentals, Navigation, Seamanship, and Ordnance and Gunnery. We get underway at 8:00 A.M. and go to noon. Then lunch at 12:40; study from 1:30 to 2:30 in a smoky, noisy, poorly-lighted room at long tables. Then we have another hour of optional study followed by hours of drill and physical training. Dinner is at six and we have an hour and a half to study afterward.

10/7/44

...Here we go again. I was interrupted yesterday. We are constantly interrupted and have little or no free time. They even take our study periods with special details and orders. We've been so busy with dental exams and odds and ends that we have had just one hour of drilling and no physical training at all...

...I have bought a pair of navy shoes at the store on the camp grounds for $5.00. They are very comfortable and would cost a civilian plenty. I can get anything you poor folk can't, including real pre-war sneakers, sweat shirts, Oh Henry bars and chewing gum galore....

10/10/44

I have a little time before noon chow, as we have been taught to say. I miss you and Joy and Jeff more every day. Your good letters are life savers...

...Yesterday our study period was given over to inoculations. It's not just a matter of getting jabbed and then going on our way. We have to march to the dispensary. In fact we march to everything, even meals.

...Today everyone has sore arms from the shots. We had three: typhoid, tetanus, and cowpox. We have more next Monday...

10/13/44

...We had some tests this week, two of which I missed because I was "mate of the deck" yesterday and had to stand watch during class periods...

...We had "night-blindness" test this afternoon...I had no trouble with it. Airplanes were flashed on a dimly-lighted screen and we had to tell the direction in which they were flying. After that we saw a movie about China showing their war with Japan from the beginning to the present. It was a documentary film filled with propaganda. All the newsreels ever filmed I would guess, cleverly pieced together to give continuity and appropriate dialogue. It included some heart rending shots of civilian victims and the effect was to instill in us, as you might guess, a desire to slaughter every Nip on earth...

I don't know why, but Dinner Cooney suddenly appeared at Infantry School at Fort Benning, Georgia in October, 1944. We had seen a great deal of him in Boston, when he was with the Air Corps.

> Dear Math & Dick
>   Thanks for your letter. In the same mail I received a letter from Chappie. The news in both of them concerning Jim's boat, etc. made me even more sure that Jim is okay. The fact that it was off German-held shore is very good news, don't you think?
>   ...There's not too much to say about this place except that we'll be through in two weeks. The work is all infantry basics and deals with infantry weapons and tactics. The next time I see you, Dick, I will be able to discuss intelligently bracketing, tracking, breech blocks, sears, firing pins, recoil mechanisms, etc.
>   By the way. What is an Amplydine?
>   Best,
>   Dinner

In the South Pacific Jeff was on another special mission. His battalion boats took an awful beating, and there came a time when some replacements were available. When they learned about 12 LCMs awaiting at Milne Bay, Jeff was dispatched with an appropriate number of boat crews to pick up the boats. Before leaving Milne Bay, Jeff checked with the Aussie weather station and was assured that conditions were right, so off he went. At this point his unit was at Tamahmera Bay, and the Japanese still held an airbase at Wewak which was on Jeff's course. As his fleet was sneaking past that area in the dark, a vicious squall blew up and scattered the formation to the four winds. The big ramps acted as sails and with their shallow draft and flat bottoms, the boats went skimming in every direction.

Despite the precarious location Jeff ordered "lights on" so they'd have some idea of where they all were. When dawn arrived, they found boats out of commission, some with tarps wrapped around their propellers, but they finally got everything together, and with the use of tow lines, etc. they limped back to Milne Bay. There Jeff confronted the weather officer who said, "Oh my, I did make a bull of it, didn't I?" Jeff's thought was "How can you be mad at a guy like that?" After all was back shipshape they set out again and the ocean was like a millpond all the way, as forecast by their meteorologist friend whose reputation was restored. But, Jeff sounded tired in this October letter from the South Pacific. After all, he'd been at it almost two years without an apparent break of any length.

> 10/13/44
> Dear Folks,
>   I am now on another one of those detached service deals and I have quite a responsibility. In the course of operations I've found it necessary to tangle with a certain amount of brass. I'm amazed at my belligerency and refusal to be shoved around. Despite being terrifically outranked I won my point on each item in question. I always thought I was one of those easy-going guys…
>   …What is Ha's address?
>   …Everything is okay, but I'm plumb wore out. I would like to at least have a leave in Sydney. Best of all, though, I'd like to see the end of the war. But it won't be so soon as all the people in the States say. They just don't know. We do.
>   I have to get back to the job now. Be Good.
>   Love,
>   Jeff

Another extract from Harry's letter via his wife, Betty. The following will again be, therefore, an extract of an extract.

> 10/18,44
>   …I'll make this brief so that I'll have time to learn my seamanship which includes signal flags, ship nomenclature, ground tackle, including anchors, rope, pulleys, etc…The guys who were

commissioned from the enlisted ranks(and there are many of them), have a distinct jump on the rest of us. There are quite a few smart guys, Phi Betes, such as my sack partner (he has the lower). Also a lot of physics teachers, and scads of engineers. I can hear Dad, saying that doesn't mean anything. Look at what Dick did against competition. And, of course, he'd be right. Well, I'll just do the best I can...

Harry

Mother and Dad offered to make the trip from Plandome, L.I. to Larchmont, NY to baby-sit young Joy and Jeffie, giving Betty the freedom to join Brother Harry in Plattsburgh for his only weekend liberty during the entire stay in upper N.Y. Here is his thank-you letter.

November 11, 1944
Dear Moth and Dad,

I have a moment before chow to write a long over-due note to you swell parents.

We just completed our Armistice Day parade which had us marching into town and back. Luckily we didn't have to stand in front of the town hall and listen to the speeches this time. It's cold as the devil today, so it would have been plenty uncomfortable. As it was, we were marching continually, and everybody was out to watch us...

I don't know yet what I will be specializing in. Our orders haven't come through and probably won't until next week...I think that I'm slated for either armed guard, or communications. ...armed guard, for which they choose j.g.s usually, would have me in charge of guns on a merchant ship and the navy crews who man the guns. If it is this, I will be sent to Gulfport, Mississippi for training for a period of 2 or 3 months. Communication officers go to Harvard for a similar period...

...Last weekend was a highlight for us. A full weekend off, the only one in our entire stay in Plattsburgh and everybody made good use of it. But, thanks to the good cooperation of you folks, my darling wife and I had a better time than anybody else. It surely was fine of you to take over that way. It involves considerable effort to make that long trip I know. We want you to know that we don't take your help for granted, and that we appreciate sincerely feeling free to call on you...

...All my weekly hour tests are over except for seamanship, and next week we have finals...

...Thanks for all your help...

Love,

Ha

It was hard to keep tabs on Dinner Cooney. He next was heard from back in Texas. As one of Dickens' god-parents, he mentions his "spiritual" obligation.

Co.C, 68th BN, 14th Regt.
Camp Fanin, Texas
11 November 1944
Dear Math, Dick, and Dickens,

I haven't forgotten you. I've been too busy to write since arriving here...My first two weeks were spent on bivouac, and hence was out of touch with civilization. I never did get that leave I was counting on, or you would have had a knock at your kitchen door, or maybe even the slug-infested cellar entrance...

Now that you have my latest address I hope you'll find time to put it to use...I miss those wonderful Sunday suppers of waffles, cream chicken on toast, that super salad, etc. with the accompanying rolling on the floor afterwards. Also I want to keep posted on Dickens' progress and I'm only sorry that my location prevents me from performing my spiritual obligations.

I had an awfully nice letter from Mrs. M. the other day. She was very optimistic about Jim as are the rest of us. I was glad to hear that and am just waiting for the day when we know for sure that Jim is ok...

Dinner

From Harry comes the first letter to his spouse as he commences training for the armed guard in Norfolk, Virginia.

December 2, 1944

The trip down was quite uneventful. Awakened at 5:30 A.M. in time to get off the train at 6:20 and board the steamer that crosses from Cape Charles to Norfolk.

At the pier at which we went alongside at 9:00 A.M., we loaded into a taxi (six of us from Plattsburgh with luggage) for the ten mile jaunt to this camp.

Our camp is a very temporary looking place consisting of one story frame buildings covered with tar paper and heated by coal stove. It's situated in a pine grove and covers quite an area with barracks, administration building, mess hall, theater, class buildings, etc…We keep our clothes and belongings in standing lockers fitted with hangers and shelves.

There are people to make our beds and take care of the stove. Furthermore, we have no inspections. We have "arrived" and are treated as full-fledged officers, having learned our discipline and indoctrination.

We can get up when we wish as long as we are on hand for the march to the first class each A.M. at 7:55. Four classes in the morning, then lunch, then four more classes in the afternoon until 4:30 P.M. after which we are free unless there are special movies or lectures after dinner.

If we want to we can live off the base and quite a few guys have wives here and are doing it. I plan to look around tomorrow, but understand that apartments and cottages are pretty poor with just kerosene stoves for heat…The food is excellent and costs $1.10 per day: 30 cents for breakfast and 40 cents for the other meals. I bought a $10 meal ticket…Tables have real linen cloths and the food is served on plates…You'll be interested to know that I can have milk for an extra .05 cents, and always do, of course…The work is going to be interesting, but concentrated and tough. Our class is crowded into a month and we have a mid-term in two weeks and a final on the fourth.

Lots of love,

Ha

Tom has some gastronomic problems with which to deal in his little piece of Italy.

December 8, 1944
Dear Folks,

This afternoon I was visiting a friend at the hospital (stomach trouble), and as I left, an orderly came in with the apparatus for an enema. So I got out quickly. The poor fellow had never had one before, and trying to explain how it felt, which is impossible, brought back those occasional bed-ridden days when I was a party to "the tube that cheers."

My gastronomic life received a rude setback today, as my pre-war Red Cross girl friend, was transferred. She was in the habit of taking me to the very superior Red Cross mess for a very superior meal every once in a while. The other day I was visited by Parker Hall's sister-in-law who lived with them in Plandome. She too is a Red Cross girl stationed about thirty-five miles away. Too far away for meals, unfortunately.

Love,
Tom

On December 12, Harry writes Dad about accommodations for his family in the Norfolk area.

Dear Dad,

I have your letters and want to thank you for arranging the family transportation.

There is no need to worry about the housing because I have gone into that with the thoroughness you should have come to expect and have acted in my customary all-too-methodical fashion. I spent two Sundays in Virginia Beach and vicinity and have talked with many guys who have been living outside.

Although I knew what each hotel offered I could not very well make accommodations without knowing when the angels would be arriving...

As for the study problem, I look for the presence of Betty and the children to be helpful rather than otherwise. So all's well. Have to run to muster now.

Thanks again,
Ha

I received letters from my three brothers that arrived close to my birthday which fell on December 16. Earlier in the month, I had been informed that I might expect orders in the near future. The orders were to take me to the West Coast. Said my commander, the top ordnance officer in the Charlestown Yard, "I hope this will not interfere with your Christmas plans."

When word had been passed on to Math, we went about convincing ourselves that it would be very pleasant living on the other side of the country, where neither of us had spent much time. It would be a new experience.

Questions crowded our minds: What if we were to end up in Washington instead of California? They say you need a car to cover the wide open spaces. Should I try to drive out, with but four days proceed time?…Is it silly to ship furniture way out there?…Just how permanent is this move?…Should Math plan to make it out there in her pregnant state?…If she has the baby in Greenwich, it will be almost a year of separation. Is this the wise thing to do?…There must be good doctors out there…we're bound to know someone if not a doctor.

And after all the questions came word that the ordnance commander had written the Bureau of Ordnance that Jackson is essential to the operation of the South Boston Naval Shipyard. It was flattering, but the commander himself advised, "I doubt if the letter will make any difference." At this point I didn't know if I cared whether it did, or didn't.

The year ended inconclusively.

CHAPTER 19

NEW ORDERS

ON JANUARY FIRST I was promoted to senior lieutenant. On January 5 I received orders: "When directed by the Commandant, Navy Yard, you will regard yourself detached from duty at the Navy Yard, Boston, Mass., and from such duty as may have been assigned you; will proceed to Seattle, Wash. and report to The Assistant Industrial Manager for duty in connection with fire Control Equipment, reporting by letter to the Commandant, Thirteenth Naval District."

I was verbally advised that I would lead a group of some 19 or 20 ratings (1st and 2nd class gunnery mates) and one ensign. We were scheduled to ship aboard a repair ship in the Pacific theater, and to be transported by helicopter to ships of the line which were having difficulty with their fire control equipment. We were to repair their systems as needed. It was a very "iffy" assignment, I thought. Faced with the reality of a tour of sea duty, I suddenly was not sure I welcomed the opportunity at this particular point in the Pacific war, and my personal life.

I was granted a seven-day delay leave, and four-day proceed time when I received the final date of detachment from the Yard commandant.

Although my thoughts were obviously of the future, I could not expect to divorce myself from the present. The USS *Springfield,* a new light cruiser back from her shakedown cruise, was busily preparing for her next trip—to the Pacific. She stretched along Pier #6, her gray camouflaged hull basking in the winter sun. As usual, there was much to be done. I had been called to a conference in the captain's cabin. I joined the captain, the gunnery officer, Johnny Dee, the General Electric representative, whose company manufactured the directors, and various senior civilian yard representatives.

"We have violent oscillation in the forward main battery director when the ship changes course," said the gunnery officer.

The captain said, "We can't be expected to hit a target unless on an even course, and we can't be on an even course when under Jap fire. So the situation must be corrected as fast as possible." He looked at me.

"But sir, we can't simulate a ship changing course when she lies here at the pier," I said.

And so it was decided that during the test run scheduled on the morrow that ordnance observers would be aboard. I was ordered by my boss to make the trials, and oversee the work.

It was a cold and dark January morning at 6:30 A.M. when I saluted the colors aft and asked permission of the officer of the deck to board the *Springfield*.

Not having had time to eat breakfast at home, I hustled forward to the wardroom, and the steaming hot coffee, the fried eggs over, bacon, toast and jam.

There were the usual bos'un's whistles and accompanying announcements as lines were cast off and the ship nosed out of the harbor. There is something very definite about the quartermaster's voice over the announcing system that blares forth in all compartments of the ship though somewhat lost this morning on the cold wind-swept deck.

The voice concluded by saying, "Condition affirm is now set!" Hatches banged shut, watertight doors swung closed. The ship was being readied for a day at sea.

As I put the last bit of jam on the remaining corner of toast, I felt the ship start to roll just a trifle. I knew we were through the nets and starting to pick up speed. I remembered, uneasily, that the captain had mentioned the presence of German U-boats in the area the day before. He had refused to try any trials with the ship in reverse.

"I'll be damned if I want to be caught backing down in the middle of the ocean," he'd said.

Two ships had been sunk three days ago just north of Boston not far off shore. The Nazis were still managing a dangerous strike on occasion.

I was joggled out of my thoughts by the realization that there was work to be done. I was off for the plotting room, far down in the ship's hull where the armor is the heaviest. It serves as a nerve center for the main battery's 6-inch gun turrets

As I started toward the familiar hatch, I remembered that it would be tightly dogged (closed). Condition affirm had been set. The most direct way down was the emergency escape hatch, a long narrow trunk that contained three small hatches en route at appropriate decks. The ship had started to roll and pitch, and the wind could be heard as it whistled through the superstructure, even below decks. I grabbed the first hatch, turned it loose, and eased my 210 pounds into the small opening. My feet instinctively sought the metal protrusions, a foot rail that ran along the side of the trunk. I started down. As I pulled the hatch shut above me, the small bit of light that it had afforded was shut off. I was in the pitch dark, a black hole of Calcutta. Down, down, down the ladder, gently bumping one side, then another, in rhythm with the ships' rolls. I reached the next hatch and groping in the darkness, I broke it loose, slid through and endeavored to tackle the second part of my perilous trip. Alas, I had forgotten that the foot rail was on the alternate side of the trunk. My feet were dangling into black space, looking for the rail, and I hung like a ham on the hook of an abattoir. My body banged against the enclosure, and it was that precise moment when I heard the quartermaster's impersonal voice, "Now hear this, now hear this. All hands will wear life jackets…there are German submarines operating in the area!"

I hung helplessly wondering where I would get a life preserver, assuming, that is, I could make my way out of the escape trunk. I persevered, through the final hatch, and found myself in the warm inviting glow of the plotting room. All hands were huddled around the massive range-keeper which occupied the central part of the compartment, some standing in front of the switchboard, or pacing back and forth with dangling cords attached to earphones.

I approached the gunnery officer and said, "Hey Temp, where do I get my life jacket?"

In his best southern drawl he said, "Aw, if we get hit you won't need a life jacket down here, Jack. Stay loose."

As the morning wore on, and as our tests were running, the little spark on the error recorder danced and sputtered. The ship rolled, the air was hot and getting foul, and we all sank lower and lower as we hung over the plotting board discussing our findings. I looked at the GE's Johnny Dee. Not a good sailor, he was ashen white, rolled up in a corner of the room, his head in his hands. But he had performed his miracle, and we were yet to see if his findings were correct. But now it was time for chow, an excellent excuse to go topside for a bit of fresh air.

We all felt better after eating. The skipper had said that he would maneuver radically on the way in, so there was not much we could do until the time came for the final testing. I spent the time with the gunnery officer in his compartment, being regaled by his tales of previous service in the south Pacific. He had left to check on something or other, and reappeared and started pulling on his foul-weather gear.

"Better hang loose," he said. "We're gonna try some full speed full rudder turns, and I'm afraid this bucket might turn over." Naturally I laughed at such a preposterous thought. A fine new ship like this turn over…?

But the quartermaster had his say. "Now hear this, now hear this, all hands will wear life jackets, pronto."

It was but a few minutes later that I was summoned to the big test. I hopped into my heavy coat and up, up, up I went, the main deck, the flag bridge, the navigating bridge, the forward control station, and finally the main battery director. A savage wind tore at my face and I felt as if it might rip off my nose or an ear. And my heavy jacket was breached, by the strong gusts finding their way through the folds of warmth. I made my way into the director's hatch, slipped on the battle phones that hung from the handwheels, and when a voice said "Forward director…plot testing," I replied, "Forward director, aye."

I turned on the motor when the word was given. As the ship swung violently to port, heeling over radically as she did, I trained the director. As I looked through the scopes, the horizon danced and whirled before my eyes. But the director ran as smoothly as could be. There were a few more tries at this as the ship swung to starboard, then port, then back to starboard. With arms and legs aching with the cold I finally got the word that the tests were satisfactorily completed, and I made my way down to the warmth and comfort of the wardroom.

In time we pulled into Boston and the Yard. It was dark, but not too dark to observe the coating of ice that enveloped the handrails on deck, ice that sheathed the superstructure up to the bridge where the spray, whipped by the wind, froze as it struck the solid metal. The fo'c'sle had three inches of frozen slush lying in an uneven covering along the deck.

It was from this ship that I had acquired a fine heavy duty sea jacket. It had the name of the ship's gunnery officer stenciled across its back, but it managed to keep me warm during that brief journey, and has done the same over the years as it is my favorite cold weather jacket. It reaches to my knees, and has a hood. It was a matter of *cumshaw* that brought me the coat. I have forgotten the details, but it was an honorable exchange.

It was not an unusual practice in Navy yards to deal for favors. Generally it was a matter between the ship's officers interested in acquiring an "edge" and the civilian yard birds. But on many occasions it was an exchange between the Navy personnel in the yard and on the ship. For instance, a gunnery officer might desire another pair of 50-mm machine guns for his ship. Navy regulations stated that no additional fifty's were required aboard a ship of this class. Hence, the gunnery officer was out of luck if he attempted to go through the proper channels. But, there are always means of "beating the system." In this case, for instance, an ordnance officer might be aware of a pair of such guns taken off another ship that were in storage. So through the various channels available to him, he goes about securing these mounts and arranging for them to be mounted on the requesting ship. In appreciation for this favor the requesting gunnery officer might grant his benefactor a thank you gift, such as a winter coat which was issued to all ship's officers. It would be the assumption that said gunnery officer could get a replacement coat, whereas the Yard officer could not The above is a simplified example of "cumshaw." It is not always as simple, direct, or, if you will, innocent. Indeed, the exchange of services or goods can take the form of out-and-out barter, even suggesting some unscrupulous or criminal exchanges. But it all carries the obscure name of cumshaw, and in its simplest form it is a way of getting things done in a hurry, to the mutual satisfaction of the two parties.

* * *

In the interim, Jeff's Co. C., in New Guinea, had taken part in what for him was the final landing. This was at Biak Island. It was fiercely defended by the Japanese. When the convoy arrived off Biak, the beach was in a mist which soon thickened by the smoke of the Naval bombardment. There was no wind, and the humidity held the smoke down on the beach. As a result the first wave of boats hit west of the proper beach. The error was discovered as the smoke cleared slightly, and the troops swung east to the planned station.

Jeff's company was not in the first waves, but had a part in evacuating some of the Allied troops cut off by the Japanese, and then to supply the forces as they counter-attacked. Jeff relates one episode in which a Japanese flyer had abandoned his burning plane and taken to his parachute. An enthusiastic gunner in Jeff's LCM started firing at the flyer, as he floated down, which Jeff recalled, "Was simply not done. You don't shoot at a guy in a parachute." However, Jeff recalls, he did not restrain his gunner as he was aware that the flyer was well out of the range of the 30-mm caliber machine gun, and therefore no damage could be done.

It was rumored, Jeff recalls, that Colonel Charles Lindbergh, who had been tarred as a leader of the "America First" movement relative to his references to German air power, was taking part in the aerial thrust at Biak, flying a P-38. This rumor was never verified.

A letter from the South Pacific written at year's end but the first such received in 1945 finds Jeff lamenting missed Christmas greetings.

28 December 1944
Dear Moth & Dad,

Holy cow! All this time and no mail from me, no excuse as usual, but a weak explanation: 2½ months of detached service which found me on the go, and seldom near a post office.

Missed Christmas greetings, etc.; missed arranging for gifts to all from me. Missed the boat all around!

…Now that I'm back with the unit I find everything changed; we are strictly rear echelon guys, with an officer's club, nurses, and all kinds of lush surroundings. We have dances, go aqua planing, do some drinking, see U.S.O. shows, and indulge in precious little work. What a change from detached service! I'm pitching right in and enjoying it…

…Please send me Ha's latest address, and that of Bets and the kids too. I can't write because I don't know where…

Love,
Jeff

It was on January 13th, 1945, that Mrs. Grace Page, a wife, learned by a telegram from the Chief of Naval Personnel, via the German Government, that her husband, "John Layden Page, Radioman 3/C USNR of MTB #509, who was previously reported as missing is now a prisoner of war." The Navy said in conclusion "letter follows."

It did follow on 23 January, advising that the report did not give Page's camp location. "This conforms with the usual practice of the German Government not to report the address of a prisoner of war until he has been placed in a permanent camp. Past experience indicates that his camp address may not be reported to this office until one to three months have elapsed from the time he was first reported as a prisoner." It was suggested that pending receipt of his permanent address, mail could be directed via the International Red Cross at Geneva, Switzerland. The letter was signed by Harold F.

Bresee, Colonel C.M. P. Director of the American Prisoner of War Information Bureau.

And on February 3rd, the same colonel advised Mrs. Page that "information has been received which indicates that your husband is now interned at Dulag Luft Hospital, Germany." She was advised she could communicate with him postage free following the usual instructions. And in the final paragraph of the colonel's letter he states, "One parcel label and two tobacco labels are issued every sixty-day period, without application, to the next of kin, for the benefit of the United States prisoners of war interned in Germany."

Mary Chap dutifully passed along this information, and all that came her way, to the other wives or parents of all the crew members. She performed a vital secretarial service, and was the primary source of any information that was available re: the 509, from whatever source it was received.

In the meantime, early in the new year, Tom tries to set the record straight. An honorable young man calling it as he sees it. He is still in Italy with his bomber wing.

2 January, 1945

Dear Folks,

I wish you wouldn't lump Jeff and me together as "suffering overseas." It's certainly unfair to him, and it makes me feel a little sheepish. The only hardships we suffer in common is being away from home, and being tired of the whole thing. Otherwise I think I can say I have no real hardship over here.

I sleep in a nice warm room in a stone building. The room is clean and quite neat and nice-looking, my bed is comfortable, with a nice mattress and plenty of blankets. There are wash basins, toilets, and hot showers in the next room. The food is about as good as anyone gets overseas, and the mess hall is comfortable and warm. In the next building to mine is our club, with a well-stocked bar, and I can get books of all types, that I can read. There are movies every night, and occasional USO shows, and I have a chance to see such artists as Catherine Cornell, Jascha Heifetz, and big-time Italian opera companies. There's a laundry, a tailor shop, and a barber shop right here on the base, and additional comforts in the towns nearby, which are easy to reach. There is relatively little military stuff going on, and the past week I've seen two letters from guys back in the States, one at March Field, California, and the other at Mountain Home, Idaho. Both said they'd just as soon be back here.

So that's why I ask you please not to mention Jeff's and my hardships in the same breath. His set-up is a whole lot different.

You might be interested to know that I now have breakfast in bed. One guy in the room gets up early (in connection with his work), and turns on the stove, and brings back toast, coffee and fruits. By the time he gets back the place is warm and the radio is on. Oh, I tell you, it's a rough war!

Love,
Tom

Jeff follows his December letter from the same locale as his previous note, where things have apparently gotten much more agreeable, and who knows, maybe as pleasant as Brother Tom's in Italy. This one is written from Biak Island, the same locale in which an earlier battle had been fought and won by the Allies. It was the custom to quickly build up such areas, which, in a matter of months, became thriving bases for future thrusts. As such, they were peopled by support units, such as medical staffs to man field hospitals, supply facilities, Red Cross personnel, etc. His letter opens with a remembrance of our parents' wedding anniversary on January 10, but he speaks of a "country-club" atmosphere in Biak with girls, shows, mail, and other amenities.

11 January 1945
Dear Moth and Dad,
Yesterday I thought of you especially hard, though you had no way of knowing, thanks to my inexcusable failure to write congratulations. I'm worried about myself. I've been missing too many important dates...
...Everyone remembered me on Christmas...
...And what in the hell did I do? Not a damn thing for anybody. Thanks Moth for covering up for me and giving gifts in my name.

That's typical of you. Always protecting your boys. Thanks, too, for sending the gift to Kay and Bill Schulhof. Kay wrote a fine letter of thanks to me. She composes a swell hunk of correspondence…

…Still a country-club atmosphere here, with dances, drinks, and sack time. I'm going to make a conscientious effort to taper off and wear a hair shirt for awhile.

…Moth, that 145 hours must be a record. Please don't do that much again. When Tom and I come home we want you to still be young and beautiful as ever. Take it easy, please. You too Dad.

Love,
Jeff

On January 15, Bud Brett, from whom little word had been received of late, wrote from Hollywood, Florida, where he had been stationed for a year. In 1942, Bud had been sent to San Francisco to radar school, as the *Honolulu* had just been fitted with its first radar. In the meantime, the *Honolulu* had suffered a torpedo hit in the Solomon Islands and was limping back to the States for further repairs. Brett was retained as an instructor until the ship was refurbished. He went with the *Honolulu* back to the South Pacific. Later, when a new radar school was being set up in Hollywood, Florida, Bud was specifically requested, and plucked from his ship to become an instructor at the school. After a year in Hollywood, Bud was ordered to new construction in Boston. The "new" U.S.S. *Helena*, a light cruiser, was to be his ship, and he was to be the combat information officer. She was built in Quincy, and fitted out in the South Boston Navy Yard, shortly after I had left the Yard for Seattle. Bud never did serve on the *Helena*, as he was replaced with four ensigns to work in the radar field, and the war mercifully ended his tour of active duty. He became a lieutenant commander three days before the war ended.

The letter below was written in Hollywood toward the very end of his tour at the Hollywood Radar School.

Jan. 15, 1945

Dear Dick,

I've been anything but prompt in answering your letter, and I am hoping this will reach you before you move on. I'm very anxious to hear more about what the future has in store for you. It was only just a few days ago that I got word from the family that you had called and given them the word that you were expecting orders.

I was rather surprised to hear this as I was under the impression that you were pretty well set. It certainly is too bad that it should come now when you and Math are awaiting the arrival of a playmate for Dickens. I think the latter is terribly exciting.

I know that you all must have had a perfect Christmas and New Years. I had hoped so that I would be able to get home, but Uncle Sam said no. Gosh, it's been a long time since I have spent a Christmas with the family. I had a fair time down here, but it's nothing to rave about. It hardly seems possible that a year has passed since I arrived in Hollywood.

…It's been a good year but I imagine that come April I'll find myself on the way out again. I'm hoping to get new construction around Boston. A CL or a CA (light or heavy cruiser). That would give me a chance to be with the family…

…Give my very best to Math, Dickens and all your families, and send me the dope.

Bud

Tom comments in the following letter about Brother Harry's duty in the armed guard, as well as passing on how he spent his latest three-day pass.

15 January, 1945

Dear Folks,

I just got interviewed in connection with taking the test for a Warrant Officer appointment in communications. But I found that they are only interested in the very technical end—and of course all I know is my code work, so that is that.

I also just came back from a three-day pass, which accomplished three functions. First to pick up a few odds and ends for the code room, also to visit my sick friend (a duodenum ulcer), and to have fun. In the latter connection, I saw the opera "Rigoletto," and despite my second row orchestra seat from which I could clearly count the chins on the soprano (about 5), I enjoyed it a great deal; even more then I had enjoyed "Aida" on a similar occasion some weeks back. My seat cost 75 lire (cents), which wasn't bad.

From the little I know of the Navy, Ha has a very nice job. Coming across on a liberty ship I had some opportunity to talk with Navy gunners, and for one thing, they get the best food available, since they get Merchant Marine stuff. Also, by now, the danger is greatly minimized, and the cruises only last about four months. The only tough thing about it is the comparative pay checks of the Merchant Marine who draw down plenty for taking the same risks as the sailors. They are the most overpaid bunch in the world, although, of course, you can't take any credit away from the old merchant mariners who were on the Murmansk run. But now, they make thousands for doing nothing and taking no risks.

Excuse me for missing your wedding day on the 10th. Hope it was a happy one.

Love,
Tom

Brother Harry had not yet hit the Atlantic. He was still in Armed Guard training in Virginia. He had visited the same Dam Neck Firing Range that I had participated in months before.

January 20. 1945
Dear Folks,

Everything continues fine with us and the time is flying by. Today I started my last week as assistant battery officer and next week at this time will have my own crew to train. So four weeks from Saturday will find me all through down here and on my way to Brooklyn and Larchmont. Unless, of course, the Navy decides to change things and that isn't entirely out of the question either.

During this past week I was assigned to the Dam Neck firing range as an "observer" of the armed guard crews shooting at sleeves towed behind planes and small radio-controlled Model planes. We had to watch and grade the different crews on their work and our criticism was brought to the attention of the crew members next day to enable them to correct the mistakes. Each crew trained here gets to fire 3 types of guns. It's an opportunity for them to use all the stuff we teach them during the first few weeks of their 4-week course.

I benefited from that assignment because one day around a gun being fired is worth weeks of practice at a loading machine. Unfortunately, however, we had only 3 days of the 6 at the range, due to poor weather and low ceiling.

Love,
Ha

Bill Webster dropped us a note inviting us to his father's farm in Lenox, Massachusetts for a weekend of skiing. He was anxious to get our two kids of a similar age together. His wife Bunny was also pregnant with their number two child to match Math.

Jan. 24, 1945
Dear Dick,

Sorry not to have written sooner—Christmas holidays and a rush of things at the plant so I just had no time...As I didn't get my vacation last summer we are leaving February 22 for two weeks at Lenox. Bunny and I were wondering if you, Math and Dickens could get over there for the weekend of the 24th. Perhaps we could do some skiing. I don't recall when Math's baby is due, but if it's not expected that week-end we'd love to see you guys...

We saw Freddie and Marcia (Borsodi) before Christmas. Their second girl was born then, five weeks early, but perfectly okay. Freddie is now in England on a four month's trip, demonstrating jets to the brass...

Best,
Web

A letter from Captain Chet Loomis arrived. We hadn't heard from him in some time.

Hdqts NAFD—ATC
1250 AAF BU
APO 396, New York, NY
January 27, 1945
Cher Dick,

...Yes, I have heard that Jim Mathes was reported "missing," and hope to hell that by some chance he may have been picked up and in the hands of the Germans.

I hope you don't leave for sea duty, if you are scheduled to, before I get home. I sure would like to have our little families get together for a week somewhere. As luck would have it, you will probably leave about the time I return, which is about June...

...Jean and Teddy are spending the winter at Captiva, Florida, where I wish we could all get together. It's a swell place for the kids and a good spot to get away from it all...

...I have been leading a routine existence here for the past few months except for a four day trip to the Azores. I sure felt like staying right on the plane and going through to New York...

...Christmas was, as you might expect, quite dull although I didn't spend it in the desert as I did last year. However, wherever one is, Christmas is not the same unless you are with your family and I hope I shall be with Jean and Teddy next December...

...The war news is looking much better and the Russians are really pouring it on now. I'm afraid they are going to make us look sick if they get to Berlin and we are still grinding away. Of course the western front is tying up a large amount of men and materiel that might otherwise be used in the eastern front. Also if the German Air Force hadn't been whittled down by the AAF and RAF to the second rate outfit that it now is, they would be raising plenty of hell elsewhere.

Well Richard, I must write the little woman a sugar report and then to bed. My regards to Math and Dickens and lots of luck to you if you leave before I return.

Chet

On the very same day we heard by V-mail from Dinner Cooney en route to France.

Lt. J. S. Cooney
Ex. Off. Co.
APO #15717
c/o Postmaster New York, NY
Jan. 27, 1945
Dear Math & Dick,

At last I'm on the way. The ship is rolling so much that it's pretty hard to write. Furthermore, the impersonality of V-mail makes it pretty boring to start with.

I'm awfully sorry to have missed you three (or 3½) when we were up in Boston. I was looking forward to having you meet Johnny. She's a wonderful egg and I know you'd like her…

…Let's have a letter from you when you find time. I will write a real one later.

Dinner

CHAPTER 20

ON TO SEATTLE

ON FEBRUARY FIRST I departed on the New York Central Railroad for the first leg of my trip to Seattle.

I wrote to Math the very first night

"Perhaps I'd better start this letter with the conventional traveler's gripes: Bouncing train, scratchy pen, and all that stuff. There was a bumpy stop in Albany and a nostalgic moment as we crossed the main street of Schenectady. I remember the florist shop where I had purchased some flowers for you, so many months ago, to commemorate the up-coming birth of Dickens... We've just passed Utica, NY now but already I miss you both very much."

By February 3rd I'd left Chicago for the far reaching flat fields of Minnesota and South Dakota. An occasional farm house and barn reminded me that it is indeed the human hand that sets out the rows of corn stalks which peeked up through the snow. The sun came up in a most beautiful pink hue from behind the foot hills of the Rockies in the desolate rolling hills of Montana. Some of the monadnocks mixed in with the sharper hills look like huge loaves of bread. Snow fences and cattle fences divide the land.

I saw wild pheasants, flushed by the train, glide over the tracks and into the bush, and cattle and sheep by the score. In closer proximity, I was amazed at the number of babies on the train, most of whom were evident only at meal times.

At every stop along the route there were "handouts" given to all service men. Either a bevy of girls carrying baskets of oranges, cigarettes, stationary, matches, postcards, doughnuts, etc. Or a "canteen" with welcoming signs advertising free food and goodies.

I had been approached by a shore patrolman aboard the train. He suggested that I was the "senior officer aboard" and as per custom, had to give him my name and station. Should anything out of the ordinary occur, I was told, the SP would report to me for orders. Aha, my first command.

Once in Seattle I managed to get a room in the New Washington Hotel for the night of the 5th, which I shared with an ensign in the Coast Guard.

The next morning, I awoke on the late side. I was misled by the late sunrise. As I was not due to report to my new post until the morrow, I had arranged to spend my first day visiting Dick Haley and his wife Jo. Dick was one of my ten fire control training associates. He was a Bostonian who had landed at Bremerton Navy Yard, which was off Seattle, on an island in Puget Sound. I boarded a 10:10 A.M. ferry. Such a lovely trip!

The ferry, large and substantial had soft chairs arranged around its enclosed second deck. Big fat seagulls swooped in front of the large plate glass windows, looked in and had their say in shrill cries. The islands that were scattered about were, for the most part, sparsely inhabited, and tall evergreens covered the hills, with a backdrop of the Olympic Mountains.

The ferry wound through the islands, and through a narrow channel where the submarine nets were strewn. It hardly seemed like a commercial trip, this crossing of Puget Sound, but more of a delightful excursion. It took an hour, and I was met warmly by Jo Haley.

We dined that evening at the Officer's Club and I was amazed and pleased at the warm reception that I received from the officers and their wives. "So at last we're meeting Dick Jackson!"

Haley had apparently blown an early horn in my behalf. I saw some old friends: Lou Naeker, an associate at Newport and Washington DC, a Ford Instrument specialist whom I knew from Boston, and one from Waterbury Pump Co.

I took the 9:00 P.M. ferry back to Seattle, chatted a bit with my roommate and prepared to report in to my new job on the morrow.

I described my first impression of my new job as "rosy" in my almost daily letters to Math, back in Greenwich. True to our first understanding I am in a "flying squad," but this is not exactly how it had been visualized for us. The Assistant Industrial Manager's Office is an adjunct of the Bremerton Navy Yard, representing the yard in Seattle proper. My job was to test and analyze fire control troubles on the ships which came into the various private yards in and around Seattle. My assistant, Ensign Bob Zespaugh, arrived in mid-February. He was a fairly green ensign, and not at all conversant with fire control. I was told there would be an experienced crew of 15 enlisted men at our disposal, three f/c chiefs, five 1/class, five 2/class and two 3/c gunners mates, all in from service with the Pacific fleet.

This appeared to be a fire control officer's dream. With such a gang of highly rated F/C enlisted men, we could be a top organization. Frankly, I wasn't at all sure that we could remain busy with only CVE's (small carriers) destroyers DE's etc. and no battleships or cruisers. If I had a gang like this in Boston, we could have done a whiz-bang job.

But the bosses in the office made the job particularly promising. Captain MacPherson—the Assistant Industrial Manager—was a big friendly guy who I learned was a mustang. A mustang is an officer who has come up through the ranks from a seaman. He was warm in his greeting, as was his executive officer. The latter, Captain Lillard spent a good deal of the first day at my elbow, and endeared himself to me forever by encouraging me to bring my family out to the coast. He suggested that I take all the time necessary to hunt up proper quarters for my family as I worked into the job.

Under the exec came the planning officer, a commander who seemed equally as affable. All this was beyond my fondest dreams, and much unlike the strict military protocol in the South Boston Yard hierarchy.

Ten days later it was again Captain Lillard who found me quarters in the College Club in Seattle. It would be impossible to count the number of different roommates I had at this friendly haven. The room I occupied had four beds, and the turnover was almost daily with military officers of the Navy, Army and Coast Guard. I was surprised at the number of married fellows who went out on dates with the local girls, both married and single ladies. It generally meant that one or two of the beds in the room were unoccupied, which made for quiet evenings.

I had noticed that Captain MacPherson had spent a good deal of time introducing me around the office as "My new gunnery officer." Apparently he had never had an ordnance officer on his staff, and he was most pleased. I spent the first few days in the office, doing little if anything, and took the liberty of leaving on occasions to follow housing leads. It was 4 P.M. on the 11th of February and I had left the office early to respond to a possible rental, following which I was scanning the housing ads in the *Seattle Times* at the College Club.

The loudspeaker on the wall summoned me to the phone and it was Captain Lillard calling. He requested that I report to the AIM office pronto. "The skipper wants to take you to the conference in the Bremerton Navy Yard tomorrow. He wants to give you 8:15 A.M. ferry tickets and all the needed information."

I was on board the ferry at 7:45 on the following day, and sat in the bow where I had been told the skipper liked to sit. At 8:05 the skipper came on board in all his gold finery. There was an exchange of salutes and then we sat together. Captain MacPherson is a nice looking, fatherly man, with just enough "fuddy-duddy" and peculiar mannerisms to qualify as a captain. He leaned over confidentially and asked me where I'd been trained, where I served last, where was my home, etc., and then he said, "I hope you don't mind my asking these questions, Jackson?"

"Not at all, Captain."

I noted his nervous glances toward the gangway and I heard with cold fear, his mention of the admiral. And sure enough, the admiral

of the Thirteenth Naval District arrived with his aide. Up jumped
the captain, and up I jumped. There were the usual exchanges and
my introduction as "My new gunnery officer," by the captain. All
was sealed with a handshake.

The aide departed briefly, and upon his return, said, "I told the
ferry captain to take off, sir." The admiral nodded.

As the captain and the admiral talked I sat in terror on the captain's left, against the gunwale of the ferry, at the end of a long pew-
like bench of many. As the trip progressed I pretended to be absorbed in my paper, reading but not comprehending. I heard the
discussion of the current welders' strike, and about the captain's two
sons, and all those things that captains talk to admirals about. As
the admiral spoke he leaned confidentially toward the captain, and
the captain was pushed toward me, and I was pressed tightly between captain and bulkhead where I remained jammed, for the
hour's trip.

As all things must, the ride came to a close. We had to walk to a
waiting car, ceremoniously chauffeured by a be-medaled marine.
The aide scurried to the admiral's left, where I recalled, he could
draw his sword out of the scabbard to defend his senior officer, that
is, if it were the olden days and he carried a sword. He paraded
along in perfect step with the admiral. Not to be outdone, I made a
headlong dash for the captain's left, but he had chosen the left lane,
close to a wall, giving me no room to walk on the "sword side." And
then the old boy noted the protocol of the admiral's aide, and he
stepped out to the middle of the path, and motioned me to approach his left side.

There was a tense moment when we approached the car. Who
gets in first? The admiral of course. And once again the kindly
captain guided my movements. I was the last man in, sitting in
front.

At the Yard we went to the manager's office where I shook the
hands of countless captains, one more admiral who was the Commandant of the Yard. And then, the skipper decided that I would
benefit by visiting the ordnance shop rather than the meeting, so a

lieut. commander was summoned to show me about. I was told to proceed back to Seattle at my convenience sometime before noon, which is precisely what I did after my tour of the ordnance shop. Free at last, I pulled out a first cigarette and pulled in the smoke luxuriously. Alas, who should be bearing down on me but Captain MacPherson, returning from the meeting. I hastily stubbed out my cigarette and dutifully returned to the Adminstration Building at the Yard where the captain had a few final duties to perform. There were a few more captains to meet, to whom, of course, I was introduced as "my new gunnery officer."

At long last we went to the ferry for the ride home. The USN car was before us but the driver missing. I set about looking for same, but the captain, standing with his hands behind his back and rocking up on his toes said, "What say we walk it, Jackson, eh?'

I said, "Fine, Captain. It's a nice day. Fine…"

The captain solicitously grabbed my arm to steer me right or left on our brief walk. We boarded the ferry, and as we passed the food counter he said, "How about a sandwich, and a nice glass of milk, eh?"

I said, "Fine, Captain, fine."

He had chili, and I a mustard sandwich with a stray piece of egg mixed in. We both enjoyed a glass of milk. All the while the captain regaled me with a rehashing of his career; in the Philippines just before the Japanese arrived, and Shanghai's International Settlement. As he talked, with his arms wrapped around his body, he leaned like a conspirator, in my direction. We ended our meal, each having a piece of pumpkin pie.

Once back in the office, I entered his office at his request. He cautioned me on not facing the afternoon sun because my eyes might become sore. During my brief stay, he whirled around in his chair with his feet on the radiator, his field glasses to his eye, he looked at a Liberty ship leaving the harbor. "Don't mind me," he said. "I have to keep a check on these ships."

It was a good introduction to my kindly, new boss.

The month of February was primarily spent in trying to feel comfortable with my new job. Having never had an ordnance officer in this office, the other planners breathed a sigh of relief with my arrival and dumped all the ordnance work into my lap in a heap, without really bothering to break me into the system. It became apparent that I was really becoming a planning officer. I was happy with the additional work, and secure in the knowledge that no one in the office had the expertise in ordnance, much less fire control, that I possessed.

I was also taking on the role of a mother hen. My enlisted men who appeared in time, had nothing to do. I organized a soft ball team among them and they played a few games around the city. They did a bit of work for me at the yards, but it was not really necessary. Primarily they kept me busy with Red Cross ladies who were constantly approaching me as the responsible officer. The men spent their free time, for the most part, in bed with various women, many of whom became pregnant. We finally managed to get most of the men reassigned, retaining, as I recall, two of the first class gunner's mates who were of great assistance, along with Ensign Zesbaugh, to whom I more or less taught the trade.

In the meantime, I was receiving my share of the copies of February's correspondence from the various areas. Brother Harry was finishing up his training in Virginia and getting ready to put to sea. His wife Betty and the two children were billeted with him in a near-by hotel in Norfolk.

February 4, 1945
Dear Moth and Dad,

Here I am in my old barracks. This is my official address because I never did give up my bed and locker even though I sleep here only on nights that I have the watch. I have it tonight, going on at 9:30 P.M. in a couple of enlisted mens' barracks and carrying through until 1 A.M.

Matter of fact I was on watch this afternoon, from noon to 3:30 P.M. and its one heck of a way to spend a Sunday afternoon. I certainly have no complaints, however, because I've had all these weeks with the family and they've been perfect. Yes sir, thus far old Hadsie has felt none of the hardships of war. I'm a regular commuter nearly every night by 5, three square meals a day, a safe stretch in the good old USA that totals 2 months in Plattsburgh and 3 down here. When I do get to Brooklyn on the 23rd according to schedule I may be around longer still.

I have completed my first week as battery officer. I seem to have a good bunch of men. Not the smartest in the world but cooperative and hard-enough working. I have two crews with a gunner's mate and 3 coxswains...

...The guests at the hotel change constantly as officers are detached and move along. A lot of our friends are gone but there are still some around. A new class of officers came aboard on Friday, so you see there's a big turnover, both at the hotel and the base.

Love to everyone,
Hads

From Brother Jeff in the South Pacific came a birthday letter to his twin, Harry.

6 February 1945
Dear Ha,

Up comes the magic month once more and up with it comes an annual chance to tell you how good it is to be your twin...

...Well, Sir, Happy Birthday to you Hadsy, and may we be saying that to each other for many, many, years.

...You know it's funny, but I never look at the 16th as my birthday. With you it may be coconut cake, and with me chocolate, but way down deep it's very much a joint affair and that's why there's a special meaning when I say Happy Birthday to you, and so it will be forever...

...This is my first letter since your addition to blue suits, (or is it mostly khaki or gray) and herewith my delighted congratulations. A guy who has given up as much as you have deserves especial commendation. I'm proud of you sportsman.

...I'm sending a box of belongings home. In it is my only souvenir—a grass skirt (brand new, custom made, no bugs) which I mean Joy to have. It's supposed to be a little girl's size. For Bets and Jeff, all I have is my love, but wait 'til I get home.
Jeff

On the day of his birth, Jeff sent a letter to the folks from the Philippines, where he was now stationed.

The Philippines
16, Feb. 1945
Dear Moth & Dad,

...Actually, of course, I am happy enough and acutely appreciative of all my blessings. It's a good old world and everything's going to turn out alright and I have no doubt but that my next 33 years will be graced with good fortune, happiness and everything nice.

Life here is a speck more interesting than in our previous stops. The Philippines are interesting and friendly. They are happy little people, and most appreciative of our efforts toward their liberation. They all speak pretty good English, and all think America is wonderful. A surprising majority of the common people seem to be strongly opposed to Philippine independence. They seem to like being our little brothers.

Schools which during the Jap occupation were closed, are now open and it's kind of heart-warming to see the little tykes walking happily to classes with paper-covered books under their arms. They wear regular American clothes, except no shoes (save an occasional pair of wooden clogs of the shower-room type). The girls are immaculate and their little dresses are always clean and freshly ironed. They wear pig-tails usually, although others have some success with curlers. The boys are typical of boys everywhere. Many are scouts and all the kids are amazing and unaffected as children all over the world. Too bad they have to grow up and fight wars.

Some of the older girls are attractive and are getting quite a play from the soldiers; some on a professional basis.

Lots of love to you both,
Jeff

A brief V-mail letter from Dinner Cooney, now in Germany, was forwarded from our Cambridge address. He apparently was in the middle of the action.

Lt. J.S. Cooney
Co. B, 139th Inf.
APO #35
Postmaster, NY, NY
2/17/45
Dear Math & Dick,

    I wish this could be more than V-mail, but will try and do better next time. That's all I can find just now at 1:20 A.M. We are stationed in a beat-up German farming village and have been here for about a week... I'm living with part of my platoon in the basement of one of the wrecked houses. I have already dodged several kraut machine gun bullets and mortar bursts. The V bombs pass over head all the time. It's damned interesting but the terrific waste of war is far more than I ever imagined, and makes you sick to think about.

    Please write.

    Best,

    Dinner

I received a nice letter from Mother. She wrote to us in Seattle regularly. This one came in mid-February. She refers to the difficulty in the travel to the hospital. Mother never did learn to drive a car, primarily because Dad thought she was too excitable, a charge that could well be questioned. As a result, she struggled most of her life to find transportation to the markets, or to anywhere. It was particularly difficult to travel to Mineola, in the middle of Long Island, during wartime limitations. In conclusion she notes the death of Dinner Cooney's Dad.

February 19, 1945
My Precious Boy,

    What do you know. I am going to Hobe Sound March ninth unless I get an S.O.S. that any of my sons are due between March 9 and April 9.

    I am very tired and feel the need of sunshine for my old joints. So I've made up my mind to clear out of here.

    I really have worked very hard between this house and the hospital the entire winter, and now that it is so difficult to travel to and from the hospital, I decided it was the propitious moment to take a complete rest. I only wish Dad could join me...

...You surely are having troubles about this housing situation. But I feel certain that you will find a treasure before the family arrives. If there is one to be had in Seattle, you will be the lucky boy...

Today I went to Cooch Cooney's funeral...He was so young, only 53 years old. And they were such a devoted pair. Why can't some of these old devils die off, instead of the good people?...

...Keep well, darling, and good luck with everything.
Oceans of love and kisses,
Moth

Tom is still getting passes to Rome. With the war in Europe winding down, things appear to be loosening up a bit in the ranks.

23 February, 1945
Dear Folks,

I am just back from 6 full days in Rome, a real privilege and a great deal of fun. As you've probably read, both the Air Force and the 5th Army have large rest camps available, and the town is literally given over to the GI's. Consequently there is a holiday spirit in evidence, and together with the genuinely cosmopolitan and cultural atmosphere in Rome, it makes for quite a wonderful time. Every facility imaginable is available to us, from women on up (or should I say down?) The Air Force even has reserved a well-stocked wine cellar for the boys. I managed to catch one opera (*The Barber of Seville*) and see a concert and ballet. It was the first legitimate ballet I'd really ever seen, and it really rang my bell. Other visits included an art gallery they've put together for us, and the zoo where the chimpanzee has been trained to stand at attention, and give a Fascist salute...

Love,
Tom

CHAPTER 21

A PRISONER ESCAPES

MARY CHAP kept everlastingly at the job of trying to locate her husband. She scoured every newspaper available to her and followed up on every possible clue. One of her objectives was to somehow contact Rdm 3/c John L. Page, the only known prisoner of war from the ill-fated PT #509. She knew that he was incarcerated in Stalag Luft 3, in Germany.

In early March, Chap noted a brief article in the *New York Times* to the effect that an American flyer, George Haas, who had been missing since August 2, 1944, had been reported in a prison camp in Germany, recovering from injuries. This item attracted Chap's attention for two reasons.

1. The date of August 2, 1944 was just one week before Jimmy Mathes' encounter with the enemy and she thought that if Haas had been missing for seven months, it gave hope for Jim.

2. She recognized the name of Haas. Jim's sister Fuffy had a roommate at her Connecticut school named Joannie Haas. Could this flyer be her brother?

She thought that perhaps Haas might be in the same prison camp in Germany as Page, and if such were the case, and if she could get word to Haas, he might be able to contact Page. She decided to make a phone call to Joannie Haas's mother's home in Westchester to check the relationship. If her guess was accurate, she could perhaps make contact with Haas.

Joannie Haas answered the telephone. After some preliminary conversation, the Haas girl announced that her brother was not in a

German camp, but was at home at that very minute, and would talk to Chap. They made an appointment to meet on March 4 only after Chap was sworn to secrecy to protect the accomplices of Haas.

The following facts came from their meeting: Haas was shot down on August 2, 1944, and made a forced landing near Granville on the west coast of France. The territory was then held by the Germans. He was taken prisoner and transported to a hospital on the Island of Jersey. He was given good care and kind treatment. After he had recovered he was assigned a bed in the prison camp on the Island of Jersey next to the bed of John L. Page, Rdm 3/c of PT #509. Page had also recovered from injuries sufficiently to leave the hospital. Page had been shot through the lung, and indeed had thirty wounds and a broken arm, which were all professionally cared for.

During their confinement the two men discussed the battle between the PT 509 and the enemy. The following are the facts not heretofore known by Chap. In the early stages of the battle, Lieut. Pavlis, the executive officer of PT 509 who was at the wheel of the boat, was either killed or wounded so that the PT boat was without a helmsman and "ran wild." It crashed into the side of the enemy ship completely smashing in the bow of the 509 and making her helpless and unable to continue the battle. As she was close alongside the enemy ship, the enemy was able to use small arms and threw hand grenades aboard the 509, setting her afire.

Subsequently the bodies of five enlisted men washed ashore on the Island of Jersey and were buried there. Haas was not sure of the names, but he was positive that there were no officers among them.

In all the conversation between Page and Haas, Jim Mathes' name was not mentioned. Haas, of course, did not know that Jim was aboard the 509, but had the name of Mathes been mentioned, he surely would have recognized the name on account of his acquaintance with Fuffy.

It is reported that PT 509 killed fifty and injured many aboard the enemy ship on which there was a complement of 450 men, before the battle was completed.

On January 8th, Haas escaped from the Island of Jersey by

embarking in a row boat in a storm, being driven by the gale to the shore of France. He reported all of the above to the American forces, and was returned to the U.S.

Haas also reported that the *Vega*, the Red Cross ship, had reached the Island of Jersey on January 4. The Germans stated that the ship had not brought any Red Cross parcels as the prisoners had hoped it would. Of course, the *Vega* had brought such parcels but the Germans, starving themselves, had enjoyed the lot.

Despite what appeared to be this extremely reliable information, other sources of information were being passed along, some of which was more encouraging, and hence seemed expedient to follow.

A telegram sent on March 21st to Mr. Chapman, from his contact, J.W. Shillan of the British Motor Boat Manufacturing Co, Ltd, who had been pursuing contacts on the Isle of Jersey said the following:

> HAVE TODAY INTERVIEWED LESURIER WHO RECENTLY
> ESCAPED FROM JERSEY. HE STATES THAT THE ONLY AMERICAN
> NAVAL OFFICER NOW IMPRISIONED AT FORT REGENT, ST.
> HELIER IS PROBABLY JIMMY MATHES. HAVE AIRMAILED YOU
> DETAILS TODAY. AM ENDEAVORING TO INTERVIEW OTHER
> ESCAPEES.

The follow-up letter stated that Shillan had managed a lunch with escapee LaSurier. The latter had come from Jersey on November 11, with two companions. LaSurier said that another boat got away on November 10. This last was possibly the boat in which George Haas escaped, though the date does not tally.

> 21st March, 1945
> My dear Chap,
>   It took LeSurier twenty-four hours to do the journey to
> Granville, France, through several misfortunes...
>   Monsieur LeSurier, knew about the action between the American P.T. and a German Armed Ship, about last August. From what he told me the P.T. rammed the Gun Boat, and the only Naval

Officer saved was the Commander of the vessel, and I think I am right in stating that Jimmy was in charge.

...The story in St. Helier is that the P.T. Commandant jumped on to the German boat when the ramming took place...

...I could not find out anything about any other members of the crew, but mentioned to Monsieur LeSurier that Page had been rescued and was also a prisoner, but he knew nothing about Page, who I take it was not a commissioned man...

...I was also told that the Islanders have for a long time past been giving food and a few luxuries to the twenty American and British prisoners who are at present on the island. These boys are nearly all Airmen, and have been there since D-Day...

Another thing I discovered was that PT boat which was in the charge of the American Naval Officer now at Fort Regent was definitely sunk and a number of bodies were washed ashore a day or two later. None of them were commissioned men, neither is there an American Commissioned man buried on the Island.

There is no way of our communicating at the moment with the Island. I am told that even the Vega crew and the Red Cross people were not allowed ashore, which is, of course, just spite on the part of the Germans...

Obviously the above, though encouraging, was misinformation. Mr. Shillan later, on May 8, discovered and transmitted the information that Page was the lone survivor of the P.T. crew, and that he had since been taken as a prisoner to Germany. There appeared to be no commissioned naval officer of the 509 on the Island of Jersey.

On March 2 we received a plaintive postcard from Dinner Cooney.

Dear Math & Dick,
Looking forward to hearing from you one of these days. We're now in Holland again after a few weeks in Germany. Please let me know about all the additions to the family. My very best to you both and Dickens.
Dinner

From Brother Tom came the usual complaint about his standing in the Army. He has long contended that he should be promoted to sergeant, and obviously, on the basis of his following letter, he should get his promotion.

> 2 March, 1945
> Dear Folks,
>   …By the way, I understand that I am now the section chief in my office. This doesn't change anything, it just means that I have a tiny bit more work. It means that I should be a Technical Sergeant (5 stripes) but I'll stay Corporal I'm sure. I have sergeants under me, too. The whole thing is kind of discouraging because when you live in a vacuum, any kind of change like promotions begin to assume proportions which are out of shape. But the hell of it is, it doesn't bother me much as long as people understand.
>   Love,
>   Tom

In the February issue of the magazine, "Air Force," an article appeared called "Shock Waves At 600 MPH." It described Wright Field's recent experiments in compressibility at high speeds and reported the achievements of Major Frederic A. Borsodi, who while diving a P-51D from 40,000 feet was the first man ever to see a compressibility shock wave on an aircraft wing. He later installed a camera in his plane and became the first man to photograph such a phenomenon.

Previously we had heard of Freddie's death in England on January 31, in connection with his test run of the new American jet which he was demonstrating before the American military leaders in the United Kingdom. Bill Webster passed on some of the details on Freddie's death.

> Hillcrest Farm,
> Lenox, Massachusetts.
> March 9, 1945
> Dear Dick and Math,
>   Sorry you couldn't make the skiing in Lenox, which I almost missed, myself. Five days before leaving I got into trouble with one of our experimental planes and had to jump out. I got out okay but

sprained an ankle when I landed. Because it was an experimental plane, the Company was quite concerned (over the plane, not me) so I had a series of conferences with experts, Navy Officials, and N.A.C.A personnel had to be arranged. This all took time, and I didn't leave until a week later.

...I don't know if you learned of many of the details of Freddie's accident. I'll tell you what I heard from Fred before he left and then from talking to Marcia a couple of days afterwards.

I ran into them all in Dayton a few days before Christmas. Marcia was still in the hospital. Their second baby, a girl, not a boy as reported in some papers, was born five weeks early. A small one, but perfectly okay. Fred left on December 26 to go to England with two colonels and six very new and experimental jet planes.

They were to demonstrate these ships to the Air Force heads in England and then, as Fred said, "To look for a fight with some of the German jet ships." He only expected to be gone about three or four months.

The accident occurred on January 31st while demonstrating to the Allied brass. Another plane happened to see the accident which occurred at about 3,000 feet. The plane was in level flight going pretty fast when the tail failed. The ship immediately started tumbling and Fred went in with it. Nobody will ever know, of course, why the poor devil didn't get out. He's jumped twice before and if there was any chance at all I know he would have made it. I kind of think that the cabin jettison device failed to work. At high speeds, these new bubble-type canopies cannot be opened by hand so an emergency cabin jettison device is used. One never knows how these darn things are going to work until they are tried.

Freddie had done a marvelous job at Wright Field. In less than a year there he became chief of the fighter flight test branch. He performed a number of very difficult tests and was, in fact, making a name for himself, not that that made any difference to him. I learned all of this, not from him, but from Marcia, other pilots and the magazines. There is an article in the February "Air Force" about some dives he did. Also, while I was in Dayton, a writer from the "American" Magazine was interviewing him for an article scheduled to appear in the May issue. It certainly doesn't seem right for that guy to go...

...We took the train to Hanover and stayed at the Inn for three days. The old place (Dartmouth) has certainly changed. There are 250 civilian students, a freshman class of 40, and 900 Navy/Marine trainees. Fraternity houses and many dorms are closed up...

...I entered Billy in the Class of '65...

...I had a letter from Dad yesterday in which he said he talked to Mr. Mathes and learned of the very encouraging news about the prisoners of war on the Island of Jersey. We can't help but feel that Jim is there and well. It just wouldn't be the same without him around again...

...I'm sorry we couldn't get together in Lenox for some skiing. Take care of the little Mother.

Best,
Web

Still on the subject of promotions, Tom writes his mother with a caution, and word on the promise of good things to come.

March 17, 1945
Dear Moth,

I'm extremely glad to hear that you're taking that well earned rest, and doubly glad that the place is so nice. Someday I'd like to take a look at Florida. I've heard so much about it.

I just heard some mighty encouraging news, but I won't believe it for sure until I see the orders. The General finally took note of our sad plight, and as a consequence I will be a sergeant in a few days, a staff sergeant in a few weeks, and possibly a tech Sgt. later. But as I say, this sounds too good to be true and remains to be seen.

I spent a quiet birthday yesterday. I saw a pretty fair movie and a fair USO show.

What news of Jeff? Any credence to that hint that he might be coming home? He certainly deserves it.

Weather around here remains wonderful, which is fine with us.

Love,
Tom

I went to Lake Washington Shipyards across the Lake from Seattle in early March, a distance of about 20 miles, to chat with the Vice president of the company launching a new ship, and a few others. The drive across Lake Washington, my first on the floating bridge to Mercer Island, was beautiful. The sun shone and it was warm. The tall evergreens and the blue lake with the inevitable backdrop of the snow-covered Mount Ranier was majestic, and lovely.

Math had asked about the weather in Seattle, and I had responded in a letter in early March, "It is predominantly warm, comparable to our April weather. Quite a bit of rain, which really amounts to a continued fine drizzle. This lets up in an hour to two, then starts again. The air is damp, but not cold, and quite hazy. It gets a bit nippy at night…

"…The grass is bright green the year round, and when out in the country where there are miles and miles of green patches tucked in amongst the bluish green of the evergreens, it is lovely. I was in Everett, supposedly a major city in Washington, and it is a surprisingly small town. Its main street and stores are the absolute core, and one comes upon them almost by surprise, suddenly from the hinterlands surrounding the town."

March 11 turned out to be a banner day. I made an arrangement, finally, to rent a house, only 75 yards from the campus of the University of Washington. I thought I was paying an arm and a leg for the rental, $150 monthly, but as my deadline was approaching, and I'd had no luck previously, I thought I better grab this opportunity before all was lost.

I looked forward with intense impatience to the arrival of my family.

CHAPTER 22

A FAMILY REUNITED

APRIL, 1945: Dampness was in the air, and the sky was heavy and dark, but my heart was singing joyously as I made my way to the railroad station. I was meeting Math and Dickens on their arrival in Seattle.

It was a long fifteen minutes that I waited on the windy platform. In due time the train puffed into the station, and I took up a watchful position near car 51 while the luggage was being passed out the door from one hand to another. I looked at the windows of the train, and though the grime of the voyage and the dark backdrop made it hard to see, I spotted a small familiar face peering out. It was Dickens, in his new spring coat, which I remembered had been big for him when purchased some three months ago. His face looked leaner, and older, teeth were more numerous, and his happy smile more mature. Math was holding him up to the window, and she was smiling too.

I could see Dickens mouthing the words, "Daddy! Daddy!" over and over, and then looking back at Math and pointing his crooked finger out the window in my direction. I noticed the fellow passengers in the car look at Dickens and then toward me, and I could see their understanding smiles. It was like a play in pantomime, because the heavy glass made it impossible to hear, but not to see.

We were a happy family as we rode through the main streets of Seattle toward our new home in the University district. It was one of those important events that sweeten the flavor of living, not necessarily only for the moment, because it is kept locked as long as memory lasts.

* * *

The war was moving along, and as it moved it appeared to be picking up momentum. Like a huge glacier dragging rocks and earth with it as it tore up the cities, towns, and the countrysides it left the broken remains scattered in its path. Casualties grew daily, as in Europe the Allies closed in on Berlin after their second breakthrough over the Rhine and onto the plains of Germany, while the Russians hovered at the very doors, east of Berlin. In the Pacific the bloody battle of Iwo Jima was won, and a new one at Okinawa, just 400 miles from Tokyo, was being enjoined.

The *Admiral William L. Capps* (AP21) a large Navy transport made her way into the docks of Seattle from the Philippines. Her cargo was made up mainly of American evacuees from the Japanese prisoner camp at Santa Tomas in the Philippines, liberated some weeks ago by the attacking Yank army.

I went aboard her to inspect her ordnance, to lay out the repair and overhaul work for the present availability. The executive officer invited me to lunch, and while we ate he told me just a bit about these people who were heading home at long last, after so many months of hardship under the Japanese.

There was one little fellow, about 4 years old, who came aboard with his tummy bloated to abnormal proportions. Malnutrition was the cause, and this is only a technical way of saying starvation. The exec was glad to say that during the trip home that little fellow rounded out into fine normal shape.

There were lean men, he said, whose ribs protruded pitifully through their sagging flesh; there were women who looked lean and drawn but not so bad as the men. And there were many children who looked more normal than their parents because they had been fed the best food, and the most food.

The people had reported that for the most part the Japanese left his prisoners to their own devices. Civilian courts were established to govern, and apparently there was a great necessity for this as stories of drunkenness, of men invading the privacy of women, or women forcing their attentions on men. There was the struggle to obtain food, and here, as always, money seemed to play an important roll. For the most part, those who were willing to go "native," to kill and eat stray dogs and cats that existed, faired better. It was very noticeable, said the exec.

A big raw-boned lieutenant commander who was sitting on my right produced some pictures that had been taken on the journey. They graphically illustrated what I had just been told. I was most impressed by pictures of the little fellows who frolicked about the captain's legs, or gathered with glee at the "Father Neptune" ceremonies to commemorate the crossing of the equator. They looked characteristically happy and enthusiastic and yet became a trifle pathetic when I thought of their years of abnormal living. I suppose some of them will bear the scars of their early experiences throughout their entire life.

There was the old sergeant who had died on the voyage, suggesting in death, how terribly hard it was particularly on the older people. There were also the young sickly children who reflected their inability to survive under such circumstances.

Two days later, on April 11, in the largest headlines of the war, and over the air of every radio station in the country, came the word that President Franklin Delano Roosevelt had died. When I heard the news I was shocked. It seemed hard to believe. Never having been a political supporter of President Roosevelt, I was amazed at my immediate mood of despair, the emptiness that crawled through the pit of my stomach. What do we do now, I thought, and marveled that I could be so moved. The mood of the country was prepared for the war with Japan after the attack on Pearl Harbor, and people shall probably never know what role the president played in this early phase. But the president was a symbol of power to the entire world, both friend and foe alike. His successor, Vice President Harry S. Truman, was not generally conceived to be a strong leader, and the task he faced, not only with the conclusion of the war, but the winning of the peace, was gigantic.

We heard from Tom in early April. The weather was pleasant in Italy, and he was popping popcorn.

> 4 April 1945
> Dear Folks,
>   By the time this letter arrives I guess Moth will be out of Florida and back in Plandome, so that dispenses with the Hobe Sound address.
>   The weather is increasingly warm, and life is running along as pleasantly as possible. Last night we popped popcorn; rough war here.
>   After all the sound and fury surrounding my promotion, I seem to be still a corporal, so I guess it's the same old story...
>   Love,
>   Tom

Brother Harry's first trip as an armed guard officer was under way. He was apparently having trouble with sea-sickness.

He was on the *Anniston City*, a cargo vessel that pre-dated the Kaiser World War II liberty ships by some few years. Here is a brief excerpt from a letter to his wife Betty.

> Lieut.(jg) Harry R. Jackson USNR
> Armed Guard
> S/S *Anniston City*
> FPO, New York
> April 5, 1945
>   ...This old ship is really rolling, so the writing may be even worse than usual. Heavy ground swells, they call them. By this time, however, that balance mechanism in my inner ear, or wherever it is located, has caught on to the crazy movements the vessel makes and my stomach has been behaving nicely. I had a difficult first two days though.
>   It's hard to understand why I'd have any trouble, too, because the weather has been perfect and the sea relatively calm. It had been hot as the dickens and was over 90 degrees on the bridge yesterday. We're quite far along now; nearly half way in fact.
>   The crew is shaping up well enough. I have been busy straight-

ening things out, taking inventory of gear lockers, ammunition, etc., cleaning guns, and doing many other necessary jobs. I have had no excitement at all.

    Hads

Mother sent Math and me one of her long newsy letters, detailing her rest in Florida, and declaring she was back again to nursing at the hospital.

April 16, 1945

My Dears,

    I enjoyed your letters no end…

    …Well, our Harry boy is on the high seas somewhere. I somehow can't realize that he isn't with his little family, poor dear. I only hope his stomach behaves. It is a most deadly feeling to keep churned up while tossing about…

    …Dad has the grounds looking marvelously. He had been working hard every Sunday for quite a few weeks and they surely reflect his hard efforts. I am amazed at his pep. He still works three nights a week, but I must say the garden work is good for him…

    …I started my hospital duties immediately, and hope to keep with them to make up for lost time. They are sadly in need of nurses at Meadowbrook Hospital.

    There are two new classes of nurses aids in Manhasset, but all refuse to go to Meadowbrook to work. They claim it's too far away and too hard.

    I really can't understand it, for I find it a very nice hospital and feel that a nurses aid works hard regardless of the hospital…

    Hugs and kisses,

    Moth

From the tone of this letter from Tom one can sense the war in Italy is about over. He has not even complained about his rank of late, though all in that direction appears to be status quo.

20 April 1945

Dear Folks,

    It's only 2:30 P.M. but I've already had what passes for me as a very busy day. I got up for breakfast (powdered eggs), had a catch, played handball (have a swollen right hand), traded my cigarette rations for beer, had the kid at our club shine my shoes, and went up for a short but pleasant flight to a nearby base. I go to work in about 30 minutes.

A fairly funny (or pathetic, depending on the outlook) thing happened at the nearby outfit, which had to transfer 19 men to the infantry. The usual procedure is to tell the guys the night before, but this results in their all getting dead drunk. So the outfit decided to withhold the names of the 19. Consequently every guy thought he might be one of the 19, so the entire outfit got drunk...

...The only really new thing of late is increasingly wild rumors as the European war draws closer and closer to the finish. The only thing that sounds right to me is that I'll see the Pacific, but whether I'll get home first or not remains to be seen.

Love,
Tom

Jeff writes from the South Pacific in a guilty mood as usual.

22 April 1945
Dear Folks,

Just a quick conscience-stricken bulletin to proclaim that I am well and happy enough despite the customary period of long silence...

...I am at present commanding a mixed group of about 200 men on a kind of detached service deal and have been kind of hopping...

...Moth, your rest sounds like a perfect change. If only Dad had shared it with you!...

What is Ha's address?

Boy, am I behind in letters...

Gang of love,
Jeff

The mixed group of about 200 men that Jeff mentions in his letter turned out to be the crews complete with several ensigns and a lt. (jg), of a string of Navy landing craft, which he commanded. He was stationed on the Island of Cebu, and the Navy boats had to get back to their ship at Leyte. A hard and fast Navy rule forbade them to travel without at least a rank of a senior lieutenant to lead them. There was none available at the time, so Jeff's first lieutenant bars apparently qualified him for the command. It was a simple enough trip, he recalls, in and around the islands, and all in friendly territory. He says that the Navy men were seething under an Army command, but to the Army's credit, they did not "rub it in."

Harry writes a letter home from the Armed Guard station on the SS *Anniston City*. He is on the way back from Chile, where the cargo of nitrate, a vital substance in the manufacture of ammunition, was unloaded in Norfolk, Virginia…

April 27. 1945
Dear Moth & Dad,

We're at the halfway mark on our way back to the States and I should have a chance to mail this long over-due letter this evening when we dock for a few hours to take on fuel oil and water.

We made one brief stop early this A.M. at which time, among other arrivals, a nice man came aboard with a sack of mail which produced twelve letters for me exclusive of the usual USN official stuff. Moth's swell letter came along with copies of Tom's and Dick's, to you folks. Seven were from my darling wife with enclosed contributions from Joy and Jeffie. So you see, I've been reading all morning. I'm sure no one on board did as well and I do appreciate it.

I have come to realize how important letters from home are. Nobody can know until he has been away for a while. When the while has been as long as my twin Jeff has endured it must be of tremendous importance to receive mail. Here, for example, after one measly month out, these men in the gun crew can hardly wait to hit port. When they do the first thought, oddly enough, isn't to get ashore, it's "is there any mail?" I say oddly because, although I'm that way, I didn't think these kids who indulge in antics that aren't for me would feel that way about it…

…At first there was a lot of real work entailed in taking inventory and getting guns in shape. There have been three armed guard units on this ship in the past. They couldn't have done a constructive thing because guns and mounts were in wretched shape, gear was all over the place, out of order and with no record that could be relied upon. Ammunition was likewise stowed willy-nilly and our inventory reveals that much of it is out-dated and must be returned to the ammunition depot upon return.

Now we have the guns cleaned and painted and things generally are a little more ship-shape. The initial trip is naturally the hardest especially for a green officer. And this one was green in more ways than one even with almost perfect weather conditions…

…And now let me give you some trite but excellent advice. Don't work too hard, either of you. It's great to get things done, but…

Love,
Ha

CHAPTER 23

V-E DAY

MAY 8, 1945 was known as V-E Day—Victory in Europe Day.
The day meant different things to different people. In Seattle, occupied almost exclusively with the battle against Japan in the Pacific,
it did not meet with quite as much enthusiasm as it did in the east.
Few people talked of the end of the war in Germany, and no one
demonstrated. I put in my day with my dispatches, plans for the returning ships, and piles of job orders.

I didn't find it any different than any other day at the office, but I
knew that it might present some answers to the mystery of PT Boat
#509, and the whereabouts of its crew.

I recall finding a seat in the crowded bus on my way home. I
shook out the paper and ignored the heavy, black headlines herald-
ing the new peace in Europe. For weeks it had been obvious that
the war was sputtering to a close. There had even been a premature
surrender, similar to World War I, but unlike that war there was no
flag-waving, no excessive public elation or festive celebration in the
streets. The war with Japan still raged, and people in Seattle, particularly, could see the ripped hulls of our fighting ships, limping
home from the Pacific for repairs and sense the loss of lives that
each ship represented.

Germany had surrendered in bits, day by day; in Italy, in Den-
mark, in Norway, in Holland, and finally in Berlin. But isolated
armies still fought on commanded by fanatical Nazis leaders. Hitler's whereabouts were veiled in mystery, and countless stories told
of his death in battle, or his suicide, or of his withdrawal to Japan to

fight on. On this day, no one knew. Notorious Nazi leaders explained a few of the now historical questions in their own peculiar manner and they made good reading, but not much else.

We noticed a tiny paragraph tucked in the bottom of an article to the effect that the Nazis still held out in the Channel Islands.

Back in Greenwich, Connecticut, the emphasis on the search for Jim and his crew mates swung toward the whereabouts of the only known survivor, Rdm 3/c John L. Page, who was last known to be a prisoner of war at Stalag Luft 3, in Sagan, Germany.

A telegram to Mr. Chapman dated May 25 from the ever alert John Shillan, of the British Motor Boat Manufacturing Co. in London, said:

HAVE TRACED PAGE FROM SOUTHAMPTON TO PLYMOUTH. BELIEVE WITHIN THE NEXT FEW DAYS HE WILL ARRIVE IN AMERICA. I REGRET NOT HAVING BEEN AFFORDED THE OPPORTUNITY OF SPEAKING WITH HIM. FURTHERMORE AM DISAPPOINTED INVESTIGATIONS ON THE SPOT SHOW NO TRACE OF JIMMY IN CHANNEL ISLES.

* * *

On May the 11th, I trudged up the steep hill toward the Virginia Mason Hospital at around 5 P.M. to a very important engagement. The sun was warm and friendly, my coat hung over my arm, as I puffed up the steep Seattle hill past 3rd Ave., 4th, 5th, all the way up to 8th. And there I saw my second child, a girl, Mary French Jackson, swathed in blankets, little legs and arms sticking out on the edges, hands clasping and unclasping, and crying her eyes out. I recall being amazed at her likeness to her mother, which could only please me.

After this important meeting, and an equally important visit with Math, I hopped into a bus and went home to apprise Dickens that he had a baby sister. He was equally pleased.

Dinner Cooney wrote us from Germany in early May with a note under the date stating that the time of writing was 7 A.M. For this he requested us to grant apologies accordingly. His salutation includes not only us, and Dickens, his godson, but "Thumper," his euphemism for our second child who he had been told often kicked (thumped) within her mother's tummy before birth.

May 7, 1945
Dear Math, Dick, Dickens, and Thumper,

Your letter from Seattle reached me over a week ago and my only excuse for not answering immediately, as I always try to do, is the old trite one of being too busy, more than somewhat actually.

...What prompted this worm-catching communiqué from the E.T.O. was that this morning I reached into my duffel bag, which arrived here yesterday, to get some non-GI clothes for a change.

The underwear drawers, which incidentally darn near fit me now, bore a faint R. S. J. imprint, which several washings before, was nice and bright and seemed to say, *"Why the hell don't you return these drawers? You know damn well they aren't yours."* Now, all the initials R. S. J. can do is whisper, but the ear drums of my conscience have become so sensitive that a salvo from ten 8-inch guns could not be more impressive. Yet I continue to wear them. I have a vague feeling in the back of my mind that I am subconsciously planning to repay you, Dick, in one way or another. I don't know how it will be, but if nothing else, you will one day receive these same drawers with a brilliant JSC in them and nothing to indicate that they ever belonged to you except, perhaps, the size of them.

During the above harangue somewhere I ate breakfast. It would be interesting to note whether you could tell where the break came. No fair looking for egg stains. All of the above may give you the impression that la guerre is having a baleful effect on me. I hope not. But I have seen some damn horrible things. Many of the guys who came over on the *Queen Mary* with us have already given their lives, eyesight, legs, arms, etc. I have certainly been lucky. Right now, with things just about wound up over here, we are getting a good deal out of it. Our outfit is living in a nice little German town and have all of the comforts of home. I slept in pajamas and sheets last night for the first time since Camp Shanks in New York. It really felt good. The only thing lacking which in my opinion are the biggest things on earth anyway, are all you good people back home...

…It's now 8 P.M. of the same day. I'm tired as well for some reason or other, but there's certainly nothing to complain about here. The good war news has reached us and there is really plenty reason for rejoicing. Right now, however, we're all sweating out the CBI theatre.

Please give Dickens my best wishes for a Happy B.D. Sure wish I could see the lad…

…The army has a non-fraternization policy that no doubt you have heard of. We are not permitted to speak with, drink with, etc. the German people. It is quite a problem as you can well imagine. It is as hard to enforce as it is to obey. That is nothing, however, to our real problem that has us all tearing our hair out at this point. You will probably have read of it by the time you receive this letter and if not, soon after. I predict much discussion of it as it's definitely a brain teaser. That is, the question of D.P.'s (Displaced Persons), both P.W.'s and slave laborers—Russians, Poles, French, etc. Some of them have been prisoners for five years, have been mistreated, have had their homes destroyed, their loved-ones killed by the Nazis. Now, they are free. What would you do in their place? Damn Right! They do it too, and it's up to us to try and curb it until the several million of them can be sent home. This is a stupendous job. All of them must be classified, clothed, fed, and have transportation provided. They run around looting, pillaging, robbing, kill hogs, hens, cows, and in general raise HELL. We are doing our damndest to stop it. Some of them have weapons (even machine guns).

I hope the end of the war here has a good effect on the yellow boys we're trying to wipe out in the SW Pacific. The Krauts are really finished. They're a whipped bunch and we have them exactly where we want them. They are really afraid of the Russians and Poles, which is advantageous to us when we want to move into their homes to set up a local guard post. They eagerly give us their best accommodations. They have a beautiful country, especially this time of year. The prettiest I've seen was in the Ruhr Valley when we were working on that pocket. It almost looked fake, it was so perfect…

My very best to you all,
Dinner

A few days later, I received a letter from my Mother, in her classic and lovely hand-writing. It was dated the 10th of May. She was obviously working too hard, but this is the way she spends her life.

My Dears,

Yes I do love you dearly, even though my letters are few and far between. I think of you oh so much and write you in my mind daily. But somehow the days get away from me before I accomplish all I plan.

I now write nine letters per week; three to Jeff, Tom and Ha, say nothing of the odds and ends one has to write in a business way. So you can see how this eats into one's hours each week.

These three fellows are so many miles away from home and haven't their cozy family to help them endure their hardships, so I feel I must keep their morale up by giving them news of home.

Ha should be coming home shortly but Bets hasn't heard from him so she really doesn't know much concerning his whereabouts. One thing he did say was that he still gets very sea sick when the old ship tosses.

Poor fellow. I know exactly how miserable he must feel. Dad seems to think that his stomach will adjust itself after it becomes accustomed to this kind of travel...

I worked all day at the hospital and came home in the miserable rain, a dead person. But, I am happy to say I have written letters to all my children tonight...

...I have pledged myself to be on call each week from Monday midnight until Tuesday midnight at the Mitchell Field Military Hospital. When they have an influx of boys return we are called and immediately rush over to help them. They call us any hour. It might be at 2 A.M. or at midnight whenever the planes arrive. So far I have been over twice and I have seen plenty. Many of these boys have been in German prisons, and my heart goes out to them. But they are good sports and delighted to be back in the States. With good care, they can be nursed back to health.

You can well imagine how I am spending my days, between my hospital duties and my household chores. I can't even get a woman to clean for a single day. They think that this house is too hard to work in. The ceilings are too high and too much to be done...

...Isn't it wonderful about the German situation, but I can't get much excitement out of it. I will certainly be delighted when we learn that Jimmy is O.K. and that the Japs have been beaten.

A lot of love to you all and kisses too. And God Bless you all.

Moth

From the Isle of Capri we hear from Tom.

12 May 1945
Dear Folks,

I am writing from the Isle of Capri. All of a sudden they decided to give me a week's pass here. Needless to say it's really an ideal place, particularly so for a guy who's fed up with Army life.

As you probably know the Air Force has taken the Island over as a rest center. We stay in very elaborate hotels with box spring mattresses, sheets, pillow cases, baths, etc. The meals are delicious, and served with great aplomb by very correct waiters who use the one hand spoon-fork method of serving that Jeff used to favor.

I am mildly surprised and delighted to find that my 2½ years in the army has not completely done away with my background. Things like napkins and waiters I am still able to take in my stride.

The scenery is really wonderful here, with fine swimming, innumerable bars, plenty of girls (Wacs, nurses, and the various civilian women). The weather is ideal, and there is absolutely no rank distinction. In fact, I think we common men have a better deal than the officers—damnest thing I've ever seen—and wonderful.

Love,
Tom

Now back in the States, Brother Harry writes a congratulatory letter on the arrival of our number two. He is not at liberty, for some unfathomable reason, to disclose his port of call. Time would indicate that he was in Norfolk, Virginia, which meant he had a few trips through the Panama Canal, since he embarked from Brooklyn, NY.

U.S.Navy
Sunday, May 13, 1945
Dear Math & Dick,

I talked with my dear wife over the telephone last night and heard the good news that Mary French Jackson arrival presents...

...As that opening sentence indicates and as you have undoubtedly been advised I'm back in the U.S.A. But far from home and the big question is whether I'll get there before departing once more. Certainly hope so.

The trip was entirely uneventful as far as contact is concerned. Destination was Tocofilla, Chile for nitrate which is presently being unloaded with the conveyor belts humming even as I write...

Much love,
Hads

An unexpected letter from Mason Green was received with his congratulations on the birth of Mary French. Mason was my first boss at the Aetna Insurance Co. He, and the old Navy Chief, Art Ives, and I worked on the underwriting of the State of Texas in my first job with the company.

48 Elm Street
Windsor, Connecticut
May 19, 1945
Dear Dick

It's welcome news, the arrival of Mary French Jackson on May 11th, and at least she skipped one war, that with Germany. You and Math certainly will remember this month of May with two such events in one short week...

...Things at the office are rather difficult. But it appears now that there may be some men returning and available to help out if they are content for a bit of humdrum life...

...The announcement card was generously circulated at the office as you can well understand and one and all always seem so pleased to learn of and from Dick Jackson...

...I wonder whether you have plans to return to the old Aetna for a breather after the war? In that connection I cannot picture

you boys being exactly contented for a long time to do such work.
However it would be nice for us…

Thanks for remembering us.

Sincerely,

Mason C. Green

Dinner Cooney sent us another letter from Germany. In a letter to
him, I had described a rather bizarre job that a Seattle shoemaker
had done to my black Navy shoes. The heels were raised to such a
degree that when on the level, I had the feeling I was constantly
walking down hill. Thus, I had suggested that I could only walk
uphill. He had a solution. Further, he was off in his guesstimate of
the birth of Mary French by only 9 days.

> May 20, 1945
> Dear Math, Dick, Dickens and Thumper,
> Maybe today is Thumper's birthday. According to your last
> letter, Dick, I find that my degenerated calculating ability has
> brought me to that conclusion. I wish I could be there for the
> big news.
> I noted with interest your comments about the newly heeled
> shoes. You say you can only walk *up* hill and not down. Why the
> hell not walk down hill backwards? A very simple solution which
> has another advantage; that being if you want to look back at
> something you've gone by, you don't have to turn your head. You
> are looking in the right direction.
> Speaking of right directions, we are moving in that direction
> and are now in a little village called Distedde. Censorship rules
> have been relaxed. In case you might try to look it up, it's 12 miles
> north of Liepstadt. Things are plenty quiet. In fact this is no longer
> considered "overseas." The reason is obvious. You are lots nearer
> the war than we are. Right now, though, everyone is sweating out
> the C.B.I. Most of us will, no doubt, land there, but we're hoping
> to do it via the USA.
> Best to you all (3 or 4?),
> Dinner

Brother Tom has received word of another niece, but typically, he can not find his address book to write us a congratulatory letter. Now that censorship is lifted, he lists where he has been in Italy.

27 May, 1945

Dear Folks,

I'm feeling like a caged animal just set free. Now we can seal our own letters just as if we had intelligence. This letter will not be read by some ill-bred boor.

I just got a V-mail from Aunt who mentions the birth of Mary French, and I am in quite a hole. I lost the address of Dick and Math. I can't keep track of all my nephews and nieces. Anyhow, its wonderful news, and I expect to get a letter any day now telling me of Mary F's weight, and that Math is in fine shape…

…Of course we don't work very hard now, and I'm reading twice as hard as before. Just recently I stooped low enough to read *Forever Amber*, but I am making a neat recovery with the NY State Medical Report on Marijuana, by His Honor the Mayor's Committee. After which I shall swing into *Vanity Fair*.

With censorship over I might mention my exact whereabouts. We are located in what was intended to be a small town in the center of a farming area. It is about 8 miles out of Foggia. The camp is located on the main road which goes up the Adriatic side of Italy, and we are about 15 miles north of Cerignola, about 90 miles north of Bari, and about 125 miles from Naples. The latter, of course, is on the other side of Italy…

…Aha—a guy just paid me back $20 of his $50 debt to me. I love money, not just as a means, but for itself…

Love,

Tom

CHAPTER 24

RDM 3/C PAGE RETURNS

ON A SUNDAY NIGHT, June 7, 1945, just before midnight, Mr. Chapman happened to hear a radio broadcast in which John Page, RDM 3/c was interviewed. He had just arrived in New York, and was broadcasting from a ship at the pier. The next morning Mary Chap contacted our old friend, Jack Daniel, the ex-executive officer of PT Squadron #34, who she knew was in New York fitting out a new PT squadron.

Daniel immediately went to work on locating Page, and managed to find him in a hospital at Lido Beach, Long Island and received permission for Page to come to New York City. Daniel, who was now a lieutenant commander, Mary Chap, Mr. & Mrs. Chapman, and Mr. & Mrs. Mathes Sr. met him in New York at 6 o'clock in the evening.

Page detailed the following: At about 6 A.M. on August 9 at which time the action took place, a convoy of four German minesweepers was located a couple of miles off the Island of Jersey. The commanding officer of PT 509 decided to attack one of these enemy vessels by torpedo. The torpedo run was ordered and a torpedo discharged at the enemy vessel at about 700 yards. This missed its mark.

The commanding officer of the PT decided to make a gun attack at close range. It was foggy with very low visibility. The position of the enemy vessel could be located only by radar.

The gun run was started and when they came upon the enemy vessel through the fog, it was only a short distance away. The PT was going at a high speed and opened fire immediately. The enemy vessel fired a heavy broadside at the PT at very close range and it was accurate. The minesweeper was a steel-hulled vessel, heavily armed, and over 300 feet in length with a large crew aboard. Lieut. (jg) Pavlis was at the wheel of the PT and he was shot and probably killed at the very beginning. This left no one at the wheel of the PT and consequently it ran wild. As the boat was going at quite a considerable speed at the time she crashed into the side of the enemy vessel and stayed wedged into the hull of the enemy craft.

The crash killed the motors of the PT and left her at the mercy of the German ship, whose crew continued to rake the PT with every gun she had. In addition, they used hand grenades, which was possible as the boats were tightly wedged together.

The gunfire set the PT on fire. Jimmy Mathes, who was in the chart house with Page, went below to get the various ships' papers, secret orders, et al so that he could destroy them to prevent them from falling into the hands of the enemy. This was the last that Page saw of Jimmy. His last words to Page were, "Isn't this fun!" [Editor's note: This comment rings so true of Jim.]

Page went on the forward deck to try to extinguish some of the fire and was severely injured by German fire, but made his way further forward on the PT and was pulled aboard the enemy craft and taken below decks, a prisoner!

Page remembers that German sailors were working frantically with crowbars trying to free the flaming PT. Eventually they worked it loose and it probably exploded shortly after.

Page did not remember what transpired after he was taken below to the crew's quarters. He managed to count fifteen dead, and a good number of wounded. He did not hear any explosion although he believes there was one. This he could not guarantee. Naturally, he could not account for any other members of the 509 crew.

"Later, I could hear the ship docking," said Page. After they removed their dead and wounded, they took him ashore at the Isle of Jersey. He was laid out on the dock for quite a while and a couple of civilians tried to question him.

"They saw how badly I was shot up, so they didn't spend too

much time with me." He found out later they were members of the Gestapo.

He was then taken to the former English hospital at St. Helier. He remained in the hospital from August until early in January when he was sufficiently recovered to be placed in a prison camp on the Island of Jersey. His body was hit in thirty different places, one shot going through his lung. He also had a broken arm. He reported that he was well cared for by a skillful German surgeon who performed many operations on him, removing dozens of bullets and fragments from every part of his body. His final operation was not until Dec. 27, and he was released to a prison camp on Jan. 2, 1945. The problems were the food, lack of heat, and other conditions that were bad, presumably throughout the Island of Jersey.

He also mentioned that three bodies of shipmates were washed ashore on the island, all enlisted men. They were given decent burial by the Germans on the Island.

It is said that on V-E Day, Allied prisoners on the Island of Jersey, one of whom was an Army colonel, requisitioned a German tug on the island, and with the American prisoners as an armed guard, they forced the German crew of this tug to take them to the coast of France. They went to Cherbourg, then to England, and then home to the USA.

Essentially, this is as complete a story on the action of the PT 509 as has ever been detailed. Nothing is added by the official Action Report from the Commander, Motor Torpedo Boat Squadron #34, dated 12 September, 1944; nor in the "Summary of an Interview with John Leyden Page," in a Memorandum dated 2 April 1946, for the Chief of Naval Operations (Director of Naval Intelligence). A book entitled *At Close Quarters* published by the Naval History Division in 1962, details PT boat action during World War II includes the 509 action off Jersey (Part VII, Chapter 2 entitled "The English Channel- D-Day and After). It is written by Captain Robert J. Bulkley Jr., USNR with a foreword by the then president, John F. Kennedy. But it adds nothing new. There was a colorful article published in the Jersey paper, the *Jersey Evening Post*, on August 12, 1945 of a story taken from "Der Insolzeitung," which contained a translation of an article about the 509 action. This was sent to Mr. Chapman on December 12, 1945. Essentially it offered much of the same detail, although from a German viewpoint, and certainly from the viewpoint of the author, Juergen Petersen. The person who passed the article along to Mr. Chapman stated that "the accuracy of the story cannot be vouched for." The headlines read:

CLOSE RANGE ENCOUNTER
BOARD TO BOARD NAVAL COMBAT
WITH AMERICAN GUN-BOATS OFF JERSEY.

The fog between the islands was so dense that visibility was less than 50 yards. The convoy had put to sea at 3 A.M. under a clear starry sky and a late moon; half-moon shone on a calm sea. Soon after, it had a halo, and before long it became invisible. The boats themselves lost sight of each other. Their outlines disappeared in the gloom; it was only by the brighter bow-wave that the neighboring vessel could at times be made out, but then, it was already so close that the bow of our boat almost touched the stern of the next ahead so that the helm had to be shifted rapidly. It was an extremely difficult situation. It was a convoy with a precious load of men and materiel aboard. Neither was it likely that the weather would clear; on the contrary the veils continued growing denser. Nevertheless the boats stood on the course unswervingly, the men knew these regions from countless crossings. The officer in charge of the flotilla gave orders for the poop lanterns to be put on and as the small lamps no longer penetrated the signalmen stood with their large Morse Lamps on the bridge, holding them aft. The searchlights did not reach very far; the enemy could have made them out only from close range, but it sufficed for the convoy that sailed in close formation.

So the boats stood on their course. Steam whistles and speaking tubes helped keep up communication and the convoy kept up the connection. It had slowly begun to dawn. The boats had reached the Huk beyond which they had to haul towards the port of destination. The most difficult part of the voyage had been overcome. In half an hour the boats could be at the pier.

Dense fog was still hovering over the water, but daylight penetrated the veils and made navigation somewhat easier. What followed now occurred with that rapidity which is typical for naval combats. It was known that the convoy had been shadowed by enemy units for sometime, but nevertheless these enemy units shot suddenly out of their cover as if the fog had shaped them, the very fog behind which they had presumably been lying in wait during the whole night. They dashed right into the midst of the convoy. It could be guessed by the humming of the engines that there was quite a number of them; the escort vessels heading the unit could make out three boats at that moment. At first they appeared to be speed boats, but as was ascertained later, they were American gunboats. Two of them ran into the midst of the convoy and got fire immediately. A combat at closet range with all available arms started. With a crackling and clattering noise the 1.5 cm and 3.7 cm projectiles of the enemy hit the ship's side, the bridge, the upper works of the vessel, the armor plating of the guns and penetrated into the wireless operators room and the conning bridge. But our own shelling was better and more concentrated. The first enemy vessel swerved, and the second was shot ablaze and stopped soon after with a huge smoke-mushroom, but the third was rammed when it attempted to dash past the flotilla at close proximity with a speed of 60 km per hr.

When the commander saw the enemy unit he immediately ordered a course that made it impossible for the Americans to parry. A violent motion shook the vessel as if it had been hit by a torpedo. It listed slightly but did not sink. But now the engines of the gun-boat thundered in closest proximity. It was only now that most of us realized what had happened and that was probably an unprecedented case in the history of naval warfare. The gun-boat had run aboard with her bow close to the front superstructure of our vessel where it got caught. With united strength the two unequal vessels sailed "board on board" for nine minutes. Of course they did not get on with each other very well. First of all there started a fire on the American vessel and owing to a cloud of smoke and the ammunition exploding through spontaneous ignition, visibility was difficult even at such close proximity. There was a crackling of fire and enormous heat on the port side of our vessel. The guns ceased fire during these minutes. One did not feel quite as easy in this sudden quietness after that frantic noise that had stirred the air just before. But it lasted only a few moments. The sailors and soldiers who were on board threw hand genades, the shrill short flashes of fire of the machine pistols were directed against the enemy, who answered with hand grenades. And so, close range fighting started while the fire on the gun-boat grew more intense. Its engines must have received hits. The last American who was still manning a gun raised his arms. He seemed to recognize that resistance in this situation would only endanger his own vessel.

The Germans ceased fire. Again there was quietness for a few minutes. When our sailors tried to board, the Americans opened up again. But this time our four-barreled Ak-Ak on port caught him pointing from a distance of 20 metres, and put a stop to the fellow's mind to go on firing.

The sailors fetched him on board. With a shoulder wound he lay on deck and groaned when he received an emergency bandage. His comrades had already jumped over-board during the combat and swam in the water. Six of them were picked up later and bear him company in the hospital now.

The first task now was to render the fire harmless that endangered our own boat. The Officer in Charge of the Flotilla gave orders for the extinguishers to be made ready. Everyone who had his hands free helped, also the soldiers pumped water and held the hose-pipe. Soon the gigantic blaze crumpled down; only the steam sizzled on the red, hot wood. The engines of the American boat were running no longer. Without any strength of its own, the boat clung alongside and eventually it got loose, a drifting wreck. The following boats of the convoy saw it sink.

When the convoy made for port, the visibility had become clear. The fog had dissolved and the sun separated the boats of the convoy. No boat was lost nor seriously damaged. In the same formation in which the convoy had put to sea during the night, it passed the pier head of the port of its destination.

In a letter to the folks, Harry, still on the good ship *Anniston City*, related his experiences on his next trip. It included his conducting Sunday Church services, which, as his life has unfolded, is very apt. Harry has always been a very Christian gentleman. This trip originated in Baltimore from where they set sail for Buenos Aires, Argentina, with all holds empty. Thence up the Parana River to

Rosario to pick up a cargo of grain. The ship could not load fully up-river, because of the limited depth of the water. For this reason they had to finish their loading in Buenos Aires. The next destination was across the Atlantic to Stavanger, Norway, where the *Anniston City* emptied holds of its cargo. Harry recalls that they returned to Norfolk, Virginia, empty.

June 6, 1945
Dear Moth and Dad,
    We'll make a brief stop tomorrow morning to take on fuel oil and fresh water so I should have a chance to get off some mail, and I hope, pick up some.
    …The Captain has taken to calling me the "pissinger" and the "tourist."
    "What a ceench you got! You go to war at joust the right time!"
    The trip has been uneventful so far. The area we're in, the Atlantic, has been adjudged the least hazardous in the world now that Germany is out of the way, and her subs pretty well, if not entirely, accounted for. As a result we are permitted to relax to quite an extent. With no more CQ and the watch cut to one man, I have all hands working on the armament mornings and devote afternoons to study, tests, and gun drills. I've made it clear that I expect an "excellent" when we're inspected in the States on return. And there's no reason why we shouldn't get it.
    I held church services yesterday A.M. One service, a mass, for the Catholics, of which three attended, and a separate Protestant one for five. It's significant that the troublemakers didn't show up at the services and that all others did. You should have heard me reading the elaborate Catholic service and singing the Doxology. I couldn't help but think of little Joy who handles it far better than I did. Maybe I'll make a good minister before this thing is over.
    I obtained service books at N.O.B. Norfolk, from a Protestant Chaplain/Captain who was at Pearl Harbor during the attack. He gave me a big bundle of religious matter and, evidently flattered at my stopping at his office, threw in the Prayer Book that he used aboard the USS *Pennsylvania* on that fateful day 7 Dec. 1941. He was a swell fellow; big hearty, sixtyish and he-manish enough to make a good chaplain…

…What do you hear from twin Jeff? I wonder, just as we all have for over a year, how much longer they're going to keep him over there. And what about Tom?

Love,

Ha

Brother Tom's letter in June, beyond complaining of the heat, and delineating his answer to it, showed some concern about his next duty.

10 June, 1945

Dear Folks,

Today it was amazingly hot, but lately I've been staving off the heat via cold showers, and an occasional swim. I just took a shower, and opened a cold beer…

…Things seem to be more optimistic nowadays, and I am beginning to feel certain that we will eventually come home sometime in the summer. By the way, about the time you receive this letter, the 451st, which of course is my old outfit, should be arriving in the States, and should bring Tom Coyne around. I commissioned him to report to Dad with a bulletin on my health etc…

…Tonight we have a special War Department film added to the program—a little thing with the very grim and prophetic title of "On To Tokyo." This is no joke to a guy with only 68 points (although I might pick up a couple of more battle stars worth ten points.).

Love,

Tom

CHAPTER 25

THE *LAFFEY* LIMPS HOME

A FEW DAYS into June the USS *Laffey*, a 2,200-ton destroyer, limped into the Seattle port. She was twisted and torn, and her story was one of a heartless cruel war.

It was decided that she would remain at a public pier and she would demonstrate to the people of Seattle what our fighting men had to endure. It might further emphasize the need of backing the 7th War Loan Drive and the need for more ship workers at the local construction yards.

I went aboard in the morning, before the public visiting hours. I had work to do, plans to make, and information to pass on to the gunnery department. Once on board I was shown about by Lieutenant Smith, the gunnery officer. Number three five-inch gun mount was smashed, with its barrels pointed toward the sky in grotesque fashion. Shrapnel holes dotted the superstructure, depth charge racks were ripped out of shape, a gaping hole in the wardroom bulkhead left the room open to the outside, and the table was torn by shrapnel. Parts of the superstructure were missing, and the charred remains of 20-mm guns, and various and sundry parts of Japanese suicide plane engines, eloquently told the story. And in the engine room rested a complete Japanese plane, where it had been wedged in the fight.

I learned that over 40 planes had attacked the *Laffey* as she patrolled far in advance of her task force, a lone destroyer going about her dangerous duty. She was a picket ship, charged with spotting waves of enemy planes, and giving the necessary advance warning to the Allied task force. Seven Japanese planes had recklessly flown into the ship with their deadly bombs attached, and one hapless American plane had crashed into the mainmast when following a Japanese too closely. Five bombs hit the ship, rocked her from stem to stern, tore out large sections, started raging fires, killed 32 men and injured over 60. The *Laffey* had fired everything she could. She managed to down 9 enemy planes by herself, and her air cover had accounted for more.

But it is the story of the men who made the fight that strikes home. I listened while Lieut. Smith told of their return from Pearl Harbor. The exec and two officers were returning to their ship from a night ashore. A young, happy sailor approached on the run, saluted, and asked them enthusiastically where the *Laffey* was moored.

"I'm on my way to see my brother," he said with a grin trying to cover up his anticipation. "I haven't seen the sunofagun for over a year."

The exec quietly asked the sailor his name, and when the sailor had answered, the exec blanched. "Your brother was killed, son. He died bravely…"

The young sailor slumped to the ground as if shot, held his head in his hands, and sobbed. His body shook with the grief and despair.

Lieut. Shaw was the assistant engineer. He told me how a Seattle gunner's mate had manned a twenty millimeter gun until the deck was shot out from under him, and he disappeared with the entire gun mount. Shaw had just finished talking to the young gunner's sister. "It was like talking to Sullivan himself," he said. "She had the same brown eyes, the same quiet look. And I had to tell her how we lost him. She cried a little, and I guess I did too."

The communications officer's closest buddy was the first lieutenant. When the planes hit, he had gone forward to his battle station. One of the planes hit the deck, just above him and burst into flames. They never found any identifiable part of the first lieutenant. And now his wife was coming on to Seattle, and the communications officer was going to meet her at the station in an hour. "God," he said. "What can I say to poor Sue?"

One of the officers was not aboard. "We had to leave him in a hospital in Pearl Harbor," said Lieutenant Smith. "He was a smart cookie. A really savvy boy. He was hit with a piece of shrapnel in the head that opened up his skull. The doc sewed him up in Pearl, trying to put back everything that had spilled out. Now he's wacky. He kept thinking that a Japanese was in his bunk with a hand grenade. Too bad. He was such a smart cookie before he was hit."

Those were just a few of the stories, the few that I happened to hear. There were more, and many were told to tearful mothers and fathers. Stories that those who survived are obligated to pass along.

By this time, Jeff's unit had moved on to the Philippines. His first letter was from the Island of Cebu and it included copies of letters of commendation for his organization. These commemorated the three full years of service in the front area. Though they spoke of the length of service, none mentioned a furlough or a return to the States

General Headquarters
Southeast Pacific Area
Office of the Chief Engineer
9 June, 1945
Subject: Commendation
To: Officers and Men of the 2nd Engineer Special Brigade
   On June 20th the 2nd Engineer Special Brigade will commence its fourth year of service. On June 29th it will enter its third year of continuous participation in combat. It seems appropriate at this time to review what has been accomplished since the 2d Engineer Special Brigade made its first landing at Nassau Bay, New Guinea.
   You have spearheaded our amphibious advance from New Guinea to the Philippines, a distance of 2,000 miles, in eighty-two combat landings. The road back has been difficult, our progress was slow, but as our resources and skill increased, the speed of our advance increased. The contributions you have made to the technique of amphibious warfare have greatly increased our capacity for striking the enemy where he least expects us.
   Your outstanding contribution to the success of our arms has not been without its toll of sacrifice. From Oro Bay to Corregidor

the way has been marked by the blood of men of the 2d Engineer Special Brigade who died that Liberty might live. In carrying on undaunted, you have assured that your comrades' sacrifice was not made in vain.

As the 2d Engineer Special Brigade enters upon its fourth year of devoted service, I pray that Almighty God may bless and preserve each one of you who participated in the final victory you have done so much to earn.

Hugh J. Casey
Major General, USA
Chief Engineer

Similar letters of commendation were written by R.C. Echelberger, Lieut. Gen'l from Hdqtrs of the 8th Army; W. F. Heavey, Brig. Gen'l, USA from Hdqtrs of the 2nd Engineer Brigade; and Walter Krueger, Commanding General of the 6th Army, USA.

Jeff's letter was brief and included his acknowledgement of the birth of our little daughter, whom we now called "Bonnie."

23 June, 1945
Dear Folks,
    Everything hunky-dory with me...
    ...Still in the Philippines and as usual little to report. Good to learn of little Bonnie's arrival and Math's good health.
    If ever I get out of this war business I'll probably hit Seattle as the first stop, and then by gosh I'll see that slick little family in the flesh.
    Great to learn that Old Ha is coming along so well. And that Bets and brood get a chance to see him occasionally.
    Hope Tom doesn't have to come over here...
    Love,
    Jeff

Brother Tom, still in Italy, continues his "education" by reading constantly, and trying his best to evade the heat.

25 June, 1945

Dear Folks,

I've been trying hard to beat this terrific heat. Yesterday I went to the beach at Manfradonia, and today I flew down to Bari (and back) and I must say that both stratagems were successful.

It now begins to look as if I won't make the baseball season after all…Oh well, there is always the football season to look forward to.

A fairly attractive deal has presented itself, namely thirty days "going to school" in Florence. I have applied, and plan to take up journalism, and if I learn anything, that is pure gravy. Florence, meanwhile, is a beautiful and fascinating city. If I am not selected I will resort to the available "rest centers," chief among which are the Riviera (Nice), Venice, Cairo (including Tel Aviv and Palestine), and Rome. I am hoping they will open up Switzerland for us. So this sitting out the boat home does have a few pleasant features.

I continue reading like mad, and among the books already fallen are: Samuel Butler's *Way of All Flesh*, and Tobias Smollett's *Humphrey Clinker*; some of Eugene O'Neill's plays; *The Maltease Falcon*, by Dashiell Hammett; Aldous Huxley's new book, *Time Must Have a Stop*; *The Big Rock Candy Mountain*, by Wallace Stegner; and *Storm Over the Land*, by Carl Sandburg.

Butler and Smollett, like Jane Austen and Henry Fielding, really delight me. They write in such wonderfully genial and humorous fashion. All four share the opinion that most people are utter bastards, yet they take it in their stride, and continue to get a kick out of people anyhow. I don't know why it should happen that these four near contemporaries should all be of the same temperament (I guess Thackerey was too, but I haven't read him yet). But no one has approached their warm-hearted satire yet, except Mark Twain, and I guess J.P. Marquand is the nearest thing writing today.

Movies are as bad as ever, although I did see one wonderful picture, *The Lost Angel*. Margaret O'Brien gave a performance that was really staggering in its excellence.

V-Mails seem to have lost their reason for being now, as I notice they don't arrive photographed anymore. So you all might as well forget them as far as I am concerned.

Love,

Tom

This letter from Harry was mailed in Buenos Aires, Argentina, his first port of call on his second Armed Guard trip.

June 22, 1945
Dear Moth & Dad,

By the time we reach our destination a few days less than a full month will have lapsed and we're all becoming more and more impatient to get there…

…Not much to tell you. The routine is not varied much. The highlights of this week was the firing of our 3-inch 50 gun. We used anti-aircraft rounds and got ten out in fairly fast time. You wonder at times what the sense in wasting the ammunition when the chances of ever getting a shot at an enemy plane are so remote. It's too bad in a way, because these guys love to fire (I've never seen a gun crew that didn't), and they will get very little chance to do it over here. We're allowed just five rounds every ten months. Incidentally, in case you're wondering how I could have fired ten rounds in view of such a limitation, I can explain that by saying that we didn't fire at all during that first two month trip…

Wasn't it good to hear from Jeff and to learn that he's living in such civilized surroundings? By this time, though, he may be in an entirely different and less healthy setting. They move the poor guy so often. I only wish they'd move him home.

Now to Dad. I was thinking of you last Sunday, Father's Day, and couldn't help but marvel just as I always have and always will at what a successful career you are hacking out for yourself and us. An outstanding business man, an unequalled parent, and as your dear wife knows better than any of us, a husband beyond compare.

Much love,
Hads

Tom's brief July letter laments the continued heat and has a further word about his application to study in Florence.

7 July, 1945
Dear Folks,
      …Weathers hot—…
      …I wasn't chosen to go to the University at Florence, but expect
to journey to the Riviera for a week or so. Reports are that it's a terrific place.
      Love,
      Tom

Harry's next came from the town of Rosario, up the Parana River
from Buenos Aires, where the *Anniston City* took on a cargo of
grain for Norway.

July 11, 1945
Dear Moth & Dad,
      We've been in port two days and the chances are we'll be here
for still another. We are being loaded now about 100 miles from
the large city (Buenos Aires) we first docked at and its taking much
longer than expected for the good reason that they've run out of
cargo and must bring in more from the hinterlands.
      We take on the final tonnage in the City as it can't be loaded
here because it would settle us too low for navigating the shallow
river.
      We are not returning to the States but rather going to another
continent with our cargo; then, home according to present plans,
and I fear that it won't be any sooner than the fall that I'll be seeing
you all.
      This is an up-and-coming country that hasn't been touched by
the war. They have everything including meat, butter, sugar, wool-
ens, silks, etc. The latter two items are scarce and expensive as the
devil, but food is cheap as the dickens. A large and delicious steak
dinner costs just a little over a dollar.
      People here live well and dress well and the large city compares
favorably with ours in the States, although, of course, there is only
one New York. This city is modern, clean and well kept. It's population is half a million whereas the other (Buenos Aires) is over 2
million. It has two subways, street cars, the largest opera house in
the world, the widest avenue (they claim) in existence, modern-de-

signed buildings and fine stores, theaters, etc. It's really one of the finest cities in the world.

There is a good-sized American colony down here, representative of large US Corporations with their families, and they make a business of entertaining the Navy men. We were guests at their American Club, a men's social and business organization occupying three floors in a downtown bank building. The American Women's' club maintains a U.S.O. canteen on its premises. As guests of the American Legion, we spent a Sunday at their Athletic club in the suburbs. We attended a large July 4th luncheon, along with 700 Americans at the Plaza Hotel, where we heard the American and British Ambassadors speak. That night we went to the U.S. Ambassador's Opera House at the Embassy, a very formal affair for 1000 guests who in short order, and after a few glasses of champagne or scotch, were making it just a friendly, cozy, cocktail party. It was an experience to attend such a function, and especially for the four men in my crew who were along. I tried to make them realize the significance of it and I think they did. They will probably never again have such an opportunity, and I guess I won't either…

Much love to all,

Ha

Two days later Harry was back down in Buenos Aires and wallowing in a huge sack of mail. He sent off a birthday note to Mother.

July 15, 1945

Dear Moth,

Happy, happy birthday to the most wonderful mother a guy ever had. …Years seem to make no difference whatever in your appearance…

…Remarkable and good are the words for you and your life, and what you like to call your "inner self," too. You have indeed been an inspiration to your four sons…We just couldn't have been given a finer start in life and I have come to realize now that we have these two little tots of our own, just what sacrifices you made to give us those wonderful advantages.

You're a beautiful young lady, Moth. Young in appearance, spirit, ideas and ambitions, and beautiful in every way!

…We are now back down the river at the main port and what a huge sack full of mail was waiting for me…

All love,

Ha

Jeff wrote his annual birthday letter to his mother, an excerpt of which follows.

20 July, 1945

Dear Moth,

…Main purpose of this note is to pass along the annual "love and congratulations" for all that July 29th means! Happy Birthday!…

…I enclose a snapshot of our Catholic Chaplain who is the most beloved man in the Regiment. I wish there was a Protestant Chaplain in the Army who had half as much on the ball. In fact, I wish there was a Protestant Minister in the States who could inspire me. I've never encountered one yet that measures up to what I expect in a man of God. The Church could do such a heap of good. But for my dough, it's a 100% bust. Why, all this peace talk and conferencing, and League of Nationing is just so much booshwah. The whole damn solution is neatly blue-printed in Christianity. All the rules and regulations and by-laws that are needed are all right there. But the Church has thoroughly loused up the job of selling the World on the plan. It could be a great force. Too bad!

It hasn't been wasted though. Someone somewhere has succeeded in having you and Dad understand. And in turn, you two, not the preachers, have managed pretty well to pass it along to us. For this I join Tom, Dick, and Harry in humbly thanking you.

Well, maybe that's the way I mean it from the core of my heart when I say, "happy birthday, Moth." And perhaps that explains why I love you very, very much!

Jeff

CHAPTER 26

V-J DAY

EARLY AUGUST brought with it some thrilling days. From the corners of Seattle's busy down-town streets newspaper boys screamed of America's new and weird atomic bomb; the entry of Russia into the Japanese war; and on August 10, the offer of peace from Japan. In the restaurants of the city, on the streets, in the offices and in the homes, conversation was only of the events of this very day. An electric tension was transmitted from one person to another with the jabbing speed of an alternating current. Tomorrow, we figured, we may have peace!

Hearing for the first time about an atomic bomb was a powerful story that was shrouded in mystery. I was introduced to the term by a bright red banner headline in the *Seattle Times*. One bomb was reputed to be powerful enough to do the damage of 20,000 tons of TNT.

My imagination was unleashed to run beside the racing minds of my fellow officers, all engineers, all who had hastily constructed theories to describe the bomb. They said it is a splintering of the atom. They said it destroys all material things by smashing the cohesive structure of matter. Nothing remains where a city stood; nothing but dust-like particles that create a shroud for the death and destruction that has been wrought.

As yet, there has been scant information for the man-on-the-street, but we all knew that the bomb must be deadly. It was deadly enough to prod Russia into the Pacific war, and Japan out of it.

These were the thoughts that rushed through my mind as I first heard of the bomb. Instinctively, I objected. Noontime discussions found me arguing against the use of the bomb. Obviously it would bring the war to a close, and save millions of lives. But the discovery of such a force seemed to me to be greater than the war itself. Apparently the bomb doesn't kill a person in the manner that we can comprehend. It disintegrates the body leaving no evidence that there was ever an existence? It is a method of destroying life that apparently rivals the mysterious forces that instill life into a body.

Could God have ever meant us to infringe upon His prerogatives? The arrangement of matter is most certainly God's prerogative, and most certainly so when it applies to man himself.

Such a bomb provokes endless questions which come nearer to approaching the eternal questions of God himself than anything that has confronted man to date. With the limitations of man, his inherent greediness, carelessness, and ruthlessness, one wonders if such a powerful force can be controlled.

It could be expected that Russia would declare war upon Japan, when it was so obvious that surrender was imminent. Why should Russia allow the Japanese war to terminate, without exercising her right to share in the victory feast?

At this point, Japan had agreed to the peace ultimatum drawn up by the meeting of the Big Three, USA, Britain and Russia at their Potsdam conference. But she insisted upon maintaining her Emperor. It is upon this subject Russia, China, Britain and the US had to dwell. The Emperor of Japan embodied not only their leadership, but their deity. He was their God as well as their physical leader, and as such the people willingly and gloriously die for him as easily as they live under his rule. But I did not think it was he alone that motivated his people. Rather, it was the military, who used the Emperor's cohesive power to promote their purposes. So it seemed to me, that if we were to accept Japan's peace offer, the trick would be to control the "intellects," that strong group of militarists who had so successfully framed the Emperor's power. Without them, I could see Japan diverted from its evil aggression.

We lived in expectancy for a week, and on August 14, 1945, V-J Day was declared by a simple announcement at 4 p.m. over the radio. A tremendous surge of pent-up emotion was released.

I was in the Assistant Industrial Manager's Office at the time. Similar to almost everyone in the City of Seattle, I was hanging over a radio. Almost instantly, and simultaneously with the announcement whistles on every ship along the waterfront blared triumphantly. Adding to the din were countless automobile horns, along with the hysterical screams of joyous crowds pouring out of buildings onto the streets. From the windows of the tall downtown buildings floated torn up newspapers, confetti, reams of copy paper, fluttering toward the street, or eddying about the buildings. Streamers landed on bus line cables and were carried along with the slow-moving buses. People walked arm-in-arm with purposeless abandon, or individually hurried toward some apparent objectives.

In a matter of minutes our office was emptied of all but a few. When I reached the street, the paper on the sidewalk looked like fresh New England snow, and one had to dodge the masses scurrying everywhere along the way.

On Third Avenue, I crowded into a bus, barely escaping the closing doors as I shoved my way inward. From the windows of the bus I could only see scurrying legs that moved in unorganized fashion along the sidewalks. Progress was slow. Horns blew, as cars moved at a snail's pace alongside of the bus. I noticed the anxiety of my fellow standees, as they shifted from one leg to the other, impatient for a celebration.

In the distance was the martial thump of drums. As it came nearer, I saw an impromptu victory parade headed by two sailors with a bass drum, and a snare drum. Behind them marched a moving mass of heterogeneous humanity from ship-workers with their hard hats, to servicemen. Men and women were joining the throng as it paced along the main street. I noted a core of elderly gentlemen, marching quietly but purposefully.

It took the bus almost an hour to travel through the downtown area. Once in the outskirts, travel was normal. In the University shopping district, there was evidence of a celebration, but for the most part the crowd had dissipated. I hurried the few blocks to home, and found Math and Dickens were at the beach. A young girl, today's sitter, sat placidly by Bonnie's kiddie-koop reading a "movie" magazine. The quiet of the room was broken only by Bonnie's sucking her finger, and my footsteps as I approached her. I leaned over the side of the kiddie-koop and smiled. She saw me and immediately smiled back. I told her that the war was over, and I tried to explain how very great that news was. Taking her finger out of her mouth, she waved her hands enthusiastically, and I could see her kicking her legs under the sky-blue blanket. She made that quiet, yet excited, purring noise that is so often coordinated with an expression that seems to be saying something very important. A happy little girl with a bundle of smiles and the war is over.

Tom, still stationed in Italy with the air force shortly before V-J Day, is making the best use of his time. He continues to enhance his education.

4 August, 1945

Dear Folks,

Last night I got back from Switzerland which was certainly the high spot of my overseas career. It's a wonderful country, and coming after Italy, it was like *heaven*. The scenery, of course, is all it's cracked up to be, but what really impressed us was the cleanliness and the people. The houses and cities were spotless, and the kids were all spotless. The people were clean-cut looking, very good-looking and delighted to see us—buying us drinks, eyeing us curiously, and in general treating us royally. The country is also untouched by war, and traveling around in it almost made us feel like civilians again; a wonderful feeling. The beer was the best I've ever had, and we even got fresh milk, although it was rationed.

Apparently the plans regarding our outfit have changed. At least something new is afoot, because they took a number of guys out of here. In a few days our officer leaves, which adds to my work and responsibility, as I must single-handedly close down our office (a hell of a job, since any mistake reverberates through the army and to the War Department).

I bought a wrist-watch in Switzerland for $8.50. Very nice.

At any rate, it may be that my stay here will be lengthened, but this might be a blessing as to go home now would probably lead to the Pacific, which is absolutely no bargain.

Love,
Tom

Hurrah! Brother Tom is finally a sergeant! But he is not so enchanted with his promotion as not to complain about the American Legion and its like.

August 9, 1945
Dear Folks,

As you may have noticed from the return address, they finally made me a sergeant. Since I figure (and so does everyone else around here) that I should be at least a Tech Sergeant, I am not jumping through hoops, but at least it's in the right direction, a slight source of satisfaction, and a $15.00 raise. And sergeant does look a little better than corporal. In a few more months I am hoping to con my way into Staff Sergeant, since in this outfit the only way you can get promoted is to apply some sort of heat. Some army, some officers, as Ernest Hemingway used to say.

I have the Manhasset American Legion folder sent to me, but it moves me not. Long ago I decided to steer clear of the Legion, VFW, etc., for I have always taken a rather dim view of them all. Just a bunch of guys trying to relive a dead common experience, and doing it completely sans grace. (Note their conventions)

Also, they all seem to follow unpleasantly reactionary lines, and in general I distrust the big national organizations, particularly those who refuse to admit members of the Nisei 442nd Infantry Regiment, and 100th Battalion of the 5th Army. I don't know if there is much excitement in the States regarding the persecution of the Nisei veterans, but over here everyone is dangerously hot over it. These Jap-Americans are exceedingly popular in the 5th Army, having amazing records, and are great favorites with all MTO GI's. It's barely possible that I will be hypocritical and unprincipled enough to take advantage of some of the benefits that the Legion is offering, but I hope not…

…This is all for now. The weather has been oppressively hot, and still no word as to when we go home.

Love,
Tom

Dad wrote a letter sent to his sons on August 10, when the bomb dropped, and it was reputed that the Japanese were ready to surrender. Obviously the peace meant deliverance of his four sons.

August 10, 1945

Dear Ha, Jeff, Dick and Tom,

This is a banner day for Moth and me, and for all of us, if the news of Japan's surrender is true. They are such a sneaky lot, however, we dare not become too enthusiastic; but even so what has transpired thus far points to ultimate capitulation. And it doesn't sound far off.

We hardly dare hope it is true because the war's end means so very much to us. Jeff's homecoming after so grueling a siege; Tom's return from his African and Italian campaigns; Dick's relief from the steady grind of doing his swell job by perfecting accuracy of gun fire so vital to our cause; and Ha's most necessary job of getting the supplies where most needed. Heroes all! And we are proud.

We know God will see fit to deliver you all back home safely, and in good health to your Mom and Pop at the old stand in Plandome. Glory be His name! Amen!

Love,

Dad

With the bomb in Hiroshima, and the arrival of V-J Day Jeff's regiment was moved to Japan; all that is, except Co. C., the company that Jeff commanded. They remained in the Philippines. It was tough to keep the troops happy, because their duties consisted of harbor work, unloading ships. "The guys," Jeff said, "were buying a home-made Filipino brew called 'Golden Horse' and they'd get into trouble."

He had them build a stockade and under a provision known as "company punishment," he'd sentence trouble-makers to a stay therein. Some wag soon erected a sign on the structure reading, "Golden Horse Corral."

He writes on V-J Day plus 1, (August 15, 1945).

August 15, 1945

I know—long time no me. And still no excuse. But I'm in good enough health and/or fettle, so once again I say: never worry about old Mr. Bones—he'll be all right.

You probably ask about my future; when am I coming home and all that. Well, sir, you've got me. In fact nobody knows. Most of our gang are where the history is being made, but not my bully little band. We're still sitting on an Island sweating it out. A lot of the men have gone home, though. But don't set an extra place at the Thanksgiving table. Nor, probably, even the Christmas feast. Of course, we get assorted rumors about going back as a unit, soon, but I've done enough campaigning to take reports like that with a dose of salts.

So let's wait for Kismet to shape my future as he sees fit, and we shall know when we shall know.

I'm not working overly hard, but have plenty of official worries and since the chow is not of the best, I'm mighty crotchety and poor company…

Love,
Jeff

Brother Harry writes from Scotland. He is enroute to Norway on V-J Day.

8/14/45

Dear Moth & Dad,

What a happy day this is for you two. At last the Japs have been made to realize that it's time to quit! We heard the news over the radio at about 10 o'clock tonight.

I can appreciate the relief you feel because I am experiencing it myself knowing that Jeff will soon be home again. I don't think I'm taking too much for granted in saying that, because surely he can't be expected to stay over there very many more days. No one deserves to be dispatched homeward more than that poor guy, and no two parents are more deserving of being so rewarded for your patience, and the worry you have endured. Its been a nerve-wracking two and a half years for you, and you've stood the suffering beautifully, carrying on.

Meanwhile I am very anxious to know what goes on with others of our far-flung family...

Currently we are enroute to Norway from Buenos Aires. We stop off in a port in the north of Scotland, which we should reach on Wednesday for further routing instruction.

One thing I dislike about this life is the uncertainty involved. How long we'll be in Norway, and where we go from, what cargo we will carry, and most certainly, when we will get home, are all questions that I will not get an answer to for some time. Another important question: Now that the war is over what can I expect of the future? I'll have to await my return to the States to get the answer.

Any word from Jeff? Tom home yet? Hope so.

We've had perfect weather except for a couple of bad days. I can take the roughest seas without becoming sick once I get past the first day or so of a trip. I always start off unsteadily no matter how calm it is.

Hope you two are not working too hard at your various tasks.

Love,

Ha

Tom is still in Italy, but is looking toward home.

August 26, 1945

Dear Folks,

...Apparently I'll be home by Christmas. That's all we can be sure of. We are taking over the duties of the 15th AF Hdq, and so must stay here until the 15th outfit has been redeployed, which should take at least until November. But maybe I'll be able to get home sooner than that with my 68 points, although I doubt it.

The weather is getting a lot more comfortable. In fact, the other day I went swimming and nearly froze to death.

...I'm feeling too lackadaisical tonight to write anymore.

Love,

Tom

Harry writes from Stavanger, Norway.

August 28, 1945

Dear Moth & Dad,

Here we are in Norway at last after a full 33 days at sea. That is a long voyage as they go. For example, the run from here to the States, which I learned today we will make next, takes less than half as long so everybody aboard was glad to get in, especially after the bad weather we had the last two days.

We're at a little town with a population of 1,000 friendly people who invite the men into their homes for milk and fruit and fresh eggs, despite the extreme shortage of everything here. Their cute children caper around the dock while the cargo is unloaded.

We'll be here a day more, and unless plans change, then move to a larger City (Bergen) a city of 50,000 population, which is an hour's boat ride away. I went there yesterday to get instructions from the Navy, however, there turned out to be no representative. I talked with the only American there, a pleasant Army Captain who gave me valuable information but is not actually my authority.

In Stavanger there are many British officers and enlisted men, but all are being gradually sent off as the Norwegians take up the reins again. I had lunch with the American at the British officer's mess in the only hotel.

Food is especially short. You can't get a restaurant meal. There are no bars, very little clothing, very little of anything in fact. What a contrast between this poor country and Argentina, or our own. And the amazing thing is that families here love Americans in nine cases out of ten. They are anxious to entertain us in their homes.

It's a colorful, quaint city. I can think of no better words to describe it. Here I go again, talking of the "oldness" of the buildings, their peaked roofs of red tile, their picture book and movie-travelogue appearance. Streets are cobblestone, narrow and winding. They are populated by horse-drawn wagons, bicycle riders, and pedestrians who look just as they should for consistency's sake.

One boat runs daily from here to Bergen at 8:30 A.M. and one comes back at 4 P.M., so until we move to the City itself, there can be no nightlife. Once in Bergen, the men should enjoy themselves. There is a British service club where they can buy beer, the one place in town, I am told, where it can be obtained. Also a sort of

U.S.O. type club where dances are held twice a week, and movies four times a week. Then there are two regular movie theaters that show American films. So it may not be too bad.

We're all saving money here. There is not much use for it. What little is needed can be obtained by selling such scarce items as soap, shoes, suits, almost anything. They've caught some merchant mariners disposing of ship's property like coffee, et al, and I'm keeping my Navy property well locked up. Incidentally I haven't sold anything because I need all I have. I'm told soap brings 50 cents a bar, shoes (even second-hand ones) 10, and 15 dollar suits (old and in poor shape) sell for $35. We don't know how lucky we are at home. The Germans really cleaned this place out, but good...

Love,
Ha

Tom is expecting to continue his education with a trip to the Holy Land. He is making his over-seas days as agreeable as possible.

August 29, 1945
Dear Folks

Tomorrow morning at 0600 sharp, I will get into the General's very comfortable B-17 (complete with couches, easy chairs, tables, etc.) and will be flown to Tel Aviv. After a few days of inspecting Palestine, Jerusalem, et al, we will wend our way to Cairo, and return only after I have been photographed on a camel in front of the Sphinx.

Needless to say this is a pretty good deal, and it is very nice that I am able to have these opportunities to see a little bit while I am sweating out transportation home. And that, incidentally, is looking better also.

I have also managed to get transferred to the signal office. There I will be unessential, and my own boss. There's nothing to do there, whereas a cryptographer section chief would be kept as an essential man.

Everything perfectly okay here.
Love,
Tom

Tom's next letter is a report of his trip in the General's plane to the Middle East.

September 8. 1945
Dear Folks,

Now I can truthfully say that I have seen "The Holy Land" and Egypt, having just gotten back from my 5 day jaunt. We flew straight down to Payne Field, Cairo, and stayed in town for two days and that night. It's a very colorful, but dirty town, and deserves that sadly over-worked word, "fascinating." I managed to see most of the sights, including the Pyramids, Sphinx, Museum, etc., and I even rode a camel, which was best of all. Unfortunately the picture that I had taken with the Sphinx as a background, was spoiled somehow by the Arab photographer, who managed to get sun into the negative or something. Incidentally, I also had a fez on in this picture. This town, like the whole tour, was very expensive, and I spent a whole lot more than I wanted to. I have little to show for it not getting any souvenirs. Nothing there seemed worthwhile that I could see. Just about the high spot of the trip was hearing an Arab vocalist in the Egyptian orchestra at a nightclub sing "Chew, Chew, Chew Your Bubble Gum," which struck me as funny.

From Cairo we flew to Tel Aviv, which is a very modern city, or maybe I should say town. It is totally populated by Jews almost all of whom speak English. They had a big beach there, which was very nice. From there we took a biblical tour of Jerusalem. This is another modern place, although the "old city," which is the historical section is the most wretchedly, filthy, and depressing place I have ever seen, and almost completely filled with Arabs. We saw the Mount of Olives, Garden of Gethsemane, Tomb of Rachel, and other items. We also went to Bethlehem, where we saw the site of the birthplace of Christ, and where the presiding priest was from Texas. He crowed that Eisenhower came from Texas too, which seemed like a worldly sort of pride for a man in that position. He also confessed to us that he has just won $80 on a bet with a Major who maintained that Eisenhower was born in Kansas.

We then followed the way that Jesus took while carrying his cross on the way to the crucifixion, culminating in the spot that the Catholics maintain is where he was crucified and then entombed. I understand the Protestants say it was a different spot. It was all very interesting, and I'm glad that I went, but as I expected, and as so often happens, the whole thing left me flat. The rest of the time was spent lounging about Tel Aviv.

An interesting sidelight on the trip is that we flew down in the General's very comfortable B-17. Just yesterday the same ship was flying back from Bari on a routine flight, and was forced to make a crash landing in the water. Luckily it was only about a mile off shore, and no one was hurt. In fact, no one literally got their feet wet. But if it had happened over some of the more isolated stretches of the Mediterranean that we flew over, I'd have been swimming yet.

Nothing new about getting home, but all the new rumors seem encouraging and that might be indicative of the truth.

Love,

Tom

Mother received an unexpected letter from a Catholic Nun connected with Sacred Heart College, situated in Mobile City, on the Philippine Islands. Apparently Jeff had made a visit to this college.

September 9, 1945
Mrs. G. H. Jackson
Plandome, Long Island
NY, U.S.A
"May the Grace of God be with us always."
Dear Mrs. Jackson:

This will be a surprise for you to receive a letter from the Philippines and much more from a Sister of Charity.

Your son has been in our place about two months ago and they have gone to another island for a change. I have met him and his co-officers have introduced him to me as the CO or the Commanding Officer. He has not stayed for a long time in this place but we tried our best to make him feel at home. We are so grateful to them for having liberated us and in no other way could we express our thanks than by letting them feel at home. Their free afternoons they spend at our College. They become quite used to coming that they deeply felt it when the time for saying good bye came. On our part, we felt so much their departure. They were the best group of friends who came to visit our school.

…The war is over by now and you will be seeing him soon. I am always praying for a speedy return of my friends to meet their families. You are one of those included since I met Jeff. He is such a good man. You must be proud of him!

…My best wishes to you and may God bless you and bring your son earlier to you, is the earnest prayer of one who appreciates him.

I am

Very Sincerely yours,

Sister Felcidao Ocamomot

CHAPTER 27

GOING HOME

ON THE NIGHT OF September 25th I had the duty. This consisted of little more than sitting at the captain's spacious desk monitoring a telephone that probably would not ring. Looking out the windows I could watch the rain blow by, and I could see the red, green, and amber lights glisten on the straight wet streets some 10 floors below. The faint putt-putt of a small vessel could be heard as it chugged amongst the piers on the waterfront, and the dim, black outlines of ships snuggled against their wharves could be seen. The patter of the rain became monotonous, and its cadence was broken only by a blast from a departing ship that split the atmosphere like a woodman's axe into the trunk of a tree.

In a few hours I would retire to a tiny room, just a few yards from the captain's desk. I would curl up in a hospital bed, moved in for the duty officers, and I'd wake up tomorrow to another slow monotonous day at the office. It was like that every day this fall. With the capitulation of Japan, our activities in the Assistant Industrial Manager's Office had been slowed to an agonizing walk. At first it was a relief from the hectic hustle and bustle of "getting the ships out on time." But soon it was akin to solitary confinement, quietly waiting for something to happen, when you knew nothing would. It was almost as if I was on the WPA in the great depression of 1929. If I had a shovel, I would be leaning heavily upon it with a blank stare of nothingness framed on my face.

Common sense told us that it was imperative to tidy up the forces afloat. There were ships that must be decommissioned, put on an inactive basis, or peculiarly, spruced up to be turned over to the Russian Navy in conformance with somebody's special deal. We knew that men were needed for this last collective effort—the residue of war; but few of the "civilian Navy" could contemplate this effort with any degree of enthusiasm.

I was amazed at the rapidity with which the Navy, and indeed, the entire country retrenched with the conclusion of hostilities. To us, in the Assistant Industrial Manager's office there was an awareness of financial cut-backs, a gingerly retreat to the laborious peacetime machinery. Gone was the glib off-hand manner of war-born necessity. A job order was now figured in terms of dollars and cents, not in what the skipper of a ship deemed as imperative to prosecute the war.

As might be expected, the Navy red tape had become more evident. The regular Navy had appeared to take over the reins once again. More than ever, the Reserves are aware of the USN, those "guardians of the Naval heritage." The gap between the peacetime and the wartime Navy had broadened.

The compelling force that drove us as reserves to our best efforts during the war had mysteriously disappeared and nothing had been left in its place except a desire to return to civilian life. The major topic of conversation revolved around the required number of points needed for separation. Each of us waited impatiently for some positive indication that would enable us to return to an inactive status. Rumors were created, and then flung down by reality. Appetites were whet by the trickle of those hands who had the required number of points, and who would say good-bye, resplendent in civilian dress the day after discharge.

It is as if we were caught in a quiet whirlpool that ripples the stagnant water ever so softly, with a promise of eventual action. This waiting is worse than our busiest day.

Fortunately, I could return home each day, to a happy family. But even this was not as restful as one might hope. We had been told by our lessor that we must vacate our rented home, and were given a very short time to accomplish the deed. The burden fell on Math, my hustling wife, mother of two, cook, bottle-washer, and main source of finding a new home, to take the lead role. Most of our time was directed toward this last endeavor. Though casual at first, we turned down two opportunities for livable homes while we clung to the prospect of a release from the Navy. By the end of October it became evident that we would spend at least another month in Seattle. We stepped up our efforts to a frantic pitch. As a precautionary measure, we secured train reservations for home, and made advance arrangements to have our belongings packed and shipped.

In the process of house-hunting, Dickens came down with a fever. He passed it on to me in the form of a sore throat and head cold. Our telephone mysteriously became inoperative which neutralized the advertisement for a house that we had run in both Seattle papers. And finally, I failed in my attempt to "switch duty" with a comrade at a critical point in our house search. But despite this triple "whammy" the ad finally produced a tiny, but cozy house in the Madrona district of Seattle. It overlooked the broad expanse of Lake Washington, with the Cascade mountains in the background. But it had few modern conveniences although this was balanced by a very understanding and pleasant landlady. We moved in early October, and it served nicely for our final few months in the west.

In the meantime, Tom was lolling around waiting for orders to start for home.

Sept. 30,1945
Dear Folks,
    ...This base is pretty nice. It's more or less a staging area where outfits come to be broken up. Some guys go to other outfits, and the fortunate ones go to the 7th Repple Depple to await the big move home. I more or less expect to be one of the latter, but I can't be too sure. So far there's been nothing but rumors, and no one from the 49th has left here.
    The food is quite good, and there is absolutely nothing to do all day but sit around and listen to the radio, read, talk, or go to Naples. The passes are automatic. Since I enjoy all these alternatives, I am quite pleased with the place, and I hope I'll stay here until summoned to the Depot.

So far I've taken three passes; one to Cassino where another guy and I visited his cousin's grave at a British graveyard with an estimated capacity of 4,000, And they're still digging graves. I've seen Cassino before, but it was still a staggering sight.

On the other two passes I went to the Opera catching "Carmen," and "La Traviata." Both were fine although I think the latter had a bulge in performance with an especially fine soprano, one Adreana Geneive…

…Continue to use the same address to get me.

Love,
Tom

In October we heard from Bill Webster, who had read the final article in the *New York Times* about Jim Mathes. This article appeared 14 months after the 509 action had taken place. Web also relates his future plans in the following:

Oct 9, 1945
Dear Math & Dick,

Bunny and I took our two weeks vacation and returned to Columbus a week ago. While at the farm in Lenox, Mass., we saw the article in the New York paper about Jim. Math, it's awfully difficult to tell you how we feel. I was so sure in my own mind that things would turn out differently. And yet, it wouldn't be right to say that our prayers weren't answered; I'm sure they were.

I understand that when the end did come, Jim was down below making sure that the ship's log was destroyed. That's just like him, to be thinking of the important things. We can't afford to lose guys like Jim.

While on vacation I made my final decision to leave Curtis. I had been thinking about it for some time since the war ended. I will go to work for Dad. The export field is beginning to open up again, and there may be some very interesting work ahead.

I regret leaving Curtis after almost five years, and the interesting work it held for me, but we are both looking forward to moving back East…

…Well, what's the latest news from the Jacksons? How many points do you have, Dick, and how soon before you can join the expanding ranks of civilians? What do you expect to do afterwards? Aetna?

…Any chance of you people getting back for some skiing…
Best,
Web

From Jeff, at his post over the past three plus years, we hear progress toward a return home.

27 October, 1945
Dear Folks,

Here I come, sneaking out of my customary veil of silence and mystery to report that all is reasonably well with your Uncle Dudley. That is physically. I guess mentally I'm fine, but as far as the nerves go, I don't reckon I'm so good. My morale is somewhere down in the minuses.

For the past three months I've been in Cebu, on a little island just off Cebu City. And I'm heartily fed up with the place. All the rest of the Regiment except Company C is at Yokohama, Japan. We were left here as a rear echelon and expected to follow hard on their heels. They were among the first to land. But the plans changed as Army plans will and here we sit, pretty much on our own. Four or five months ago I became Company Commander and my headaches in that time have been traditional ones, and on the traditional frequency.

Actually, the company is a mere shell, most of the men and all of the officers having gone home on points. I have enough points but am expected to stick around awhile until someone decides what to do with the outfit. It looks definite that the Brigade will be part of the regular army, but I doubt if anyone from here will go back as part of the Regiment. We will all be spread around. All the men will be transferred out and I will head for a casual camp and home! But when is a big blank.

I hope it's soon because I'm plenty fed with this hanging around. It would have been pleasant to see Japan, but the boys write that it's not so worthwhile. It represents the finish line, though, the end of the cycle.

…Better close now. My guess is that about 15 November I'll be released. I doubt if I'll make it home by Christmas, though.

Lotta Love,
Jeff

By early November, Tom continues to talk about home, which has been on his mind for some time.

> November 1, 1945
> Dear Folks,
>
> It's definite, that I'm going to the depot in a very few days, so it looks as if I'm a cinch to be home by the end of the month; maybe even for Thanksgiving!
>
> ...I don't know what's happened, but apparently a congressman got on the Army's neck and finally got this theatre some boats. Redeployment in Italy lagged terribly last month. But I hear that the Navy is going to contribute battleships, aircraft carriers, etc. to help get the boys home. Which is fair enough with me.
>
> Love,
> Tom

Five days later, on November 6th, Tom wrote his final letter from Italy.

> 6 Nov. 1945
> Dear Folks,
>
> I'm all set to leave very early tomorrow morning on a troop transport with the coy name of "The Sea Scamp." It shouldn't take much more than two weeks before I am home and separated. We land at Hampton Roads, Virginia, from where I originally embarked. I think I will be sent to Fort Monmouth or Dix to get discharged...
>
> ...See you all soon.
> Love,
> Tom

After lunch on December 1, 1945 I was separated from active duty by the Navy. I recall that the separation process, at least as it was practiced in Seattle, was a pleasant experience. I came away with the feeling that this particular unit was the most efficient that I had experienced in my three and a half years in the military. It was "service with a smile," and I hopped from one desk to another. I was home by two o'clock and realized with a sudden rush, that I was now a civilian. The rain and the overcast took on a peculiar sunny glow, the oppressiveness lost in the happy aspect of going "home" to the East Coast.

We hadn't counted on such a speedy release. We had prudently planned on leaving sufficient time for what I thought would be the intricate red-tape needed to unwind from the Navy.

Our train reservations on the Olympian, the Milwaukee Railroad's crack cross-country train, were for December 7th.

I had been given a proposal for staying in the Navy. It included an immediate promotion to lieutenant commander, and serving further time in Seattle primarily with the decommissioning of the ships. My decision-time was not lengthy. I dearly wanted to be a civilian again. However, I did sign up for the "Inactive Reserve." As such I served until May 15, 1956 when I was honorably discharged as being over age in grade.

By the 11th of December, 1945, we were met at the tiny railroad station in Harmon, NY, on the New York Central line, and rode home to Greenwich on icy roads. A composite of the Mathes and Jackson clans were on hand to greet us. It was the end of a long but satisfactory saga. We certainly had no complaints.

Jeff's home-coming took a bit longer. In late November, his brief letter passed on the good news that he was homeward bound. But, as things went, it was not a direct route.

26 November 1945
Dear Folks,

Good News! Tomorrow A.M. I board an aircraft carrier bound for the U.S.A. and my old glen plaid suit. The trip should be fast and my chances are good that I'll make it for Christmas!

I entered the Replacement Depot on the 13th of November, and had quite a time sweating it out. But now all is rosy.

Have some packing to do. I'll try to buzz you from the coast with the late dope. I will check into Seattle situation in case Math and Dick & Company are still there.

So long. Love to all,
Jeff

Jeff boarded a "baby flat-top" for the ride home. The ship was commanded by a retiring Naval officer who had two desires: 1) to stop on the way for one last look at Midway Island where he had served, and 2) to get to San Diego close enough to Christmas so his crew would be held in California over the holidays, before turning around and going back for another load of army guys.

As a result the ship loitered on the way, stopping over the "Philippine deep" (the deepest point in the Pacific Ocean) where Jeff and some of his comrades went swimming. They also exchanged a basketball team with the crew of a companion flat-top.

By the time they reached San Pedro, it was too late for Jeff to get home, and he spent Christmas morning at the railroad station in Hastings, Nebraska, where some nice ladies came aboard the train with Christmas baskets.

When Jeff finally reached Fort Dix, New Jersey, the separation center, he was promoted to captain, his only promotion in the entire war. He also received his final physical. He was advised that he must undergo a hernia operation before he could be honorably discharged. But he was given a few days pass so he could go home for New Year's Day.

Jeff did report to an army hospital in Staten Island for the surgery. After that, he reported back at Fort Dix where he was put on terminal leave until May 21, 1946, which is the date on his separation record.

Jeff bears no malice toward the Army, which, some might say, gave him a pretty rough four years with little if any reward. He says:

> Looking back, it's apparent that I was extremely blessed with good luck and a relatively pleasant war experience. We always camped on shore lines, with no steaming jungles or mud to contend with. Of all the landings I took part in, only one, Biak Island in Dutch New Guinea, was actively opposed at the beach head by the Japanese.
>
> I had a great variety of special duty assignments which helped greatly to make up for the fact that I received no official leave time in my three years overseas. I have no complaints.

In all, Jeff had served in the Army from July 10, 1942 until April 17, 1946. A long time!

Brother Harry, home from his Armed Guard duty in January 1946, was assigned a job at one of the deployment centers in the Lido Beach Club on the southern shore of Long Island. The Navy had noted his civilian career in insurance, and had chosen him to advise the retiring troops of the value of continuing their military life insurance before separation. This insurance had been underwritten by the Government for each sailor while he was in the service

Harry addressed gatherings of sailors of some 200 men on the very edge of civilian life and advised them of their priorities, a choice for each to either assume the premium himself, or to cancel the insurance. It was hard to argue against the value of the insurance, and Harry recommended that the insurance opportunities should be continued.

He remained at this job for four and a half months, finally gaining his civilian status on April 12, 1946.

Epilogue

WELL, that's the way it was, for one American family, during those tumultuous four years of World War II.

Theirs is a story of few heroics, but many examples of love-of-country and devotion-to-duty, both ingredients that were necessary in families throughout this vast country to bring the war to a successful conclusion.

And then, with "mission accomplished," these civilian warriors joined the thousands of others who were understandably eager to return to family, and resume their individual destinies.

It is, after all, a simple story of America at war, an America that was blessed with the ability to leave violence behind and to get on with building its tomorrow.

Army of the United States

SEPARATION QUALIFICATION RECORD

SAVE THIS FORM. IT WILL NOT BE REPLACED IF LOST

This record of job assignments and special training received in the Army is furnished to the soldier when he leaves the service. In its preparation, information is taken from available Army records and supplemented by personal interview. The information about civilian education and work experience is based on the individual's own statements. The veteran may present this document to former employers, prospective employers, representatives of schools or colleges, or use it in any other way that may prove beneficial to him.

1. LAST NAME—FIRST NAME—MIDDLE INITIAL	MILITARY OCCUPATIONAL ASSIGNMENTS		
	10 MONTHS	11. GRADE	12. MILITARY OCCUPATIONAL SPECIALTY
JACKSON, FRANKLYN J.	22	1stLt	Liaison Officer (1930)

2. ARMY SERIAL No.	3. GRADE	4. SOCIAL SECURITY No.
O-910593	Capt	Unknown

22	1stLt	Amphibious Engineer Boat Unit Commander (1366)

5. PERMANENT MAILING ADDRESS (*Street, City, County, State*)
24 South Drive,
Plandome, Nassau County, New York

6. DATE OF ENTRY INTO ACTIVE SERVICE	7. DATE OF SEPARATION	8. DATE OF BIRTH
10 Jul 1942	21 May 1946	16 Feb 1912

9. PLACE OF SEPARATION
Separation Center,
Fort Dix, New Jersey

SUMMARY OF MILITARY OCCUPATIONS

13. TITLE—DESCRIPTION—RELATED CIVILIAN OCCUPATION

LIAISON OFFICER: Served 35 months in Asiatic-Pacific Theater with Engineer Boat and Shore Regiment as Liaison Officer and Boat Unit Commander. As Liaison Officer was responsible for coordination of training and operations between Boat Battalion Staff and units transported.

AMPHIBIOUS ENGINEER BOAT UNIT COMMANDER: Commanded a Boat Company and was responsible for the administration, training, discipline, morale, and tactical employment. Directed unit in transporting and landing troops and supplies on islands ; New Guinea, and Philippines. Served as wave leader and mission leader for landing.
Decorations: World War II Victory Medal, Asiatic-Pacific Theater Ribbon with 1 bronze arrowhead and 3 battle stars, Philippine Liberation Ribbon with one battle star.

WD AGO FORM 100
1 JUL 1945

This form supersedes WD AGO Form 100, 15 July 1944, which will not be used.

Honorable Discharge

from the Armed Forces of the United States of America

This is to certify that

Lieutenant Richard S. Jackson, U.S.N.R. (179468) Retired

was Honorably Discharged from the

United States Navy

on the 15th day of May, 1956. *This certificate is awarded as a testimonial of Honest and Faithful Service*

ALBERT PRATT
Acting Secretary of the Navy

NavPers-2664 (Rev. 5-50)

Honorable Discharge

This is to certify that

THOMAS C JACKSON   12 101 129   SERGEANT

HEADQUARTERS & BASE SERVICE SQUADRON   522ND AIR SERVICE GROUP

Army of the United States

is hereby Honorably Discharged from the military service of the United States of America.

This certificate is awarded as a testimonial of Honest and Faithful Service to this country.

Given at   SEPARATION CENTER
FORT MONMOUTH NEW JERSEY

Date   22 NOVEMBER 1945

FRANCIS L JENKINS
LIEUTENANT COLONEL INFANTRY

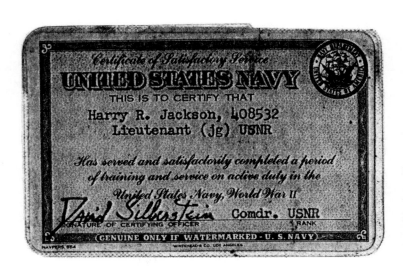

Certificate of Satisfactory Service

UNITED STATES NAVY

THIS IS TO CERTIFY THAT

Harry R. Jackson, 408532
Lieutenant (jg) USNR

*Has served and satisfactorily completed a period
of training and service on active duty in the*

United States Navy, World War II

David Silberstein   Comdr. USNR
SIGNATURE OF CERTIFYING OFFICER   RANK

(GENUINE ONLY IF WATERMARKED - U. S. NAVY)

NAVPERS 554   WHITEHEAD & CO. LOS ANGELES

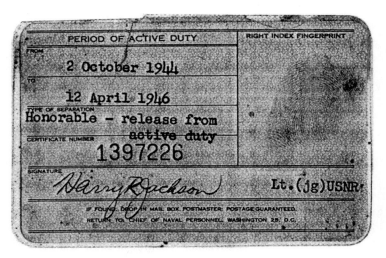

PERIOD OF ACTIVE DUTY	RIGHT INDEX FINGERPRINT
FROM 2 October 1944	
TO 12 April 1946	
TYPE OF SEPARATION Honorable − release from active duty	
CERTIFICATE NUMBER 1397226	

SIGNATURE   Harry R Jackson   Lt. (jg) USNR

IF FOUND, DROP IN MAIL BOX. POSTMASTER: POSTAGE GUARANTEED.
RETURN TO: CHIEF OF NAVAL PERSONNEL, WASHINGTON 25, D.C.

About some of the letter writers

Franklyn (Jeff) J. Jackson is now 90 years of age, and is living in Alamogordo, New Mexico with his wife Suzanne Lyon Jackson. She is the sister of Mrs. Chester Loomis, and I am happy to say that Jean Loomis and I were instrumental in getting these two lovebirds together some 52 years ago. Jeff fathered two sons, who grew up during the post-war years in their home in New Jersey. After the war, Jeff joined with his twin, Harry, as brokers in G. H. Jackson Co., Insurance Company in downtown New York City. After their father's death the twins carried on the business until selling out to Davis and Dorland Inc., a large insurance brokerage in New York in 1975. Jeff worked with the new company for some three years, until retirement took him to Alamogordo, NM. Jeff has served me as an editor for five of my six books, for which I shall be forever grateful.

Harry R. Jackson, Jeff's twin, is currently living in Larchmont, NY He was married to Elizabeth Ridlon Jackson, who died in March of 1950. He is the father of three; a daughter, Harriet (Happy), was born after the war and joined the two children, Joy and Jeff, noted in this book. He has four grandchildren. Since the war, Harry's career duplicated that of his twin as noted above, with the exception that he continued working with Davis Dorland until March of 1987. After his retirement, Harry preferred a regular working schedule, so joined the Pinkerton Security Company to keep busy, before finally wrapping it up in 1998 at the ripe old age of eighty-six.

Thomas C. Jackson, lives in South Norwalk, Connecticut. Upon his release from the Army, he married Elizabeth (Betty) Boulton Jackson to whom he had been engaged during the war years. She died in May of 1998. He is the father of three sons and one daughter. He spent his working life as a space salesman for various leading national magazines, as well as pursuing his hobbies of collecting jazz records, and observing jazz concerts. He frequently does guest shots with radio and TV stations. He continues his avid reading and spectating to the present time.

Mr. G. Harry Jackson, our father, died at the age of 86 while living in a senior development in Red Bank, NJ. He had retired at the age of 72, turning his business over to his twin sons.

Mae C. Jackson, our mother, lived to the ripe old age of 95. She died in the same location as her husband some ten years later. At the age of 63 she suffered the first of 13 different operations for cancer, all in the area of her mouth and throat. At one point, after the loss of part of her tongue due to the cancer, she spent hours in front of a mirror learning once again to talk fluently. She was a good "talker," and a woman of extraordinary courage and understanding.

Chester S. (Bud) Brett lives in Framingham, Massachusetts. He is married to Nancy (Sewall) Brett and is the father of three children, a daughter and two sons. He joined his father in the wool business upon his return to civilian status. After his Dad's death he eventually liquidated the business when the demand for wool diminished under pressure from the newer synthetic materials. At this point he went into the real estate business, from which he retired in time. Breaking up his home in later life to move into more manageable quarters he and Nancy realized that they had many antique pieces that their children did not fancy. Consequently the Bretts turned their energies to selling antiques, a pursuit that they have enjoyed at their leisure.

William (Web) O. Webster died on November 25, 2001. He was 85 years old. He was married to Alice (Bunny) Dorman, whom he met and wooed while in college. They had three sons. Following the war his father and he founded the Peruvian International Airline with surplus U.S. Army transport planes. Web was the primary pilot. Severe arthritis ended his flying career, so he turned to another business, becoming a part-owner of a company that made knit golf shirts. Tired of the New York commute he bought a failing marina in New London, Ct., before finally finding his business niche with automobiles. He started a body paint company then branched into autobody work at which he was very successful.

After the war, **Chester H. Loomis** returned to his wife, Jean Lyon Loomis, and life in his native Hartford, Connecticut. He sired two sons, the eldest of whom predeceased him. He rejoined an insurance agency formed by his eldest brother, Goodwin, Loomis and Britton of which he was a partner. Chet died on June 14, 1990. His wife has survived him.

James S. (Dinner) Cooney, was married on January 4, 1945 to Joanne (Johnny) May after returning from the war. He worked with Metal & Controls (now Texas Instrument Co.) immediately following the war. Some time later, with a partner, he started his own electronics business which he called "Pylon" It was very successful having 35 different patents. They sold out and Dinner stayed on for three years, retiring after this period. He kept busy by joining his son, Peter, in buying an American Hockey League team in Springfield, Massachusetts. He died on April 1, 1992.